HUNGRY OKLAHOMA

■ HUNGRY OKLAHOMA ■

Confronting Poverty and Food Insecurity

ROBERT LEE MARIL

UNIVERSITY OF OKLAHOMA PRESS : NORMAN

This book is published with the generous assistance of the Wallace C. Thompson Endowment Fund, University of Oklahoma Foundation.

Library of Congress Cataloging-in-Publication Data
LCCN 2025041843 ISBN 978-0-8061-9656-5 (hardcover)

The paper in this book meets the guidelines for permanence and durability of the Committee on Production Guidelines for Book Longevity of the Council on Library Resources, Inc. ∞

The manufacturer's authorized representative in the EU for product safety is Mare Nostrum Group B.V., Mauritskade 21D, 1091 GC Amsterdam, The Netherlands, email: gpsr@mare-nostrum.co.uk.

In Memory of
Dr. Steven Kenneth Reich
Anna Ramey Walker
Sherwood O. Washington

Our Father, who art in heaven,
hallowed be thy name;
thy kingdom come;
thy will be done;
on earth as it is in heaven.
—Matthew 6:9–13 (traditional)

Contents

Introduction

Truth has sharp teeth.
—Rastko Petrović

Norma leaves her mother sitting in their twenty-year-old pickup truck in the parking lot next to Thy Will Be Done. TWBD is a food pantry in Hereford, Oklahoma, that provides food for those who do not have enough to eat.* Hereford has a poverty rate of 29 percent and, because of its size, the largest number of poor in Wells County.[1] Even though it is much cooler inside the air-conditioned Butler building, Mom, as Norma calls her, prefers to wait in their old pickup sitting under a tree—despite the fact that it provides little shade from the three-digit summer heat.

From the grocery shelves inside TWBD, Norma selects only foods that do not have to be refrigerated. She carefully places cans of baked beans,

* To protect the privacy of people, places, and institutions referenced in this book, including Thy Will Be Done (TWBD), names and other identifying details have been changed. "Hereford" and "Macon," for instance, are pseudonyms. For further information about the research methods employed in this book, see the section entitled "Research Approach" following chapter 8.

green beans, asparagus, mixed vegetables, squash, and three kinds of soup in her grocery cart. Her choices seem a little unusual, because summers are predictably hot in Oklahoma. Many who are poor and cannot afford air conditioning eat their meals outside. They wait until the sun sets, fire up their hot plates or grills, and hope for a kind breeze.

Today the other guests at TWBD relish fruit popsicles, frozen yogurt, quarts of ice cream, and ice-cold melons. At home they count on electric fans or, if luckier than most, have a room with an AC that may be hanging precariously in the window frame. But it is never a fair fight. One way or the other, the Oklahoma heat rarely loses.

During the hour it takes Norma to carefully choose food from the pantry shelves, she seems in no big rush. Dressed in bulky tan shorts and a loose-fitting top, her brown bangs stop just above her bright blue eyes. Norma seems somewhat reserved compared to the other guests at TWBD. Those who come here because they do not have enough food to eat are called "guests" by the staff and volunteers.

Norma's few words punctuate long silences covered up, for the most part, by random chatter from the other shoppers, the shouts of children, and music blaring from two tiny speakers mounted on the brightly colored walls. Norma drifts down each aisle, hesitating at regular intervals in case she passes by something she needs. Twice she circles back to the canned vegetables.

Outside the wind blows from the west at fifteen miles per hour with gusts to twenty or more. But it does little to cool off Norma as she crosses the steaming black asphalt. She points to her old truck under the partial shade of the stunted sapling. It's only then that a much older woman opens the truck door and cautiously emerges.

Mom is even thinner than her daughter. She greets Norma with a pat on the arm. Mom is dressed in loose, faded shorts reaching below the knee and tired flip-flops. But this is as far as Mom's resemblance to Norma goes.

Mom begins to say something, and almost simultaneously Norma translates for her word for word. Like on the nightly national news when a non-English speaker, microphone in their face, responds to a reporter's questions, a dubbed-over voice takes immediate charge of the audio. But Mom is not speaking a foreign language, she is speaking English. The words forming her sentences are only partially understandable. Mom has no teeth, at least none visible. She is unable, as a result, to form words that make much sense. Norma is her translator.

Over time the absence of teeth has contorted the contours of Mom's face. Slack and wrinkled skin, sliding from her cheekbones in twists and folds, has with age slipped over parts of her mouth and chin. Like many Oklahomans who come to TWBD, Mom has rarely seen a dentist. When she was growing up her family could not afford this luxury. She never had proper dental care.

Norma says Mom wants to help unload the food from the shopping cart. At that exact moment Norma, while translating, pulls aside a torn blue tarp covering the truck bed. She intends to make room for her grocery cart of canned foods and other items that do not need refrigeration. In the bed of the old truck are two lawn chairs, blankets, an assortment of pots and pans, and random household items stuffed carefully into every available space. All the two of them own in this world is in the back of the F-150.

As if realizing she must finally explain their situation, Norma reluctantly says, "The landlord told us this morning we was homeless. I'm not thinking straight."

Norma and Mom are doubling up with friends tonight. After that they do not know where they will go or what they will do. Norma did not, for whatever reason, believe they were going to be evicted. Eviction came as a complete surprise. Rarely is food insecurity the only problem guests at TWBD must face.

This is one of the many vulnerable moments that I witnessed as an ethnographer at a food pantry. I share it as a candid look at the lives of those navigating the health and material consequences of economic hardship. This book goes deeper into lives such as Norma's and her mother's—to connect the problems of individuals to systemic and historical issues, to share firsthand stories of those whose lives take them in and out of poverty, and, not least, to highlight networks of care that help those in need.

Before going further, I would like to share more about myself. I think about points in my own life and family history where my own story regarding poverty could have been different. I also want to share more background because the setting of any story about poverty matters, both the history and the contemporary landscape. The story of poverty in Oklahoma includes both universal themes and those specific to place, and it's worth grounding this book in that conversation as well as my own experiences in studying poverty in the state.

My life has been very different than Norma and Mom's in Hereford, Wells County, Oklahoma. I was born and raised in Oklahoma City. Culbertson Drive was just a pitch and a catch from the old Mercy Hospital, the Oklahoma State Capitol Complex, and the rest of my very small world.[2]

I was born at the old Mercy Hospital, operated at that time by a tiny group of Irish nuns. For almost forty years my father, Dr. Joseph J. Maril, was a physician at Mercy. We, my mother, older brother, and younger sister, always got the best medical care available, including annual checkups at the dentist. But my father, mother, and their parents by no means always had easy lives. At times they faced challenges similar to TWBD guests.

My maternal grandmother, Myrtle Grace Corey, was born in 1890 in neighboring Arkansas. Her family came from very modest means. My grandmother Muzzie, as we called her, at a young age married an older man, an Irish immigrant, who lived in a hand-built log cabin in the woods. He did not treat my grandmother well. His name was R. Luther Senter, and he lived near Rogers, Arkansas, just across the state line in eastern Oklahoma. Muzzie eventually divorced Mr. Senter before moving to Bristow, Oklahoma, a small oil boom town outside of Tulsa. She subsequently married Adin Gray Corey, a Bristow train station master. Adin was born in 1885 in the Territory of Oklahoma, a full twenty-two years before Oklahoma became a state.

During the Great Depression in the 1930s, my father, the son of a struggling second-generation immigrant tailor, managed to graduate through odd jobs and scholarships from two institutions of higher education. Both were located within the same three miles that circumscribed my early childhood. Earning a college degree from Oklahoma City University, the first in his family to do so, did not fulfill his dream. My father's dream, like his father's, was the American Dream. Through hard work and diligence, he sought to achieve a secure economic future for his family, including his own parents and a sister who suffered from polio.

Instead, my father had the misfortunate of graduating from the Oklahoma College of Medicine during the middle of the Great Depression. Many of his patients in his first years of medical practice in Oklahoma City could not afford to pay for his professional care. His occasional stories—he was always a person of very few words—about graduating from medical school during the Depression were not meant to illicit sympathy. Rather, they expressed his frustration over his inability, after so many years of personal sacrifice, to support the financial needs of his parents and sister in addition to his own growing family.

My father's solution was not to give up on medicine or on Oklahoma but to enlist in the U.S. Army. In 1938 he ended up at Fort Sill in Lawton, not far from the Texas border. There he was commissioned a first lieutenant in the U.S. Army Medical Corps. After serving more than five years in Burma during World War II, he finally returned to his family in postwar Oklahoma City. Eventually he became a partner and then medical director of a small industrial medicine clinic. The clinic was on the third floor of the former Medical Arts Building in downtown Oklahoma City, catty-corner to the iconic Skirvin Hotel at One Park Avenue.

Living on Culbertson Drive, the center of my childhood geography, had many advantages that I took for granted. Any time I wanted, day or night, I could slide open my bedroom window to hear the oil rigs pumping twenty-four seven. Or, looking both ways at traffic on Lincoln Boulevard, I could cross the busy street, as I had been taught, to squeeze my face into the chain link fencing that surrounded the massive derricks. I stared in wonder at their enormous, eternally moving parts while breathing in the squalid air surrounding them.

That smell, I was told over and over again as the years passed by, was pure and simply the smell of money. But for me the constant chugging of the oil wells was also the backbeat rhythm to growing up in a tiny piece of Oklahoma City. In my wildest dreams it never occurred to me that most other kids did not live across the street from a producing oil field. Or have enough food to eat. Or receive regular medical care. Or be sent to public and private religious schools that prepared them for a college degree.

Our house on Culbertson Drive was a short distance from my father's downtown medical clinic. From where his clinic once operated for almost fifty years, it is now a quick walk to the Oklahoma City National Memorial. The memorial is a tribute to all those who suffered in 1995 from the bombing by domestic terrorists of the Alfred P. Murrah Federal Building.[3]

Until I began working in 1989 as a professor and researcher in the sociology department at Oklahoma State University, I knew something about my own family history but almost nothing about the history of my own state. That began to change at OSU when, from 1997 to 2007, I was a research associate at the Institute for Research on Poverty (IRP) at the University of Wisconsin-Madison.[4] At first I only knew random facts like that statehood occurred in 1907, or that the capital was stolen from Guthrie and moved overnight to Oklahoma City.[5] My grandfather, Adin Corey, already had filled my head with his stories of his own experiences in Indian Territory and later in Bristow. He had two pistols. One was his "working gun" and the other, which had a pearl handle, was his "going to church gun."

Only at OSU and the IRP, after first discovering the works of Angie Debo, did I begin to learn about a history of Oklahoma other than my own extended family's.[6] At least two generations on both sides of my family had been poor. My family, in those circumstances, resembled many Whites who made up the majority of the Sooners flocking to Indian Territory to join in the land runs.[7] Many of these poor migrants came from Arkansas, as had my family on my mother's side, and other nearby states. Once they registered their free land, they stuck with their claims as long as humanly possible. It did not, however, take many summers of grueling heat and blistering winters before they lost all hope for their row crops, meager livestock, and family gardens. Living dirt poor in sod huts, many eventually walked away from their free land. Regardless of how hard they worked, virgin shortgrass prairie could not sustain their attempts at small-scale farming or ranching.

I gradually learned about the many Native tribes forcibly removed from their lands in other parts of the country to what is now Oklahoma under an overarching federal policy formulated in the 1830s. In return the federal government promised them tribal sovereignty in perpetuity. For the first time I gained an understanding of the Dawes Commission and its legacy, which led to tribal lands being broken up into individual holdings in the late nineteenth century. In 1890 tribal nations were again forced to hand over their communal lands in exchange for individual allotments of 160 acres. Such legal sleights of hand, happening in many ways and on many levels, allowed Native lands to be stolen from them once more.[8]

I also eventually learned that my state, filled by a White majority, nevertheless has among all mainland states the largest percentage of Natives as a proportion of its total population. Almost 10 percent of all Oklahomans identify as belonging to one of thirty-eight tribal nations within the state's boundaries. Many of these same Natives, with notable exceptions like the Osage, who at first enjoyed great wealth after the discovery of oil beneath their allotments, have confronted undue poverty since their "removal" from their original lands. That is because those who by chance finally owned land rich in oil soon returned to poverty after their oil rights were illegally or legally taken from them. At the same time, White violence targeted Natives.

In fact, after the theft of these headrights, Natives in Oklahoma have always been disproportionately poor when compared to the majority of the White population. At the same time, a large percentage of Whites in my home state, when compared to the national average, also failed to escape poverty in the new state. When the U.S. Census first began measuring poverty rates in 1959, poor Whites, poor Natives, and poor Blacks made up a significant proportion of an Oklahoma population facing persistent poverty. Almost one-third of the total population of Oklahoma in 1959 fell below the poverty line.[9]

I was more than surprised when I confronted these historical facts for the first time. Overt violence, fueled by racism and greed, was aimed at Natives and, subsequently, African Americans. While poor Whites did not escape the wrath of those in power, Native Americans and Blacks were continually targeted. For example, among one of the many egregious events in Oklahoma history, unknown to most Oklahomans until three-quarters of a century after it occurred, is the Tulsa race massacre in 1921.[10]

Through hard work and diligence, some Black Oklahomans had created a thriving business and residential neighborhood adjacent to the all-White Tulsa downtown. The Oklahoma Ku Klux Klan did not just encourage the looting and burning of what some called Black Wall Street. Over a period of two days, they systematically murdered Black men, women, and children by the hundreds.

President Biden recently described the Tulsa race massacre and its place in Oklahoma history this way. "For much too long, the history of what took place here was told in silence, cloaked in darkness. But just because history is silent, it doesn't mean that it did not take place. And while darkness can hide much, it erases nothing. It erases nothing. Some injustices are so heinous, so horrific, so grievous they can't be buried, no matter how hard people try."[11]

My first attempt at documenting an alternative interpretation of these frequent silences in Oklahoma history, an alternative interpretation based upon perspectives heretofore excluded, began in earnest in 1993.[12] This research, funded by the Oklahoma Department of Commerce under the guidance of Sherwood O. Washington, eventually resulted in the publication in 2000 of *Waltzing with the Ghost of Tom Joad: Poverty, Myth, and Low-Wage Labor in Oklahoma* by the University of Oklahoma Press.

One prevalent social myth about my home state that I addressed at that time was the unsubstantiated assertion that Oklahoma was not and had never been a state burdened by pervasive and persistent poverty. Another deep-seated myth was that poverty in Oklahoma was primarily a problem found only among minority groups. Prevalent social myths also included the implicit assumption that those who were in poverty suffered from various personal inadequacies that then directly led to their poverty status.[13]

I now understand, twenty-five years on, that poverty in Oklahoma has an intricate and complex history that is in many ways still unexplored. This includes the historical impact upon the poor of elected and appointed officials of both major parties, Democrats and Republicans, who may have acted toward those in poverty in adverse ways.

It is foolish to assert that the bedrock humanity of any state's population, including the poor, can be addressed by a short list of nonnegotiable talking points of the political party holding power. What easily can get lost in the game of drive-through or fly-over conjecture by those who do not know much about the facts of poverty in Oklahoma is this: there remains a decontextualized historical record of poverty and the poor. At the same time, however, there is also the U.S. Census and additional fact-based research to rely on.[14]

The truth about the poor and poverty is available not only through an analysis of these fact-based data but also by listening to the voices of the poor themselves—as well as the voices and actions of the nonpoor. All these stories should be taken seriously.

Equally relevant, there is a history of caring and kindness among many Oklahomans that has largely been neglected or distorted. This is the case in part because politics frequently collides with religiosity. Many Oklahomans are faith-based.[15] One of the fundamental beliefs of Christianity—also clearly expressed in other world religions—is the biblical directive "Thou shalt love thy neighbor as thyself." Caring for the welfare of all may be held and practiced close to the chest, loudly proclaimed for all to see, or fall somewhere in between.

As is true of other Americans, there are a growing number of Oklahomans who choose not to attend a church, synagogue, mosque, or other place of worship (further discussed in chapter 8). But that does not necessarily mean that Oklahomans as a whole, regardless of faith or affinity to one political party or the other, do not or have never harbored love and deep concern for those in poverty. As a direct result, these Oklahomans have acted in positive ways to aid those below the poverty line.

It is also crucial to acknowledge Oklahoma's political conservatism and realize that it should never be free of legitimate scrutiny.[16] This political conservatism, for example, would currently appear to find considerable solace in its Christian faith. Christians are or can be, however, very diverse in both beliefs and actions. It seems otherwise only if one never takes the time to consider the remarkable history of this state and its diverse population.

Unfortunately, anyone who questions the various mainstream pseudo-certainties revolving around the poor and poverty, including Oklahoma's own Angie Debo, may become suspect themselves. Debo consistently faced public criticism and professional consequences for her scholarship. In 1994 I was warned off my research on the poor and poverty. At the time, I had a small role in the Mississippi trial of the murderer of Medgar Evers.[17] The personal threat came from a caller who identified himself as an elected state government official at the Oklahoma State Capitol Complex in Oklahoma City. He believed that my recent pro bono work in Mississippi was a waste of Oklahoma tax dollars. Contrary to this assertion, I had fulfilled all my duties and responsibilities at Oklahoma State University before at my own expense driving to Panola County, Mississippi.

The state government official who called me at my office in the OSU Department of Sociology told me he would make sure that I would be fired if I continued my research. He said that his people were going to talk with the chair of my department, my supervisor—and they did. They also said they would talk to the dean of the College of Arts and Sciences about my job status.

I had gone to Panola County to contribute to the legal team of Ed Peters, district attorney of Jackson. The trial was moved to Panola County because the racial demographics of the county in the 1990s was equally split between White and Black residents.[18] District Attorney Peter's efforts were part of a last-ditch attempt to bring to justice the alleged murderer of the civil rights activist before important witnesses passed. Evers had been vigorously organizing for the NAACP in the 1960s by encouraging Mississippi Blacks to demand the right to vote in all public elections and to have equal access to public education. Unlike other Mississippi counties, Panola had about the same percentage of Blacks and Whites who could serve as jurors.

An active member of the KKK, who will go unnamed, shot Evers in the back with a deer rifle. Evers bled to death in the arms of his wife and children. Juries composed of Whites in two previous trials of the defendant in the early 1960s could not reach a verdict in spite of an abundance of evidence.[19] As a result, the perpetrator of this heinous crime remained a free man for three decades.[20] During that time, the defendant became an active recruiter for the KKK and frequently spoke to large groups. The success of his career in the Klan was to some degree based upon his reputation for getting away with the murder of a civil rights advocate with a national reputation. There is, however, no statute of limitations on murder.

Barely a year after the defendant in the Mississippi trial in which I participated was convicted by a jury of his peers for the murder of Evers, others took up the mantle of domestic terrorism sponsored by the KKK and clandestine groups on the far right of the political spectrum. The morning of April 19, 1995, while working on *Waltzing with the Ghost of Tom Joad* from my desk at my home, I heard the blast of the truck bomb triggered by domestic terrorists. In downtown Oklahoma City, not far from my father's medical clinic, the bomb killed 169 Oklahomans, including nineteen children.[21]

The passage of time, a full quarter of a century since the publication of *Waltzing with the Ghost of Tom Joad*, now provides a unique opportunity to observe what changes, if any, have occurred with regard to the poor and poverty in Oklahoma. The first objective of this book is to document and analyze in rich detail the lives of poor Oklahomans from their own perspective. This is accomplished in part by listening to the poor who come to Hereford's Thy Will Be Done. Using the participant-observation method at the pantry over a period of three years, my colleague and I collected the perspectives of 146 individuals. The interviews and personal observations that appear in these chapters are drawn from these efforts.

The second objective is to examine how different institutions, including food pantries, government programs, and faith-based organizations, may shape and impact the lives of those in poverty. These ways may be both intended and unintended.

With my third objective I focus upon how systemic structural barriers and opportunities directly affect the lives of the poor. These structural barriers may include the stereotypes and other abundant and intentionally misleading information perpetuated about the poor and poverty in Oklahoma.

My fourth objective is to explore underemphasized or previously ignored private faith-based organizations, including private philanthropic efforts. Doing so may reveal new perspectives on how the poor can be served and persistent poverty reduced. TWBD is not the only faith-based organization created in Oklahoma to mitigate the inequities the poor may face on a daily basis.

Autoethnography, more than thirty years of lived experience in Oklahoma, also significantly impacts my research into the poor and poverty in my home state.[22] Nuns like those I knew at Mercy Hospital in Oklahoma City, for example, were vital contributors to improving the health status of those who historically were not given access to the same kind of medical care provided for White Oklahomans.

In addition to the qualitative methodologies suggested, I also utilize a longitudinal quantitative analysis of U.S. Census data to establish fact-based research about the poor and poverty in Oklahoma. Other federal and governmental documents along with studies based upon census data contribute to this work. These fact-based research studies directly address, for example, the relationship between poverty and the well-being of children.[23]

A historical approach to this research serves to contextualize the findings of the census. To this end, I consider the poor and poverty in Oklahoma within an alternative historical perspective. The groundbreaking works of Debo and others have already seriously challenged the dominant historical paradigm of state history. Recent research on the Osage along with continued research into the Tulsa massacres,[24] for example, also suggest, in conjunction with reinvestigations of other historical events, the advantage of including perspectives other than those traditionally relied upon.

A reframing of the ways inequities were confronted by the poor also must include a consideration of the role of political corruption in Oklahoma, as suggested by Debo's research. It is certainly clear that political corruption can and has impacted the poor and poverty in Oklahoma.[25]

These various methodological approaches, which include both inductive qualitative and deductive quantitative research tools, provide a strong foundation for understanding the poor and poverty in Oklahoma. For those interested, the research approach employed is described in greater detail in a separate section.

My research seeks to follow in the tradition of such work as *Nickel and Dimed* by Barbara Ehrenreich, *The Poor Pay More* by David Caplovitz, *Worlds Apart* by Cynthia M. Duncan, and the groundbreaking *Let Us Now Praise Famous Men* by James Agee and Walker Evans. But in contrast to these studies, the present research is buttressed by the use of diverse methods similar to those employed in *Evicted: Poverty and Profit in the American City* by Matthew Desmond. Regrettably, few studies by social scientists using these methods have focused upon the topic of the poor and poverty in Oklahoma.

I begin this new research with two facts I encountered in a preliminary glance at the most recent U.S. Census data on the poor and poverty in Oklahoma. The first is that one out of every six Oklahomans is poor. The second, even more problematic, is that one out of every five children in Oklahoma falls below the poverty line.[26]

The voices of those who are poor in Oklahoma need to be heard, understood, and their lived experiences in poverty seriously considered—voices like those of Norma and her mother, who have little food between them and, after one night, have no safe place to stay. My promise to the reader is that these stories of Oklahomans are told unequivocally, as are stories of the diverse efforts by different communities of care to come to the aid of Oklahomans in poverty.

1

Thy Will Be Done

In every child who is born, under no matter what circumstances, and of no matter what parents, the potentiality of the human race is born again.
—James Agee and Walker Evans

Downtown Hereford has changed in the past quarter century, for the better. Refurbished storefronts replace vacant stores. New restaurants stick out like sore thumbs. New branch banks capture the eye even as renamed branch banks, as if not wanting to seem stodgy, show off their remodeled exteriors. The major downtown churches, Baptist, Methodist, Presbyterian, Catholic, Episcopalian, Evangelical, as well all the others throughout the city, appear as vital as ever. In Hereford, most people who want a place of worship have one.

The downtown makeover is nothing, however, when compared to the growth of the business district half a mile to the west. A Walmart Supercenter holds court, buttressed by a new Staples, a Big Lots, a Lowes, and a state chain called Homeland Food Grocery and Pharmacy. Two Family Dollars and one Dollar Tree are tucked between strip malls. Nearby lurk two new Starbucks and an inaugural Panera Bread. This list does not count the four new car washes surrounded by the usual assortment of fast-food chains. But there are also new tire shops, change-your-oil outlets, and five convenience stores. Still standing is a former Holiday Inn, which at least for the moment has escaped the general Oklahoma tendency to tear down a building when it starts to show its age. Somewhat awkwardly, this old Holiday Inn has been transformed into a private technology center.

A brand-new Good Will Thrift Store stands off by itself. It hides on a quiet back street behind all the hustle and bustle of the traffic and shoppers from Hereford and Wells County. Eleven medical marijuana dispensaries manage, even though they are sometimes small in size, to stand out in this retail hodgepodge.[1] Apparently there are at least nine more dispensaries. All have catchy names. Since the state legislature made medical marijuana legal in Oklahoma in 2018, there are now more than 2,200 cannabis stores in the state.

The Strip, which lies directly across from Hereford State College, looks as if the wave of a magical wand turned the dive bars into restaurants with edible food. Other stores cater to the products and styles and brands college students must have—running shoes, casual clothes, and tanning salons galore. Fast-food chains predominate, but there are also mom-and-pop Japanese, Indian, and Thai hangouts that would have found few patrons in previous years. College students now consume sushi and poke. There is even craft beer.

Hereford, of course, was once an all-Bud town. Wells County has an alcohol consumption rate of 14 percent.[2] Tanker trucks once regularly serviced the bars on the Strip after the party-hearty student and alumni football weekends and other frequent sporting events gave way to the drudgery of Monday morning classes. Hereford State men and women who did not choose Budweiser as their beer of choice were often ridiculed, labeled effete.

Times change. Elsewhere in Hereford there are new housing developments for those who can afford it, condos, more new strip malls, and new and refurbished public and charter schools. Hereford has, in sum, all the other bobbles frequently accompanying rapid economic growth and development—even gated communities behind which the brick and stone of expensive homes, at least by Hereford standards, roast sedately under a summer's sun.

Hereford is one of only a handful of small Oklahoma cities of fifty thousand or more that appears to prosper as never before. But how has this palpable prosperity benefited those at the bottom of the economic ladder?

There has always been another Hereford, an often invisible side many residents and most nonresidents do not know much about, or would not necessarily care much about if they did know. Since poverty statistics were first collected by the U.S. Census at the end of the 1950s, Wells County has consistently ranked close to the top one-third poorest of all seventy-seven Oklahoma counties. Wells is by no means the poorest county in one of the poorest states. That distinction historically belongs to the same group, more or less: Greer, Adair, Okfuskee, Pushmataha, Atoka, and Cherokee, with a few other counties sometimes joining them.

The census defines poverty by income thresholds varying by family size and composition. The focus is always upon a family's total income. Children who live in households where the income is below certain levels are defined as poor.

Over the years, Hereford has held the dubious distinction of having one of the highest poverty rates in Wells County, almost triple the state's average poverty rate. But Hereford's relatively high rate is somewhat misleading. Students not living in the dorms on campus, many thousands of them who are not otherwise employed, may inflate the Hereford poverty statistics because of the way the census, given its current methods of collecting population data, defines residency requirements. That said, the poverty in Hereford is still much above the national average, so much so that the rumor, verified by my interviews, is that some Hereford State students and their families face food insecurity.

The formal definition of food insecurity as defined by the U.S. Department of Agriculture is "lack of access, at times, to enough food for an active, healthy life for all household members and limited or uncertain availability of nutritionally adequate foods."[3] In Oklahoma, 13.8 percent of all households experienced food insecurity from 2019 to 2021. This ranked Oklahoma as the state with the fifth-highest food insecurity in the country.[4]

While there is real poverty in Hereford that should not be discounted, this poverty may be different in some ways from the poverty found throughout the rest of Wells County. That is because Wells County has several very small communities and towns. The rural poor may face somewhat different challenges than those living in urban areas. Real needs of the rural poor may have greater disadvantageous impact than in more urbanized areas.

Unless you know where to look, Hereford's poverty is not at once evident. One big clue about the poor and poverty in Hereford is just across the railroad tracks on the west side of the city. An afternoon crowd of about seventy adults and twenty children wait patiently in line to gain entrance to Thy Will Be Done, the only food pantry in Wells County. The line of humanity seeking entry snakes at least seventy-five feet around the metal buildings housing the pantry. Everyone in line, including children and the elderly, are doing their best, like Norma and her mom, to hide from the full brunt of the summer sun. To pass the time, many in line are talking with others waiting for the doors to open. They also smoke cigarettes while they wait.

By the time the hands of the clock in the waiting room reach 4:30, these Oklahomans below the poverty line have left TWBD with plastic bags filled with food they selected from the open shelves. On this weekday afternoon in this one Oklahoma county, more than eighty Oklahomans choose food from the shelves of TWBD. But the total number of those who are provided food they otherwise cannot afford is much larger. TWBD on this one afternoon in Hereford provides food to not just the guests who come to its doors but to all qualified members of their households who are in need.

The line of adults, children, and the elderly spilled out earlier on this day from the doors of the main lobby and down three concrete steps to the level of the asphalt parking lot. Only a metal roof at the entrance provides shade to those who arrive early. Most are silent in the heat but begin to talk again as soon as they are able to stand under a patch of shade.

One lady dressed in long yellow shorts and T-shirt says, "I got here at 12:30."

"Why?" The prominent hand-drawn sign on TWBD's front door reads in a clear script, "Today Open at One-Thirty P.M."

She answers without hesitation, "Cause I don't want the choices to run out. You get better choices if you get here before the crowd."

Arriving an hour and thirty minutes before the door officially opens, she is still tenth in line. But even better, the shade of an awning protects her from the heat until TWBD opens. She knows she will sit in a comfortable seat in an air-conditioned outer lobby before her name is called. Unless the weather is really bad—triple-digit temperatures never count—there is always a crowd when TWBD opens its doors.

The line curls around the corner of the light blue, windowless Butler Building. Frozen foods and the fresh produce are kept chilled inside a portion of the building. Dry goods are stacked and stored elsewhere. At TWBD there is always enough food available in the walk-in freezers and storage rooms to restock empty shelves. They may temporarily run out of different brands or choices of food to choose from, and fresh produce goes fast, but there is always enough food for everyone. Always.

What many of those who are poor like best is that there are no strings attached to receiving this food. Plus, they treat you like you are a human being. For five years that is the way it has been. Today will be no exception.

Everyone, as suggested, is a guest at TWBD—not an applicant, not a client, not some other assigned label that may connote intended or unintended bias. After initially filling out some forms from the staff and being approved, every guest receives a TWBD card. Guests are then encouraged to select the food they want from off the shelves in a freshly painted, cheerful space resembling a compact grocery. But at TWBD the food is free and the staff are much nicer. It is as simple as that.

There is plenty of food for purchase in Hereford. But guests admitted to TWBD cannot afford the prices at the nearest convenience stores or even the more budget-friendly prices at the big chains like Walmart.

Hereford is not an example of food scarcity. There is plenty of food for purchase if you can afford it. Instead, this is food insecurity. These guests simply do not have the money to feed themselves and their households—not until they receive their next check from their jobs, from the Social Security Administration or the Veterans Administration, a pension, a private retirement fund, or from government assistance programs, including Social Security Disability Insurance, that require significant proof of economic need.

As soon as guests are ushered into TWBD, they are randomly paired with a volunteer standing in a short line off to one side, each behind a shopping cart. The volunteer approaches a guest with a smile and a few words of introduction. Sometimes the guests want to push the grocery cart themselves, sometimes they want the volunteer to do it so they can walk in front of the cart and closely inspect the food before they make their final choices.

First-time guests are always told by a staff member in the front lobby how TWBD works. They are reminded again of this same information as a volunteer greets and welcomes them. Frequently a guest is accompanied by a partner, children, friends, parents, neighbors, roommates, or possibly someone who as a favor gave them a ride. Transportation to TWBD can be a problem.

The amount of food each guest and their household receives is based on information on the three-by-five card they hold in their hand. The cards are color coded. Each card summarizes relevant information about the guest, including the size of their household. The amount of food guests may choose is always in direct proportion to the size of their household and any other special considerations, such as dietary requirements. Additionally, seniors sixty-five years of age or older are entitled to a certain number of frozen, prepared meals. Almost all the guests agree that these meals are particularly tasty, easy to prepare, and nutritious. Not surprisingly, these meals are in high demand and run out quickly compared to other items.

Volunteers make the guests feel welcome, answer questions, and help them in any way possible. Many volunteers already know the guests because they volunteer regularly. This is important because guests may have a physical disability, for example, a cognitive impairment, requiring special attention and consideration. Such information is usually either on the card the volunteer receives or is passed along by word-of-mouth from a staff member or experienced volunteer. There is an honest attempt at TWBD to determine the needs of each guest. At the same time, there is an honest attempt to provide the free food with kindness and consideration.

The guests want to pick the food they most need. The volunteers, when all is said and done, want the guests to be satisfied with the foods they select. Sometimes, not always, a bond develops by the end of the shopping, a bond between the guest and the volunteer. It is a temporary bond, but nevertheless a bond that can be renewed when the guest revisits TWBD. New guests are tentative, wary—returning guests less anxious, knowing they will not be treated badly. Those who are poor have had more than their fair share of derogatory or humiliating run-ins with service providers.

Bonds between guests and volunteers can deepen when they share their common life experiences, whether good or bad—a sick child, an unreasonable landlord, the changing Oklahoma weather, ridiculously high medical and utility bills, escalating rents. And sky-high food prices. All these common experiences and more create a glue that binds the volunteer to the individual who takes the product from the shelf and places it gingerly in the cart. Volunteers who enjoy their temporary job—and most do or they would not be there—commiserate with guests even as they provide tidbits of information about the food selections, including their favorite recipes.

From the volunteer's perspective, every guest is a little different—or sometimes totally different and, therefore, more interesting. Some guests want precise information about each and every choice they have to make. Others not so much. A few guests make it known from the git-go that they already understand the system in place and just want to be left alone to do their own shopping.

In all cases the volunteer's task is to help guests in any way possible. In whatever way volunteers choose to help guests, their help, even if in error or frivolous, is more often appreciated than not. Volunteers in turn feel good at the end of their shift because they have helped someone, even if in limited ways. Helping becomes its own reward.

Volunteers are not trained or educated social workers, they are just ordinary people: senior citizens with time on their hands, teenagers who sometimes act as if they are busy 24/7, college students, homemakers, working parents on their days off, some church members motivated by their faith, some not. The volunteers who return every week or month or during their vacations return because they enjoy what they are doing. It seems to make them feel good.

Some guests want a lot of positive attention but, at the other end, some are lost in their own needs and wants. Others appreciate a sympathetic listener. What is most clear is that smiles are exchanged and shared laughter is common between guests and volunteers. The children at TWBD run around having a good time. In the end, guests leave with carts filled with food they themselves selected and affirmation, even if unwanted, that no one has judged them. At TWBD there is a shared kindness.

Before guests at TWBD begin to make their selections on this particular afternoon, five minutes before the outside doors open, Janice, the director, switches on one of her favorite tunes. Janice hopes the music will make the guests feel more comfortable and, at the same time, possibly inspire the volunteers. Over Bruce Springsteen's "Born in the U.S.A." those around Janice strain to hear what she has to say through her white COVID mask. Today she is the only person among all the volunteers, staff, and researchers wearing a mask. As it turns out by the end of the afternoon, only two of all the guests wore masks.

Two volunteers, one young, one not, White dance to Bruce's powerful beat. If Janice or anyone else interprets the darker meanings embedded in Springsteen's lyrics, it does nothing to quell their enthusiasm or that of the two dancers.

Visibly pleased as she looks around her, eyes sparkling from behind her mask, Janice places herself at the center of the modest circle of eight volunteers. The volunteers reach forward toward the center of the circle to cover Janice's raised right hand, the same as at the start of any NBA game or Hereford T-ball practice. "On the count of three," Janice says above Bruce's loud beat as she begins to count, "one, two . . .".

They know this routine. Right arms extended as best they can, the circle of volunteers shout with an undeniable zeal, "Thy Will Be Done!"

The Guests

During my first year of studying at Thy Will Be Done, in 2019, a wide variety of individuals and their families were guests. Compared to Norma and Mom, Carol walks into the food pantry with outward confidence and aplomb. If truth be told, Carol looks as if she parked by accident at TWBD. In her late forties, she wears her business clothes well. Fashionable slacks, matching top, and sensible shoes nevertheless belie what Carol now faces. The late-model car in the parking lot, freshly washed, is a first clue. It does not belong to Carol; instead, one of her only friends in Hereford lent it to her just for the afternoon.

Carol is having a run of bad luck. Just two weeks ago, she says, "My car was totaled in an accident. I called the guy at the insurance agency. He told me I should just forget about my car." Fortunately, there were emergency responders already close by when a Hereford State student crossed several lanes of traffic to T-bone Carol's car. Carol is positive the student was either texting or talking to a friend when the student slammed into her two-year-old Ford Focus. The first responders had to use the jaws of life to free Carol from the wreckage.

Carol says she now regrets turning down their offer to transport her to the ER at Hereford Hospital, because the next morning she woke to pain in her back and neck which, two weeks later, has still not subsided. Yet Carol never visits a doctor, not only because she does not want to hear a bad diagnosis but also because she does not have the money to pay for a doctor visit in the first place. Carol feels, absent a medical diagnosis, that she has suffered some kind of injuries that are disappearing of their own accord.

Carol's insurance adjuster gives her the bad news over the phone. Her car is completely totaled. But Carol still owes three years of monthly payments on the balance of her car loan. Even more serious, Carol now has no way to commute from Hereford to her work in Edmond, a part of the Oklahoma City metroplex. When the owner of the three retail stores Carol manages realizes that Carol has no reliable transportation from Hereford, he fires her. She does not bother to describe her feelings about her long-time employer who would kick her when she is already down. After more than ten years of working at the same steady job, Carol suddenly finds herself in a predicament for which she is not prepared.

Beneath the surface confidence, Carol is flat out embarrassed to death to be a guest at the food pantry. Never in her adult life has she needed food she could not pay for. On top of that, she now worries about losing the two-bedroom apartment she leases in Hereford. She mentions no partner, children, or any other family she can rely on—not even in the short term. Carol has few friends in Hereford, with the exception of the one who lent her the car so she could drive to TWBD. Her best friends live in Edmond and Oklahoma City but seem to have abandoned her when she needs them the most. Carol is as stunned about her bad luck as if her car accident happened yesterday, not two weeks in the past.

TWBD can do little for Carol except provide her food for the next several days. The best Janice can do is to direct her to Hereford's local branch of the Oklahoma State Department of Human Services. It is doubtful that Carol will take Janice's advice seriously, at least not until she sees that she has absolutely no other options. That time is fast approaching.

Mona and her family are in a different kind of tough situation and, unlike Carol, have been facing it for months on end. It started when Mona left her home in Florida to take care of close family members here. She believes she did the right thing in coming to Oklahoma, but now as the months pass her decision has left her and her household with fewer and fewer good choices.

Mona's information card says she has a household of four.[5] But that information distorts the real situation. It is a much bigger problem than feeding four people on a very limited budget, as if that were not enough. For starters, one of those people in her household is her niece, Maureen. Besides Maureen, Mona also brought along her daughter Stephanie. Stephanie is seven years old and full of energy—boundless energy that she channels into dancing her way up and down the TWBD aisles. Stephanie's favorite food, says Mona, is sweets. While shopping, she lets Stephanie choose Rice Krispies treats, Halloween cupcakes, white and chocolate marshmellows, and chocolate milk. Mona also promises, when they get home, to share a slice of the chocolate cake she chose with Stephanie and her brother Jordan, age eight.

It is not clear if Mona is the mother of Stephanie and the grandmother of Jordan or has some other close relationship to them. She herself has gray hair and colors it dark brown. In any case, Mona is homeschooling both Stephanie and Jordan and is very proud of their progress to date. She says, "Homeschooling is better [than public schools] because they learn more and more of the right things."

Mona owns a chihuahua puppy named Big Bit. Big Bit sleeps in the same bed with Brooklyn, her husband, and Mona. Big Bit is very protective of the family. According to Mona, while she shops Big Bit and Brooklyn are both watching after Jordan to make sure he stays out of trouble.

Despite these family relationships and responsibilities, Mona is not shopping at TWBD for Mona, Brooklyn, Stephanie, or Jordan. In fact, she is shopping for her older sister, who is seventy-four. The husband of Mona's sister, although much younger than his wife, died last winter. Mona and Brooklyn traveled up from Florida with Stephanie and Jordan to take care of Mona's sister and Maureen, Mona's niece. They felt a serious family obligation. What else could Mona do?

It has not been easy for the two adult caregivers from Florida, Mona and Brooklyn, who have limited resources between them. But they had no choice in coming because her sister cannot take care of herself. Maureen, Mona's niece, cannot be a caregiver because she spends most of her time in a wheelchair. Maureen, who is possibly obese, also has diabetes.

The total number of members of Mona's household is not just the four individuals approved by TWBD but actually six people. Mona's sister and Maurice qualify at TWBD because they are residents of Wells County. Stephanie and Jordan qualify because they are children. But Mona and Brooklyn do not have Oklahoma photo IDs, or driver's licenses, or proof of residency in Oklahoma such as a checking account.

Mona is up front about her household's precarious economic situation. She repeatedly expresses her gratitude to TWBD for the food she takes from the shelves. Loading her car with food, she is very honest about the problems she now faces. In no way does she complain about the pantry qualifying only four family members to receive food rather than six. She simply says, "We really need help. We really appreciate your help."

Everyone who walks through the doors of TWBD has their own stories to tell. No two stories are the same, although certain themes among the dilemmas the guests confront begin to emerge. For instance, Nick, Jane's husband, has no intention of joining his wife while she shops for food they will both eat. Nick, in fact, never leaves his chair in the front lobby. Jane has been married to Nick for a long time. She knows good and well that Nick has no intention of retreating to their truck in the parking lot, because it is far cooler inside the lobby. Plus, running the truck, which he would have to do to take advantage of the air conditioning is, he tells her, the same as burning money. Jane knows Nick believes grocery shopping is women's work.

Without a doubt, Jane is ready to shop. She is dressed in a new Hereford State T-shirt, black jeans, and sparkles on both her shoes. A matching cap covers her long brown hair. Nick, on the other hand, skips any fashion pretense, a crown of uncombed shoulder length gray hair a backdrop to a clean-shaven face. His unruly hair is in the same league as his nondescript blue T-shirt and patched jeans—not the kind that are or were recently in fashion on campus at Hereford State, but ancient Levi's with large patches covering real holes. From beneath these patched jeans peek expensive oxford shoes shined to perfection.

Jane has visited TWBD several times before and knows exactly how she wants to shop this venue. But first she wants to tell anyone who will listen how proud she is of her two grown children and her two grandchildren, one ten, the other fourteen. Her real "babies," she also offers, are her two dogs, the oldest more than fourteen years of age. This dog, which she does not name, is her favorite. It's a combination Jack Russell terrier and corgi.

Not surprisingly, Jane chooses each of her food items decisively. Finding bacon, which is not always kept in stock, she states that it is one of Nick's favorite foods. Nick will be overjoyed to see it in their refrigerator. Sad to say, by the time we get there Jane is disappointed that there are no fresh tomatoes in the produce section. Jane also laments the certitude that, if she had arrived earlier to get in line before TWBD opened, then fresh tomatoes would have been hers for the choosing. But for reasons Jane does not disclose, they arrive just before TWBD is set to close. I hear Jane sigh, "No BLTs." She is accepting of the situation, but not pleased.

After Nick unloads their groceries into their F-150, this one white and carefully washed, the heat makes talking and much else difficult. Nevertheless, Jane expresses genuine gratitude for the food she selected. Nick, who has remained completely silent to this point, is surprisingly gracious.

Marla's attention, unlike that of many other TWBD guests, is not focused upon her children, her parents, or her siblings. At fifty-six, she is proud as punch of her two grandchildren. The oldest is two years, the youngest barely one. Shopping for a household of five for only the third time at TWBD, Marla is understandably full of questions. For one, she loves pancakes but somehow always fails at making them look good enough to eat. She asks for an opinion.

A Hereford native, Marla already enjoys shopping the produce section at TWBD. It is her favorite section because she appreciates the different greens available. She is also pleased that there is still ice cream available. And she is extremely pleased when she puts size six diapers, two cans of Enfamil, and two half-gallons of milk in her shopping cart.

Today the only bad news is that both her grandchildren must stay home from day care because they have bad cases of diarrhea. Her husband, Jermaine, is keeping an eye on them. Marla is worried about her grandkids.

"Are you going to take them to the doctor?"

"No."

A doctor is out of the question because they do not have the money. More to the point, Marla is not aware of any over-the-counter medications that might help her grandchildren. And even if she was, there is no money to pay for it.

When Marla calls Jermaine to tell him she is ready to be picked up, she gets his answering machine. Undeterred, she ends up calling several other friends, but again with no luck. Worse still, no one she knows who has a car is available to pick her up. After finishing her shopping, Marla takes a seat on the steps leading up to the front door of TWBD. Well protected from the hot sun by the awning, she crams her plastic bags filled with food next to her legs. After TWBD closes for the day, Marla still sits on those same steps waiting for Jermaine.

Women are not the only poor people who come to TWBD for food. Although far fewer than females, there are also male guests. While males are less likely to participate directly in the selection of food, there are exceptions. Harold is one of the exceptions.

At first glance Harold easily passes for a student at Hereford State in his stylish red shorts, a Hereford State T-shirt, and leather sandals. But, unlike many Hereford State male students, he is clean shaven and proudly wears the COVID haircut his wife gave him.

Harold is most concerned with saving every cent he earns. But regardless of his hard work, thriftiness, and his wife's full-time duties at home as caregiver while her husband works, Harold is still not earning enough money. He cannot at this time put enough food on the table. And borrowing money, even if it is from his family, is out of the question.

Since Harold began this job, his mixed feelings have deepened about his employer, a national manufacturer. They pay him an unusual wage in Oklahoma, more than twice the state minimum wage. In Oklahoma the minimum wage, which has not changed since 2009, is $7.25 an hour.[6]

Harold is the only wage earner in his family of three. He and his wife, Regina, decided that she stay home to care for their two-year-old baby. It is not that Harold is not grateful for his twelve-hour shifts six days a week. He's working more hours than most in Wells County and getting paid more than twice as much per hour than the average minimum wage worker in the state. But it is not enough.

Harold admits there are downsides to his job despite the pay. One downside to his job, Harold says, is that his work is "really hot and exhausting." The heat in the factory needed to produce household flooring products is the major reason he has no beard and keeps his hair very short.

Even though Harold is making a high wage by local standards, he cannot afford to pay all of the family bills on time. A COVID economy, he says with enthusiasm, has created a large demand for the products his employer manufactures. His job is very secure. The Hereford plant cannot produce enough to meet the demand generated around the country. Demand for flooring, according to Harold, is at an all-time high.

Harold feels he has both job security and is earning a reasonable wage. But serious financial problems remain. He and his wife rent a two-bedroom apartment. They would have liked to have enough saved by now to put a down payment on a home of their own—again with two bedrooms, allowing a separate room for their baby. So far, they have not been able to save much for the down payment.

One problem is the price of Hereford rentals. Rental costs in Hereford are almost as high as those in Oklahoma City and Tulsa. Local businesspersons in Hereford own rental units, but the majority in the Hereford housing market is owned by a limited number of investors. Some of these investors are local, some not.

Over time, Hereford State students have become a very profitable and guaranteed revenue stream. At the same time, their economic impact has created a higher cost of living for everyone else in Hereford who cannot afford to own their own home, like Harold and Regina. Students and others associated with the state college who require housing have become one of the city's major industries. Hereford State, the largest employer in town, provides not only jobs for its own employees but significant revenue to those fortunate enough to own rental property.

This is a very different economic terrain than the one faced by veterans returning from World War II in 1945. Their educations, including housing, were federally subsidized because of their wartime military service. Unemployment insurance was also offered, all under the G.I. Bill of 1944.[7] After the war, Hereford State built very basic housing for the needs of returning GIs and their families. The rental housing that existed off campus in Hereford was then, accounting for inflation, far less a drag on monthly student budgets than in the 2020s.

At the same time, expectations of what constitutes appropriate student housing have also changed. Returning GIs and their families did not require or expect granite countertops in their kitchens. In some Hereford apartment rentals today, students have, besides space for a queen- or king-size bed, granite countertops, big-screen TVs, in-house gyms, billiard tables, swimming pools, and beach sand volleyball courts.

To Harold and Regina these amenities seem excessive. Before coming this afternoon to TWBD, Harold thought about going to Hereford's new Goodwill Store to buy his food. He finally decided there were people who needed the Goodwill food, clothing, and other services far more than he and his family. So, he returned to TWBD.

Harold does not consider his family poor. He knows during certain times of the year he and Regina do not have the money they need to pay for necessities, such as at the end of the academic year when some Hereford apartment owners require a one-month deposit from renters for the following year to reserve their apartment, a cleaning deposit of a month's rent, or both. In theory, the latter will be returned to renters after their apartment has been professionally cleaned by the owner's staff or a subcontractor at the end of the year.

Harold can be self-critical about his relationship with money. He says that, although there is a Braums store down the street from them, he cannot afford the prices at this regional chain, especially for eggs and milk. Recently he made the mistake of spending some of his hard-earned paycheck on eggs and a few other items at Braums. Then, Harold admits, he left the eggs and other groceries in his car for six hours under a hot sun. It was a stupid and wasteful thing to do, but not intentional. He says, "Next time I won't forget the eggs."

Harold's biggest complaint is not about his wages. Today is Harold's day off, his one day out of seven each week when he does not have to go to work. He would like to spend his one day off with his wife and toddler, but here he is at TWBD.

Harold and Regina have talked about finding a less expensive apartment. But they need a two-bedroom. Two-bedroom units in Hereford, apart from those in the trailer courts on the edges of town and the dilapidated neighborhood where the invisible poor live, are in short supply and way over budget.

They have talked about Regina taking a part-time or even full-time job. What stops them cold is that child care, which would free Regina to work during the day, is not a reasonable option. The certified day care centers in Hereford are just too expensive. Child care is also difficult to find.

Regina also knows that, at least at first, she would have to start out at close to the minimum wage, $7.25 an hour. Not much, if any, of her income would be left over from her job even if they were lucky enough to find an available opening for their toddler at a certified child care facility. Neither Harold's and Regina's parents live close enough to Hereford to seriously consider taking care of their grandchild on a regular basis.

On his one day off, Harold finds himself shopping alone at TWBD while Regina stays at home with their baby. As with this decision, they do not see in general what other real choices they have.

Andrew, another frequent guest at TWBD, faces very different challenges. First and foremost, he lives by himself.

"What kind of work do you do?"

"I'm a handy-man," says Andrew.

"I know there is a big demand right now for the work you do."

"Yeah. Worked yesterday. I got a herniated disc. Got it when I was fourteen."

Unlike many of the guests at TWBD and the Hereford population in general, Andrew appears to be in excellent physical health. He looks strong and fit at twenty-five, the last person walking the aisles to have a herniated disc.

Andrew is not shy. He got it "pulling a fence post out of the ground. Yesterday I was putting in a new gas heater for a woman so it's bothering me. She lives in a trailer, and I had to lift it up, then walk out with it. Down some steps. I'm feeling it today."

As we talk, a woman dressed in dark slacks and heavy makeup comes up behind Andrew. She gently pats him on the back.

Andrew says, as he reaches for two cans of mixed vegetables, "Hi Mom." His mother remains silent, gives him a brief smile.

"How you doing?" Andrew asks her. Now his mother is patting him again, this time on the shoulder again. Andrew turns toward her, pats her lightly on her arm, then turns away again. Andrew's mother comments on his food choices in his cart, agreeing with some of what she sees, chiding him about other selections. Regardless of what she says, Andrew agrees with her.

I push Andrew's grocery cart out to his fifteen-year-old red Honda Accord in the parking lot. His mother comes out five minutes later. In spite of the heat, Andrew stands by his car waiting patiently for her to appear. Unasked, he says before she appears that they do not live under the same roof, but obviously she and Andrew have a close relationship.

Although I thought I turned my phone ringer off before starting my shift at TWBD, it rings loudly in the heavy air.

"Shit" is what comes out in frustration. I apologize for my phone, explaining that when I am teaching in the classroom I always tell my students to turn their phones off. But every once and a while my phone goes off, making me feel really stupid.

"You ever have that happen?"

"Yeah," says Andrew, eyes sparkling. "Happened while I was in court."

Unlike Andrew, Larry lives with his mother. It is the last thing he wants to do. He thought he never would have to. Larry must depend on TWBD because he had an unexpected, life-changing medical issue. He was working at Walmart when he had his heart attack. After finding out Larry had a heart attack, Walmart, according to Larry, fired him.

With pride in his voice, Larry describes how he learned that Walmart was not allowed by law to fire him because of his heart attack. And when he tried to return to Walmart after his heart attack, Larry says, he was told that they would never hire him again. According to Larry, once all the litigation was finally settled, the manager who allegedly fired him was himself fired.

Since then, Larry has been receiving Supplemental Security Income (SSI) because his total income and assets, in spite of his version of the Walmart settlement, are not enough to provide him basic needs including food. The SSI program is designed only for those with very limited assets who are disabled, blind, or sixty-five years of age or older.[8] Before they are accepted for SSI, applicants are required to provide a variety of documents verifying their economic status.

With scraggly shoulder-length gray hair, oversize jeans riding low on his hips, and nondescript tennis shoes, Larry at forty-six has his own distinctive look. His 2008 T-shirt, the date imprinted near one armpit, is from a Native American casino named "Seven Clans." Seven Clans Casino, owned by the Red Lake Band of Chippewa Indians, is in Red Lakes, Minnesota. Larry cannot be mistaken for any of the thousands of students who daily trudge across the Hereford State campus carrying textbooks and a laptop in their backpacks.

After a brief conversation—Larry has been to TWBD many times before—Larry's speech quickly becomes more difficult to understand. Not as difficult as Norma's mother but still at times unclear. The cause is ambiguous. It could be because, like some other guests at TWBD, he is missing a lot of his teeth. But maybe it is complications from his heart attack. It is better not to ask.

Larry has SSI, but it is still difficult for him to make ends meet at times. This is, at least in part, because Larry also takes care of his mother. He says, "I try to take care of her just like she took care of me when I was young." Even though Larry admits that he is far from the best cook in the world, he cooks every day for his mother. At TWBD he qualifies as a two-person household. He also receives, because of his mother's age, frozen meals set aside for seniors. All Larry has to do is toss them into the microwave. For Larry, these precooked meals are a godsend. The only thing is that at TWBD, as Larry points out, the two of them qualify for only six senior meals each month.

The Volunteers

It is not by chance that there is a place in Hereford, Oklahoma, for guests like Norma, Regina, Mona, Jane, Marla, and their partners. Or for Harold, Andrew, and Larry. Thy Will Be Done was established in 2018 by members of five different churches in Hereford. These churches, First Baptist Church of Hereford, Presbyterian Church, First Methodist Church, St. Peters Catholic Church, and Voice of God, all previously supported their own programs to address those in need in Hereford. These efforts, ranging from putting together food packages during religious holidays to collecting food and money for church members in times of crisis, were based upon a realization that poverty was pervasive. It was a real problem that could be faced at church services by those sitting next to them.

Some church leaders and members of these same five Hereford congregations also realized the lack of general consensus in response to the needs of those in poverty. This was particularly the case among community leaders in Hereford, including elected and appointed officials, law enforcement, business owners both big and small, and the town's largest employer, Hereford State College.

The five churches stepped into this relative service vacuum motivated by church leadership and congregant activists sharing the Christian directive to love thy neighbor as thyself. These religious leaders and their congregants believed it was their duty as Christians to make a difference in the lives of all Hereford residents in need, regardless of their religious beliefs or any other differences.

Ministerial leadership at all five churches, in coordination with several Hereford church members with special expertise, eventually joined forces in response to an egregious death on the streets of downtown Hereford. A committee of concerned church members from all five churches worked, under the guidance of church leadership, for almost two years to develop common goals and objectives to address the issues they defined as crucial. Eventually a joint committee representing all five churches established a tax-exempt 501 (c)(3) nonprofit.

A board of directors with three-year terms was elected under the legal guidelines required. A president, treasurer, and secretary representing the combined interests of the five participating churches were then elected from the board. Monthly meetings of the board are now supplemented by committees primarily focused on fundraising events and other ways to support TWBD financially. Currently there are more members of these five congregations who want to help than there are places on the board of directors. There is, in fact, a waiting list of those who would like to join the board to care for their fellow Hereford citizens in need.

The first task of the board of TWBD was to choose a qualified and experienced director who was familiar with the community. In turn the director, with the support of the board, selected an assistant director and an operations manager. These three positions, in addition to several half-time staff jobs at TWBC, form the leadership making the majority of day-to-day decisions.

The new director, her staff, and the board also realized that financial support was crucial. So too was the direct participation of volunteers from all five churches. Foremost, however, was the acknowledgment and support of this new not-for-profit by both the broader Hereford community and private and public service providers in the community. Those already providing services to the poor included a loose network of private and state-supported service organizations and institutions. The creation of TWBD at first challenged the credibility of some of the existing attempts to feed the poor throughout Wells County.

By 2019 this food pantry provided a wide variety of food and other necessities to more than 10,000 households in Hereford and Wells County. In 2021, TWBD's annual report stated that it served 11,000 households. In 2021 these households composed about 25 percent, some 26,000 individuals, of all residents living in Wells County. Through its new mobile food truck, an additional 2,800 people also were served in this same year.

This joint effort by a handful of Hereford churches, along with the support from the wider community, cost about $2.8 million in 2020. Only $6,000 of this revenue came from grants, which were private. The rest was raised by the combined efforts of the five churches from a variety of sources both inside the churches and in the community. All were supervised under the guidance of the board of directors. According to TWBD's annual financial statement, TWBD did not receive one dollar from local, state, or federal government.

The Demographics of Poverty

Both Thy Will Be Done and those who directly benefit from its creation may be more and less than demanded or expected. No human-made nonprofit organization created by the nonpoor is going to be perfect in achieving its goals. In a similar fashion, the guests at TWBD may not always be who nonpoor Oklahomans think they are. Both organizations and humans are usually more intricate and complex than at first expected.

Women account for about 63 percent of the total sample of individuals we worked with at TWBD. Guests Norma, Carol, Mona, Jane, Harold, Andrew, and Larry are White. Marla is Black. In my sample at TWBD, Whites account for 87 percent of the guests. Blacks, Indigenous Americans, Hispanics, Asians, and other races account for the remaining 13 percent. The guests by age at TWBD in the same sample are more likely to be middle-aged adults; about 15 percent are sixty-five or older.

In many respects Wells County is an example of a typical Oklahoma county, its population being majority White. The majority of guests who walk in the front doors of TWBD are Whites as well, Whites who are poor and do not have enough food to eat. This is not to discount the Oklahoma poor who live in some other counties in Oklahoma, minority populations with much higher percentages of Natives, Blacks, and Latinos. The largest actual numbers of Latinos in Oklahoma live in Oklahoma City, Tulsa, and the surroundings of these two metropolitan areas.

Before any guest of TWBD is allowed to shop for food, they must meet certain requirements. Each guest, before they can receive food or any other service offered by TWBD, must have a valid identification card, meet poverty income levels for their household, and be a resident of Wells County. A typical identification card is a driver's license and social security card for adults along with a local school report card for children. All members of the guest's household must be identified. There is an income scale that guests cannot exceed. For a one-person household it is a total income of less than about $2,200 a month, or $26,400 annually. For a household with four individuals the cutoff line is an income less than about $4,500 a month, or $54,000 annually.

The TWBD income level requirements are not the same as the federal definition of poverty. By federal standards, an adult who resides in Oklahoma in 2022 who annually earns less than about $13,500 is considered poor, and a family of four with an income of less than $27,750 falls below the poverty line. But the reality is, as suggested by TWBD guests and much of the research literature, that the federal poverty rates do not always make sense when it comes to food security and other issues faced on a daily basis by those with very limited incomes. Individuals who make slightly above the poverty line still can suffer. For this reason and others, the U.S. Census also counts those whose income is 125 percent, 150 percent, and more above the poverty cutoff. These individuals may face some of the same problems related to poverty as those who fall below the poverty line thresholds.

The eight guests we met above, contacted during the first year of study at TWBD, along with their nuclear and extended families, are examples of Oklahomans who in many ways do not conform to the dominant stereotypes of poor Oklahomans. First and foremost, many of them may have one or more health issues. Norma's mother has long since lost her teeth and with it her ability to speak clearly. Carol was in an accident that demolished her car and left her with as yet undermined injuries. Andrew, not yet thirty years of age, still suffers from a herniated disc injured when he was fourteen. While working at Walmart, Larry had a heart attack. Marla and Jermaine cannot afford to take their two children to the doctor, nor do they have the money to pay for prescriptions. Possible obesity and excessive weight as determined by the Body Mass Index appear common among guests.

At the same time that health issues may affect their daily lives in adverse ways because they cannot or do not think they can afford medical care, these same guests also may go out of their way to help family members with health issues or other significant problems. Mona and Brooklyn moved their family from Florida to Oklahoma to take care of her nephews. The devotion and kindness of several of these families toward their loved ones—in the face of their own limited resources—speaks for itself.

Several of these guests also face emergency circumstances that may be temporary but over which they have little or no control. Carol was not financially prepared for the economic repercussions when a Hereford College student crashed into her car. She not only lost her car, not yet having paid off the loan, but also her ten-year steady job in another city. Andrew reinjured himself while on the job.

Some of these eight guests are certainly guilty of making bad choices or decisions. But the price they pay can be ultimately far different from that paid by the nonpoor. Mona and Brooklyn, for instance, did not fully appreciate the financial consequences of moving from Florida to Oklahoma.

The poor are not the only ones who may make bad decisions, decisions that may be major, like moving the family from one state to another, or relatively minor, like Jermaine's. Jermaine left Marla to sit in the full heat of an Oklahoma summer with several bags of free food from TWBD, including frozen items. Andrew strongly hinted that he had been or still was, one way or the other, at odds with the legal system. He seemed, in fact, proud of the courtroom happenstance to mention it directly in front of his doting mother.

The poor are frequently charged with being lazy, including too lazy to work. While several of these guests have full or part-time jobs, still they may find it a struggle to make ends meet. Andrew earns twice the minimum wage in Oklahoma, but still his family cannot afford to rent a two-bedroom Hereford apartment. Nor does it make economic sense for his wife to work, because her wages would be eaten up by the cost of child care.

These and other facts about the guests at TWBD initially suggest that their lives are complex, family relationships often intricate, and the personal characteristics of household members diverse. Whether it is the love they share for each other, their willingness to take care of those less fortunate than themselves, their work ethic, a sense of right and wrong, or all the emotions and values hidden behind their street faces when they do not trust who they are dealing with, the guests at TWBD are in many ways no different than anyone else. The immediate humanity and warmth of many of these guests as discovered by the volunteers are undeniable, tangible. The guests are grateful, some exceedingly and some with a whisper, for the food they receive from this food pantry. They are also relieved by how they are treated by staff and volunteers. At TWBD the poor are treated with dignity and care.

2

Poverty Is Not a Personality Flaw

It's the damn Oklahoma weather and those construction supply stores that don't keep their word. Otherwise, I'd be doing fine.

—Guest at Thy Will Be Done

There are numerous misconceptions about the poor in Oklahoma. One major presumption among many Oklahomans is that alleged personality traits of the poor contribute directly to undermining their past, present, and future economic successes. Red flag. In general, impressions of the nonpoor about those in poverty often rely upon the embedded societal stereotypes of dominant cultural myths.[1] On occasion, to be completely fair, the impressions held by the nonpoor may also derive from having grown up poor themselves or from sporadic contacts with the poor. But these experiences and memories do not always provide clarity.

Persistent and pervasive poverty thrives in Oklahoma. One measure of this condition is food insecurity. Oklahoma ranks as the sixth state from the top in terms of the percentage of its population who do not have enough food.[2] In our state one in six adults including seniors are food insecure. Furthermore, one in four Oklahoma children do not have enough food to eat on a regular basis. This fact and the prevalence of food insecurity among adults have motivated a network of food banks in the state to take action. As a result, "Oklahoma food banks provide[d] enough food to feed more than 160,000 Oklahomans including 59,200 children in 2023.[3] One of these food banks is Thy Will Be Done.

Stereotypes of the Poor

Many low-income Oklahomans passed through the doors of Thy Will Be Done during my three and a half years of fieldwork Every one of them brought their own personal and family experiences with them. Those who came for food often openly voiced and shared their explanations of what it was like to be poor.

Undoubtedly the birth lottery plays a large part in who is poor and who is not in Oklahoma, as it does elsewhere. This fact is frequently not recognized by those who by luck hit a jackpot family. Of course, it is beyond our capacity to select the families into which we are born.

Peggy lives alone in a studio apartment in a complex fronting a major thoroughfare running through Hereford's burgeoning westside business district. Everything she needs, including groceries, theoretically is within walking distance. Proximity to shopping is not the issue. Peggy understands that, despite having spent most of her life raising a family and working hard to support them, there are times when she still does not have enough money to purchase food. This is despite the fact, according to Peggy, that she does everything she can to cut corners and save money.

First and foremost, Peggy does not own a car. Instead, she walks where she needs to go or relies on friends for a ride. Walking to stores, nevertheless, is difficult for Peggy. But not because of her physical limitations. She is very spry for her sixty-seven years. The truth is that there are no sidewalks near her apartment complex. Lack of sidewalks is a common problem throughout Hereford and makes it harder for Peggy and others without cars to take advantage of much of what Hereford has to offer to shoppers. For Peggy the six-lane bustling boulevard next to her studio apartment is almost like an impenetrable wall.

The speed limit is forty-five miles an hour in front of Peggy's apartment house. From the early morning to much later hours than Peggy keeps, motorists drive considerably faster than the speed limit allows. Peggy has good reason to fear the traffic, especially the younger drivers from the high school and Hereford State University. She wishes she could live somewhere in Hereford both more affordable and walkable day and night.

At four feet eight inches in height, Peggy is scrupulous about her appearance. She spends time to make sure her gray hair is just the way it should be. The same with her wardrobe. At TWBD she dresses in Nike shorts, Nike shoes, and a shiny black baseball jacket. Most guests here wear inexpensive clothing with few frills—or, at the other extreme, their Sunday best. Peggy tries to make a fashion statement every time she makes an entrance to the food pantry. She likes to show off her trim figure.

Beyond having fun, Peggy also cares deeply about her family. They include her adult children along with her sisters and brothers. She does not mention a partner. All her family live relatively close by but are not within walking distance for Peggy, again because of the overall absence of sidewalks. So, Peggy's family tries their best to visit her whenever they can.

Peggy is an air force brat who moved with her father, mother, sisters, and brothers from one base to another before finally settling in Hereford after her father retired. She now has two adult daughters in town and another who lives fifteen miles away. Several of her brothers and sisters (it is not clear exactly how many siblings are in her immediate family) also have recently settled in Hereford.

If Peggy is entertaining family, she also must have plenty of snacks on hand. As far as Peggy is concerned, the sweeter the better. The extra candy and other foods Peggy collects she gives to her neighbor and Andra, her neighbor's three-year-old daughter.

Although generous to others, Peggy lives on a very tight budget. She is aware of the money she saves by not having a car, including maintenance and insurance. She rented her studio apartment with an eye on the relatively low monthly charges in comparison to college student rentals. As Peggy works her way through the aisles of food at TWBD, she does not complain about her apartment rent or, for that matter, anything else.

Instead, she is quick to grab two large plastic bags of kibble before steering her cart down the remaining aisles, followed by a bunch of puppy pads because it's not always possible to take her two dogs outside to poop and pee at night. Peggy has no back yard, front yard, or other space at her apartment complex designated for pets. After dark she does not feel completely safe walking her two Chihuahua mixes, even just around her well-lit apartment complex. The drivers on the busy Hereford boulevard, she says, act as if her two small dogs do not exist, even if they stay on the shoulder of the busy road.

Vetted as a household of one and also a senior by TWBD staff, Peggy takes time to pick her frozen meals carefully. She, like others at the pantry, prizes the frozen meals over almost every other item.

Peggy is not tight-lipped about her years working in fast-food chains. When all her children finally were in school, she immediately started back to work. At McDonalds, Arby's, or whatever franchise employed her, Peggy always worked the jobs no one else wanted. Over the years, whatever her bosses asked her to do, Peggy went along with it. She never said no because she always needed the money for her family. She could not afford to say no.

Despite her hard work, Peggy has little to show for her many years of employment at minimum wage or slightly above it. Although her one-room studio apartment is just across a busy street from numerous stores and shops, most of the time Peggy does not have the bank account to shop in their aisles—even if she felt safe enough to cross the bustling avenue.

Peggy likes to joke around with her youngest brother, the one who drives her to TWBD. In his late fifties, he jumps out of his truck when she approaches his vehicle in the parking lot. Immediately spying a chocolate pie among his sister's plastic bags as she helps unload the cart, he pretends to keep it all for himself. He and Peggy share a time-worn laugh.

By any measure Peggy has not had an easy life, but she does not dwell on it. Instead, she enjoys dressing up whenever the occasion demands and frequently when it does not. But this philosophy of life takes her only so far. Despite a very positive approach to making the most of what she has, Peggy's often cannot afford to shop at the low-cost chains across the street from her studio apartment. This afternoon, if not for TWBD, Peggy will soon not have enough food to eat.

Compared to Peggy, Elizabeth seems weak, vulnerable, and a victim of bad luck over which she has little control. Today is the first day after Mother's Day in 2020, a Monday. The day finds Elizabeth among the first to walk through the glass doors of TWBD. Dressed in no-frills black slacks and a lavender top, she takes a few hesitant steps toward the grocery cart offered to her. Elizabeth's white handkerchief is already out, tears flowing down her cheeks—tears that Elizabeth cannot stem.

Last year Elizabeth's husband died of cancer on Mother's Day. They had been married for fifteen years, a second marriage for him, the first for her. Bedridden for the past three years, he had received all his care from Elizabeth, night and day. Elizabeth knew how to provide for her husband's health because, although she is now retired, she worked for many years as a nurse in a permanent-care facility in Hereford.

Elizabeth's husband had three sons by his ex-wife. According to Elizabeth, the ex-wife and all her sons virtually ignored him once he married Elizabeth, including the three years when he was bedridden at home. Her husband had been a surgical nurse at the hospital in Hereford and earned a good income. But their mutual savings eventually disappeared because of all the medical bills.

To make matters worse, when Elizabeth's husband died his ex-wife and the three sons somehow managed to take over his immediate personal affairs. He was cremated as he had directed, but then all his ashes were given by the funeral home to his ex-wife and sons. Only at the last minute, says Elizabeth, did the ex-wife gratuitously give her a small jar of her husband's ashes. Elizabeth now takes out this vial of ashes from her purse. Holding it in one hand, she apologizes for crying. She continues to cry even as she chooses her six frozen senior meals.

Besides grief, which still at times overwhelms her, Elizabeth has faced other problems. In her mid-sixties, she used to weigh almost three hundred pounds and wore at least 4X sizes. Now she is a size 4. Elizabeth says she is now very careful about what she eats.

Elizabeth also has few teeth but, unlike Norma's mother, her words are understandable. (Lack of access to health care in Oklahoma is discussed further in chapter 5.) She is blunt about her situation. Recently Elizabeth took in three homeless people from Wells County. She provides them with a free place to live. In return, the three are there, she says, to keep a close eye on her because she was recently put on suicide watch.

In the parking lot, Fred helps Elizabeth load her groceries into the back of his old black truck. Elizabeth came with Fred, along with Fred's ex-wife Jeanette. All three of them are guests at TWBD. The three of them, according to Elizabeth, are good friends. But at the same time, Elizabeth says Fred will not stop pressuring her to be with him. This is because Fred told Elizabeth he wants her to take care of him when he can no long take care of himself—just like when Elizabeth took care of her husband.

Nancy and Sid's lives as adults, unlike the challenges with which Elizabeth must contend, are really just beginning. Students at Hereford State, the two are in a relationship requiring both patience in the present and planning for the future. Nancy is from Seiling, Oklahoma, a community of less than one thousand in Dewey County in the northwestern part of the state. Sid, in contrast, is from the Tulsa suburbs. Both are now sophomores at Hereford State. They met their freshmen year and are now inseparable. They want to keep it that way.

Nancy has a pierced nose. So does Sid. Both wear jean shorts and bright T-shirts. Still taking required general education courses in their sophomore years, the couple have not yet declared their major fields of undergraduate study. Nancy thinks she wants a "practical major" that will lead directly to a good-paying job—like computer science, she thinks. Sid leans toward English literature. He feels it will not land him a high-paying job in today's market, but he does not care. Graduate school is where Sid wants to go, job or no job awaiting him after he earns an advanced degree.

It is the very first time Nancy and Sid have come to TWBD. They are not shy or reluctant when they see all the free food conveniently shelved. They do, however, seem a bit stunned at first when they realize that they can choose whatever they want. Each time Sid or Nancy puts another item into their grocery cart, Sid turns and says to their volunteer, "Thank you." Eventually he understands that his gesture is unnecessary.

Stopping at a freezer filled with packaged chicken, beef, and pork, Nancy explains, "We're saving our money for an apartment." At the present they each live in student dorms with a roommate.

"How much do you figure the rent is going to be?"

"At least $1,000 for a one-bedroom. Including utilities." That monthly price tag is the going rate in Hereford for the basics. No amenities. No big screens, granite countertops, or gym on site. Just the basics. Nancy and Sid don't care. All they want is to be with each other and have a roof over their heads.

Halting in front of the canned vegetables, Nancy leans over the grocery cart to consider her choices. As a two-person partnership, they are allowed two cans of vegetables or two big bags of pasta or rice. There is white rice in a smaller bag, brown rice in a much larger bag. So far today only one other guest has chosen brown rice. Nancy becomes the second person to do so.

Nancy says with no hesitancy, "I really don't know how to cook." Neither does Sid. They don't care. They will figure it out.

Nancy and Sid need no help getting their plastic bags of food to their car. Clearly, they have planned in detail for their future. Sharing an apartment their junior year, however, will probably prove more demanding than they imagine. To their credit, they are limiting the money they allot for food and other expenses so they can put their savings into an account at one of the new banks in downtown Hereford. This way they hope to save enough over the fall semester to pay one full month's rent up front required to reserve an apartment for the following year.

Nancy and Sid refer to the extra month's rent as the "cleaning deposit." The cleaning deposit in the Hereford rental market is an additional charge often impossible to recover from the landlord even when renters do their best to leave the apartment exactly as they found it. The Hereford "pet deposit" works much the same way.

Last semester Sid and Nancy also put away a portion of their recent summer wages in their joint bank account. Their financial plan during the first semester of the next academic year is to have enough in the bank to make it through two full semesters. Both will again work summer jobs—hopefully, they both say, at more than the going $7.25 an hour minimum wage.

It may turn out that they come up short, so their backup plan is that one or both will take a part-time job along with their regular course load. Working eighteen to twenty hours a week or more while carrying a full academic course load, they both realize, is going to be tough. Maintaining high grades—they are both good students—will not be easy. But their goal, which is to avoid piling up student debt, is admirable. They both have friends who borrowed money for college only to find the debt on their loans after graduation to be a burden.

Despite all their planning, Nancy and Sid do not have enough money to buy the food they need. They must rely, at least temporarily, on TWBD. They are likely, given what they say, to return to the pantry throughout their junior and senior years. When asked, they do not know if any campus food security programs address their needs.

Nancy and Sid are legally adults. As adults they must face the outcomes of the choices they make. This includes their financial decisions. Both sets of their parents want to help support them financially. Nancy and Sid, nevertheless, want to make their own decisions and, if and when it comes to that, their own mistakes. If further down the line they choose to continue their educations, a lower grade point average means they could be less likely to get into the postgraduate program of their choice or to receive a scholarship or other form of institutional financial support.

In Oklahoma's economy, it is far from easy to have a life partner in school and be a full-time college student. Having children further complicates getting a college degree. Marci knows all there is to know about having children while navigating her way to the stage at college graduation. Forty-one years of age, she shops at TWBD for a household of three. Marci is the mother of four children, with two still living under her roof. She is divorced and relocated to Hereford when her husband abandoned her and the children.

Marci feels lucky to have, as she puts it, "escaped an abusive marriage." Up until the very end of her marriage, she saw no options for a different kind of life. Her abusive husband finally left her for another woman when he found out Marci had breast cancer.

Part of Marci's reluctance to leave her marriage was because they lived in a small town outside the city of Lawton. In Comanche County in southwestern Oklahoma, where Marci was born and raised, everyone knew everyone else's business. Even given her terrible marriage, it was hard for Marci to leave her husband, because that meant leaving a life she had always known for a completely unfamiliar world.

Marci's husband is on the tribal rolls, but when he left her and their four children for another woman Marci stopped receiving financial help from his tribe. Money was not forthcoming either for the support of her four young children or for the medical bills Marci soon faced because of her cancer diagnosis.

The position taken by her ex's tribe is not unusual. Among some tribal nations it is standard. Though Marci's husband is on the tribal role, by federal law the recipient of certain guaranteed rights and privileges, Marci is not Native. Those on the tribal roles are the only ones who qualify for tribal benefits. Such laws exist to exclude those who may seek to take advantage of the full legal rights and privileges to which only tribal members are entitled. The history of Natives in Oklahoma is unfortunately crowded by long lines of individuals who were not Natives but intentionally sought to receive the same rights and privileges of those who were.[4]

Before the breast cancer diagnosis, Marci had been the major wage earner for her children and deadbeat husband. When she moved to Hereford to live with her sister, she eventually received support from Hereford's Mission of Care. Mission of Care is chartered in Wells County to serve the special needs of the homeless and their families. This service provider is funded by the U.S. Department of Housing and Urban Development.[5]

After Marci moved to Hereford, another Oklahoma tribe, not that of her husband, stepped in to provide additional financial support and other benefits to her and her four children. This was fortunate, because at that time Marci's faced serious medical issues related to her breast cancer.

More recently Marci was diagnosed with thyroid cancer. She says it is now at stage four, the most advanced stage. She has been told she must have three more operations after the one she already underwent.

Before the bad news about her thyroid cancer, Marci had managed to create a new life in Hereford for both her and her family. She went back to school at Hereford State College, eventually earning a college degree. However, with the full responsibility of raising four children, it took her much longer to graduate than the average student. Degree finally in hand, she found immediate work at a local mental health facility.

Ironically, Marci knows TWBD quite well because in the recent past she accompanied her own clients to this same food pantry. Now, she says, void of self-pity, she herself must rely on this same provider to those who fall below the poverty line.

Today at TWBD, Marci wears an old breast cancer T-shirt and jeans. Her T reads, "Sisters Don't Let Sisters Fight Breast Cancer Alone." Within a few weeks she is scheduled to have the first of her additional thyroid surgeries at a Tulsa hospital where, unlike at the Hereford hospital, doctors specialize in her specific medical needs.

At least one of Marci's two adult children also is having a difficult time in Hereford. Ten feet down the same aisle, her son Ralph also shops the shelves at TWBD. When Ralph turned eighteen he moved out of Marci's house, and he now lives with two other friends. For reasons that are unclear, he qualifies as a guest at TWBD.

Mary Ann and her husband, Hank, also face multiple problems within their own family directly caused by being poor. Some of these issues are also apparent in other generations of family members. Just when Mary Ann and Hank seem to have taken control of their lives and their immediate future, other family obstacles always seem to appear.

Mary Ann and Hank do all of Heather's regular food shopping. Heather is Mary Ann's sister. In addition, while Mary Ann shops for Heather at TWBD, Hank, who is a disabled vet, shops for their own family of five children. At TWBD it unfortunately takes Hank twice as long to do the family shopping as someone who does not have his disability. So, Mary Ann takes one grocery cart for Heather's TWBD food, and Hank gets another for their own nuclear family.

Mary Ann moved her sister Heather from Tulsa to Hereford so she could care for her on a full-time basis. Heather is incapable of looking after herself because she has a cognitive disability. Mary Ann and her husband have five children, four boys and a girl. Counting her disabled sister, there are eight in their household.

No more than a few minutes into shopping, Mary Ann takes a phone call that quickly makes their TWBD shopping and the rest of their day more arduous. Their daughter, who is enrolled at Head Start, is sick. The Head Start teacher tells them their youngest child is violently throwing up. They must immediately come get their daughter from school.

Mary Ann stops her TWBD shopping, finds Hank on another aisle, and tells him the news. After sticking his half-full grocery cart in a nook where it will not be disturbed, Hank leaves TWBD. Later he will return, if he can, to continue his shopping. If not, some other arrangements will have to be made.

Mary Ann says she is not surprised about the phone call from Head Start. Just two days before, one of her sons had come down with the stomach flu, though at the time the daughter seemed fine earlier in the morning before school.

Mary Ann and Heather are part of a large family who are originally from Tahlequah in the far eastern part of the state. Mary Ann comes from a family of four sisters and one brother. One of her brothers has three girls and one boy. When all the family last got together for Thanksgiving the previous year, their grandmother counted fifty-two adults and children. At the time, every family member at the table, representing three generations, fell below the poverty line.[6]

One of Mary Ann's sisters worked for Head Start in another town. Her sister felt lucky to get the Head Start job, but Mary Ann says they soon fired her because she was accused of leaving a child alone in the bathroom. According to Mary Ann that was not the complete story. Her sister left the boy alone in the bathroom because she had to take care of another child who was getting into serious trouble. Mary Ann's sister told the boy she was going to leave him in the bathroom, and she would be right back. She also told him to pull up his pants and stay where he was. The boy did neither.

Mary Ann is still very upset that Head Start fired her sister. She is critical of the Head Start program in general, but not the one in Hereford, which she says takes good care of her daughter. If it had been her, Mary Ann says, she would have set her sister's boss at Head Start straight right after the incident.

Mary Ann also tells me, a few minutes later, that she knows she has a big mouth. At times she tells others exactly what she thinks of them even though her behavior gets her into trouble. That's just the way she is.

After completing her shopping, Mary Ann waits impatiently in the parking lot for Hank to return. In one grocery cart, which she was not able to push by herself, is food for Heather. The other cart, meant for Mary Ann's family, less than half full, remains under the eye of a staff member while Hank picks up their sick daughter at Head Start.

When Hank finally returns, he can't find a parking space close to the entrance of TWBD. Mary Ann walks with great difficulty to their car. Her husband is going to take Mary Ann and the TWBD food for Heather back to their house, then return on his own to complete his shopping for their family. Meanwhile, Mary Ann will attend to their sick daughter. As a result, they will not have the time, as they had planned, to check on the status of their overdue utility bill before the city office closes at 5 p.m. Mary Ann is worried their electricity may be cut off.

Mary Ann and Hank cannot always help their other family members in all the ways they would like. Nor, given their own financial limitations, can they at times contend with their own money issues. Paying for a doctor consult about Mary Ann's possible obesity, for example, is not a financial option.

After the TWBD food for Heather and her family is unloaded into Hank's car, Mary Ann takes extra time to thank those who helped them shop. She does so with genuine grace, then slowly and carefully climbs into the front passenger seat of their car. The rest of her afternoon is going to be very busy.

Hank is not the only vet who regularly visits TWBD. James is not disabled like Hank. His life, nevertheless, has not been easy. He first signed up with the marines in the early 1970s during the Vietnam War. After his commitment to the marines was completed, James enlisted in the army.

James is stoop shouldered and very thin. He speaks with a quiet voice. When he arrived at TWBD, he carefully locked his bike to the metal railing at the entrance. He is very passionate about his bike. These days he only feels at his best when he is riding, or working on, or just talking about his bike.

James recently retired from Hereford State College, where he worked as a custodian for more than twenty years. Being a custodian at an Oklahoma institution of higher learning is not, he says, a cushy job. First there is his shift supervisor, who always leaves tasks for James that no one else wants to tackle. Then there is everyone else in his assigned building—professors, secretaries, teaching assistants, and students—some of whom feel free to tell him what work he must immediately do and sometimes also how to do it.

These sometimes contradictory instructions can become commands or even the threat of filing a complaint to his shift supervisor. Occasionally over the years someone followed through with their threats. This meant that James was eventually notified by his supervisor and forced to fill out a bunch of useless paperwork that was then sent up the bureaucratic line. James says that was always the last he heard of the complaints.

In return for this job hassle James earned, after more than twenty years on the same job, $12.50 an hour along with modest benefits. His compensation after two decades was roughly five dollars above the minimum wage. His retirement ceremony consisted of punching out on the clock from his final shift.

James's gimme cap, impossible to miss, reads, "Coffee the first thing." It sits atop long gray hair the same color as a twelve-inch, unkept beard.

"Isn't it awfully hot with your beard and hair? Especially in the summer?"

"No. Ask me about kids and dogs."

"What do you think about kids and dogs."

"Kids are too much responsibility. So are dogs."

"Married?"

"What do you think?"

James is all about his bike. It serves as his only transportation and provides options and opportunities in his daily life he otherwise could not afford. A useful example is doing his shopping in Hereford at the least expensive grocery store, which is three miles from the door of his one-bedroom apartment. After years of military service and working as an invisible janitor, James's best words are reserved for that bike. He shows off the disc brakes, which he proudly reveals are harder to repair than calipers. He does all his own bike maintenance.

Today James, as usual, comes prepared to TWBD. He has been here many times before. Now that he has carefully stuffed all his food items into his backpack, he is ready to return to his apartment. He selected each food item, as he has so many times before, at least in part for its weight. The lighter the better. Any loaves of bread or irregularly shaped food items he places in plastic bags tied to the handlebars.

James has nothing good to say about riding a bike in Hereford on a daily basis. He relates that students at Hereford State and the high school text while driving much too fast. The last thing they are looking for is James on his bike. The Hereford rednecks are no better. They mistake James for an old hippy. They yell at him, occasionally throwing garbage in his direction.

About some of the professors, James says, "They think they are entitled to act any way they want to."

And the students? "Well, they can be worse."

Although James is passionate about his bike, the truth is he would prefer a car if he had the money. Save his bike for long rides when the traffic is less of a problem.

James at first might come off as a curmudgeon, but he is more a pragmatist who has long since accepted the consequences of the hand he was dealt. He does regret lacking the money to replace all his missing front teeth, which his ragged beard and mustache almost cover up. On the other hand, he is proud of the fact that, unlike some others, he still has some teeth left and can still chew his food. Sweets, especially any form of chocolate, are another one of James's great pleasures. Chocolates go down extra easy with good coffee.

Loaded up with food from TWBD, James is at first a little wobbly when he sets off on his bike. Leaving the parking lot without a look back or a wave, he quickly gains both momentum and stability. Regardless of daily adversity, James is resilient. His endgame, however, is undefined. What happens when the time eventually comes that he cannot ride his bike?

One would think that Ahmed, because of his position at Hereford State, would be the last person one might expect to see at TWBD. "I'm getting my Ph.D. in hydrocarbon research." He makes this statement to express his pride in achieving a lifelong goal. At the same time, he also openly wonders why the institution and country he admires and to which he is committed do not provide him with enough money to feed his family during the summer months.

This is Ahmed's first time shopping at TWBD. Three years ago, when his major professor at a Georgia college took a new position at Hereford State, Ahmed and his family, as is the academic custom, faithfully followed him to Oklahoma. Ahmed was at first surprised by the news that his mentor was moving to a new institution. It had never occurred to Ahmed that this was even a possibility.

As Iraqi nationals, Ahmed and his wife and three children, ages eleven, nine, and six, never wanted to move to the United States. Ahmed took the gamble because a Ph.D. in chemical science from an American university is a ticket to a promising and secure new life. Ahmed's wife was even more fearful of their second move to Hereford State in Oklahoma. Her English is much better than when she first arrived in Georgia but, like Ahmed, she finds that many locals are impatient when she speaks English with an accent.

Most of the professors in his new department do not seem to appreciate all the cultural adjustments Ahmed and his family contend with on a daily basis. Grad students in his department, on the other hand, are more sympathetic and generous, at least in part because over a third are themselves international students.

Ahmed lives in married student housing on campus in a two-bedroom apartment just a short walk from his professor's lab and Ahmed's classes. One major problem is that Ahmed's summer fellowship is not enough to pay all his regular bills. He and his family do not have exceptional expenses. They are careful with their money, but the fellowship is their only source of income.

Ahmed's family food bill is much less than that of most other American graduate students with families. Vegetarians all, he purchases no meats or other expensive foods for his family. Their diet is rice, pasta, vegetables, fruit, bread, tea, and an occasional sweet dessert. They rarely go out to restaurants. Even if they could afford it, local Hereford menus offer limited vegetarian alternatives.

Not surprisingly, at first little appeals to Ahmed on the TWBD shelves—especially the frozen vegetables with expiration date long since passed. Despite hearing that such dates do not necessarily mean the food is no longer safe to eat, Ahmed passes on all the frozen vegetables. He also seems offended that TWBD would offer such food to its guests.

Ahmed's grocery cart remains empty except for bread, one cake, canned vegetables, soups, and a few household items like toilet paper. Then he reaches the fresh produce. He bags his limit of two heads of lettuce, spinach, three kinds of squash, okra, white potatoes, sweet potatoes, and broccoli. Carefully placing the fresh produce in plastic bags, he then rests each bag in his grocery cart in such a way that none of his food is likely to be crushed. Then Ahmed spies the fresh fruits: cantaloupes, watermelons, apples, and oranges. He sorts carefully through the fruits, selecting the best he finds.

At Hereford State, Ahmed and his family have fallen through the departmental cracks. The school does not pay him enough money throughout the year to cover his bills or to feed his family adequately. No one, according to Ahmed, not a single faculty member in his new department or university administrator, has stepped forward to help. It is far beyond Ahmed's limited knowledge of local culture to ask for help from those who he assumes are expected to provide it. Ahmed is not only confused and embarrassed but angry. He does not know what, if anything, he can do. His lurking fear is that unintentionally he will say or do the wrong thing. Then he and his family will be summarily sent back to Iraq.

Mike, the opposite of Ahmed, does not mince his words. Whether you like what he says or doesn't say, he is going to tell you what's up. He should not have to be coming to TWBD on a regular basis. "It's the damn weather and those big stores that don't keep their word. Otherwise, I'd be doing fine."

After he quit high school early, as soon as he was old enough to take the commercial license test Mike went to work as a long-haul trucker. The money was good but, after only a few years of a life on the road, Mike "screwed up his back." Realizing that his back problems would only become worse if he kept driving, he changed occupations to concrete finishing. Not only was the work easier on his body, at least at first, but he had more time to spend with his wife and kids.

When Mike eventually began to develop new job-related health problems as a concrete finisher, he again showed the foresight and gumption to make yet another transition. After more than fifteen years of experience as a finisher, Mike became an independent businessman supervising his own small crew. By trade Mike now calls himself what he is, a cement contractor.

As a cement contractor, Mike does it all. "Driveways, sidewalks, patios, you name it." Everything but foundation work. Foundation work is a totally different kind of work, he explains, requiring an investment of capital in expensive machinery, not to mention the skills and experience required. For foundation work, Mike would need to hire a bigger crew with a different skill set he himself does not have. Mike knows what he does not know. Also, his insurance would be sky high with such a change. Mike will never take the leap into foundation work because he knows his limitations.

On the far brighter side, Mike already has a total of ninety-two jobs lined up through the rest of the spring and the end of August. He's not bragging, he says, just telling it like it is. Nevertheless, for now Mike's money has run out again because it has been raining off and on during the last week of March. A cement contractor requires, according to Mike, one dry day of weather before work can begin or pick up again on an unfinished project. His work also requires dry weather on the same day he works. Today Mike has no job lined up because of yesterday's rainy weather. The forecast is not encouraging.

Mike repeats his litany. "It's the damn Oklahoma weather and those construction supply stores that don't keep their word. Otherwise, I'd be doing fine."

What Mike means is that he considers himself a self-made man, an independent businessman who is proud of what he's accomplished. On the money side of it, he's worked over every detail to maximize profits. He also prides himself on staying a step ahead of work-related injuries. Reflecting back, it was a wise move to quit driving a truck when he developed back problems. It was equally smart to quit doing concrete work when his knees started giving him trouble.

What Mike did, and he is nothing if not proud to share it with anyone who will listen, is make the best of a potentially bad situation. He knows the concrete business up, down, and sideways. He now hires two of the best men he used to work with, men he has known for years. His crew are not just good at what they do, they are dependable. In the kind of work Mike does, you have to have dependable people.

For every job, Mike charges the same, unless it is a special kind of job requiring more time and extra materials. His underlying principle is always KISS: Keep It Simple, Stupid. Five hundred dollars on the button is what he charges for almost all his jobs. He knows exactly how long the jobs will take and what materials he needs to buy. Keeping one eye on his overhead, he keeps the other on the prices his competition charges.

After Mike pays his tiny crew their share, plus the cost of materials, gas, and any extras, he walks away with around $120 a job. His crew know it's a fair deal because Mike is the one who finds the jobs, handles the customers, buys the materials, completes all the paperwork, and takes all the financial risk. He trusts his crew but is always there at the work site just in case something goes wrong.

Including transportation time to the job site, on average Mike says he works ten hours a day. The way he calculates it, he brings in $12 an hour. It's seasonal work because of the weather, so there are times of the year he is working seven days a week, other times he is off for weeks. Still, he's earning close to twice minimum wage. To boot, he is also saving his knees and back from getting any worse than they already are.

Over the years Mike's goal has never changed: to provide his family with the basic necessities. Sometimes, regardless of his attention to the quality of work and all the other details, what he earns is simply not enough. The weather is one obstacle—and a regular target of Mike's cursing. Concrete and rain do not mix. But it isn't just the weather. Another real aggravation keeping Mike up at night is the materials needed for each job. He orders his supplies to be dropped off at the job site at the start of the workday. But the acute pain in the rear, according to Mike, is when he and his two crew show up at the job site and the necessary supplies are nowhere to be found.

Mike pays cash in advance for his supplies, plus a delivery charge. That is what the chain stores always demand. What stinks "like a son of a bitch" is when Mike and his crew get stuck at the job site with nothing to do. The damn chain stores do not keep up their end of the deal—a deal Mike paid for in advance. He would take his business to the smaller retail stores, but their prices are way too high.

Sometimes Mike ends up waiting most of the day for the materials he paid for in cash to be delivered. Even when the supplies he purchased are just a few hours late, Mike says that it can totally screw up his work schedule. Sometimes, he says, the materials never show up. Through it all his crew wait there right with him. It's frustrating and unfair. Mike knows the suppliers would never treat one of the big builders like they do him. Mike knows he is small-time, which is why the chain suppliers tell him he must always pay his money up front. But what can he do?

Mike's partial answer to Oklahoma's weather is a second gig he devised on his own. When it gets too wet for concrete work, he signs up with a nationally known insurance company to replace damaged home roofs with metal roofs. This kind of roof is popular in Oklahoma because of its low price compared to shingles, especially when considering the time, the cost of labor, and the expertise required.

But to put on this kind of metal roof, Mike must have a day with almost no wind. If the Oklahoma wind starts up, putting on a metal roof becomes next to impossible and also dangerous. If you try to put on a metal roof when it's windy, which requires nailing it in place as you go, you can get seriously injured. Mike's next biggest headache in his seasonal roofing business is confronting old roofs or multiple layers of roof shingles on some houses. Removing an old roof, depending on its condition, takes extra time, which directly translates into a smaller profit.

Mike has nothing nice to say about the big insurance companies that pay for a new roof to replace one damaged by an Oklahoma storm. "I had an insurance company once I did the work for, but I didn't see the check for nine months." Every penny counts. Most of Mike's work is in the Tulsa area. If gas at the pump goes up like it sometimes does, his profits shrink proportionately.

Mike just turned fifty and his Type 2 diabetes is beginning to bother him. He also has problems chewing his food. He says he cannot afford the price of dentures and does not know if he ever will. Medical insurance, he tells me, is too damn expensive. So here he is at TWBD shopping for a household of five because he again ran short on cash despite having two different jobs.

Mike has a steady partner at home, along with an adult daughter who is going through her own hard times with two kids and no husband to share the load. One of her biggest challenges is a new baby, but the baby's father is unreliable at best. So, at least for now, Mike shops for a family of five. He doesn't know how long his daughter and her children will be staying with them. But while they are, Mike believes that it is his duty to take care of her and her two kids the best he can.

This all may explain why Mike is dressed the way he is on this particular day at TWBD. For Mike it is another day of bad Oklahoma weather keeping him from his concrete work or roofing gig. Perhaps to show his frustration at what he cannot control, he wears a pair of old blue pajama bottoms and a faded red sweatshirt torn in several places. Looking at him, you might think Mike is a poster boy for a deadbeat. You would be wrong.

Overweight and Obesity in Adults

A cultural stereotype that concludes that only the poor should be held accountable for their poverty does so in part by assuming that those who end up in poverty do so because they are or have become overweight or obese. Obesity, along with excessive weight, is stereotypically taken as proof of sloth: only the weak-willed overeat, then become overweight and possibly obese. Once overweight or obese, goes this way of thinking, individuals who are poor or become poor are far less motivated to escape their poverty.

Again, this stereotype assumes that being overweight or obese is the direct result of a personality flaw or cluster of individual inadequacies unique to those below the poverty line. Those inadequacies allegedly can include individuals who cannot resist certain high-calory foods or perhaps the habit of eating too much too often. Overweight and obesity thus become proof sui generis of why some individuals are poor or fall into poverty. Accordingly, these overweight or obese individuals are directly responsible for both their condition and the consequences of their economic status—poverty—that accompany it.

According to this line of fractured thinking, there is little to be done for overweight or obese poor because they are incapable of doing much for themselves. There may also be an assumption that those overweight or obese are incapable of working or, if they work, necessarily less capable than others.

There are indeed guests at TWBD who appear to be overweight or obese. Some have children who also appear to be overweight or obese. "Overweight" and "obesity," it should be remembered, are medical conditions defined in terms of the Body Mass Index (BMI). BMI is an individual's weight in pounds divided by the square of their height in feet. The purpose of the BMI is to screen for excess fat in adults, just as in children, because of possible recognized health problems and future health risks.[7]

According to a comprehensive study, Oklahoma has the third-highest percentage of obesity in the United States. Only West Virginia and Kentucky have higher rates.[8] In adults, being overweight or obese correlates with Type 2 diabetes, a serious health risk. This is true whether one is poor or nonpoor. The trend of the obesity and overweight rates in Oklahoma is apparent. Although already very high compared to all other states, as this state's population increases adults and children in Oklahoma with serious weight issues are becoming more numerous.

Data collected from TWBD does not include measurements that would determine who among guests is overweight or obese and who is not. To ascertain those facts, weight and height of guests would have to be collected to establish the BMI. According to the U.S. Centers for Disease Control and Prevention, if an adult BMI is less than 18.5, then it is within the "underweight range." If 18.5 to <25.0, it is within the "healthy weight range." An adult in the "overweight range" has a BMI of 25.0 to <30.0. Finally, an adult with a BMI 30.0 or higher is within the "obesity range."[9]

Being an overweight or obese adult is not a character flaw. Being overweight or obese, whether poor or nonpoor, is instead a health issue that can have serious health consequences. Why are we overweight and obese? Several theories have been posited. One focus of study is the well-being of the fetus in utero. A second area of study is the impact of cheap food upon low-income children whose parents live in food deserts. A possible genetic component as well as other environmental factors have also been considered. Biological and socio-environmental theories about the causes of overweight and obesity remain open to more research. Most recently, those who are obese but nevertheless metabolically healthy have been studied.[10] In short, the root causes of overweight and obesity in adults, as well as in children, are far more complex than often realized. Those who are overweight or obese, regardless of economic status, do not deserve to be stigmatized.

Guests who appear to be overweight or obese, such as Mona and Mary Ann, demonstrate some of the complexities that contradict simplistic stereotypes. Jed is another example. Wearing jeans, black T-shirt, and thread-bare brown shoes, Jed shops for both himself and his mother. He is in his early forties, his mother Lula twenty years older.

Jed takes care of his mother, he says, because his three sisters will not lift a hand to help her. Lula cannot take care of herself and, to make matters worse, is prone to falling. Since he has no other family to count on, Jed does what he can for Lula because he knows a bad fall can put her in the hospital. During COVID, Jed also knows, a hospital is not a good place to be if you are a senior and have health issues.

Jed has no interest in fresh vegetables and fruits at TWBD, even though this particular day the produce section is bursting at the seams with numerous choices from tomatoes and carrots to two kinds of lettuce, fresh sweet potatoes, and four kinds of fruit. He finally takes a few ears of corn and fresh strawberries, but with little enthusiasm.

Despite what one might be led to assume if stereotypes were accurate, Jed seems more or less content with his living arrangements with his mother—as he seems with his life in general and his weight. When it comes to food, he makes it clear that he knows he eats too much. But he does not feel being overweight or obese is a negative characteristic. He is not defensive about it. He suggests that a bunch of Americans are fat. Says Jed with a wink, "Like the forty-fifth president of the United States."

Joey and Kathy, both younger than Jed, also appear to be overweight. They live in Likens, a small town a thirty-minute drive from the doors of TWBD. At first, I mistake Joey for Kathy's son, but it quickly becomes apparent that they are a couple. Joey is tall, around six foot two. His weight appears in the range of 400 pounds or more. Kathy is much smaller in height, maybe five foot four, but her weight appears to be in the range of 250 pounds or more.

Kathy is as active as Joey seems sluggish. Based upon their conversation as they move down the aisles, there seems to be a strong bond between them. At the same time, they are given to constant bickering. Kathy knows what she wants in a cereal. It is not what Joey wants. She searches for a cereal low in calories and intends to add fresh fruit to it. Joey, on the other hand, says the best thing to start his morning is a cereal that tastes like chocolate and is very sweet. By TWBD rules, a household of two gets one cereal choice. Joey reaches for the sweet chocolate cereal. Kathy remains silent, but it is clear by the look on her face that she dislikes his choice.

What matters to Joey, he says, is the taste of food. Next comes volume. If it is a choice between three pounds of frozen wings and five pounds of frozen ribs, he would pick ribs over wings every day of the week—even though ribs are not his favorite food. Kathy does not agree with most of Joey's selections at TWBD, but she constantly defers to him.

Perry, another regular guest at TWBD, appears to go well beyond Joey in making decisions that adversely affect his own health and well-being. If not clueless, at the very least he seems to take no responsibility. As he tells it, he was once a promising high school football star. He was so good he was a two-way player—center on offense, nose guard on defense. After graduation, he expected to be offered football scholarships from several state colleges and universities. During his senior year, however, Perry seriously injured his back. The Friday night injury ruined his chances of receiving a football scholarship. A football scholarship, Perry bemoans eight years later, would have greatly reduced the current college debt he is legally obligated to pay to both Hereford College and the bank.

Now Perry is in his fourth year of working for a Hereford chicken franchise. It has been his only job since graduation from Hereford State. Perry stands about six feet in height and appears to be around 400 pounds or more. He offers that he has a ruptured disc from his old football injury in high school, but only recently has it begun to really bother him. It particularly bothers him after he has been sitting in a chair for long periods of time.

For the past three years Perry has worked at the same Hereford fast food chicken franchise on the Strip. He says there are several different reasons he works there. But the main reason, according to Perry, is that he is not interested in looking for another job. His employer provides a 50 percent discount on all food Perry buys during his shift break or after he has finished his shift. Since he earns $8.00 an hour, seventy-five cents above the minimum wage, a 50 percent food discount is, he hints, a big deal.

Since graduating from Hereford State, Perry has put on even more pounds than when he attended classes. He tells me that he recognizes the discounted food he purchases from his employer is high in sugar and fats. At TWBD, Perry seems to have trouble walking while he makes his food selections from the shelves.

Most of his free time, both day and night, Perry spends in his special gaming chair in his studio apartment. He enjoys competing with other video gamers around the country and the world. Most of his expendable income goes to purchasing the special brand of gaming clothes, shorts, and T-shirts he always wears. While Perry appreciates the amenities of his studio apartment, he rarely has the time to use them. The best thing about his apartment, according to Perry, is the easy walk to his job.

Perry is a fry cook. Everything he needs to do at his job requires little movement from one place to another, because the restaurant kitchen area is tiny. Because he lives so close to his job, Perry frequently volunteers at the last minute to work extra shifts when other employees do not show up. This week he is going to put in over forty hours because of his extra shifts. That means his employer will have to pay Perry benefits, which normally Perry does not receive. Usually, Perry is allowed to work no more than thirty-nine hours a week at the most.

Perry seems only mildly concerned that he cannot afford to pay down his student loans. He mentions that his parents live in a small town not too far from Hereford. In a real pinch, Perry may be able to borrow money from them. But not a big lump sum that would zero out all his student loans.

Perry also seems to realize that, if he continues to follow his sedentary lifestyle, he may soon face diabetes, not to mention more serious back problems. In addition, he has increased chances of other health issues related to eating most of his food from his place of employment.

Perry has the habit of ordering his favorite meal during breaks at work or after his shift. His favorite meal, Perry says, is a bowl of fried chicken chunks mixed in with mashed potatoes and corn. He knows this meal has about 1,200 calories per serving, and sometimes he eats more than one serving at a time. But the price all customers pay for this meal is $5.00. With pride Perry tells me he pays only $2.50.

Children of the poor in Oklahoma, like their parents, are also very vulnerable to overweight and obesity. About 30 percent of all Oklahoma children are overweight or obese, a rate that has increased since 2003. These two conditions correlate to a higher incidence of Type 2 diabetes and other health risks. These same data also show that as Oklahoma children age they are more likely to become overweight and obese. Obesity and overweight are, according to the Oklahoma data, more prevalent among Black and Latino children than Whites. At the same time, since Oklahoma Whites are the majority of the population, more Whites are overweight or obese than minorities.[11]

Being overweight or obese during childhood is defined, as it is for adults, by the BMI. The purpose of the BMI is, as with adults, to screen for excess fat, which in children may lead to known health risks. Over my visits of three and a half years at TWBD, there were many children, regardless of race, who appeared to be overweight or obese.

Children who are diagnosed with Type 1 diabetes must monitor the sugar in their bloodstream and take additional amounts of insulin in addition to that produced by the pancreas. When not diagnosed, Type 1 diabetes in children exposes them to a higher incidence of heart disease and stroke, as well as other health complications.[12] At twelve years of age my own sister, White and nonpoor, was diagnosed with Type 1 diabetes. Very soon afterward she became obese. Eventually she was beset by other serious conditions that led to her premature death.

While there is at this time no cure for Type 1 diabetes, it can be managed. Experts suggest that children with the disease eat a balanced diet that controls for foods high in sugar. At the same time, diabetic children should be encouraged, according to the experts, to be physically active throughout the day. If children follow these general directives, their diabetic symptoms are less detrimental to their long-term health.[13]

As with adults below the poverty line, children of the poor are frequently assigned by society certain personality characteristics that allegedly account for their being overweight or obese. A popular misbelief is that poor children who appear overweight or obese are that way because their poor parents receive excessive government subsidies. Research suggests, on the contrary, that there are other causes of Type 1 diabetes in children. In fact, the exact causes of Type 1 diabetes are not clearly understood, but according to the research community genetics and environmental factors both appear to play a role in the process.

What is clear, however, is that overweight and obese poor children can become one more reason to shortchange the poor and their families. The question some in the public ask is how families below the poverty line can be genuinely poor if some of their children are overweight or obese.

In contrast, similar public concern about the root causes of these same medical conditions in the nonpoor does not become a political critique of these children or their families, even though families with expendable income have far greater health care access and solutions to overweight and obesity. My sister, for example, was never blamed, nor my parents, for her diabetes.

A double standard exists with regard to overweight and obesity in the poor and the nonpoor. A bank president may not be criticized for being overweight or obese. He or she is far less likely to be accused of having a weak character or some other alleged personality deficiency that supposedly caused their condition. This is true even though this nonpoor person, the bank president, has far more alternatives available with which to resolve their health issue than the person who falls below the poverty line.

As suggested by the first guests at Thy Will Be Done we contacted in 2019, as well those guests in the study during the second and third year and a half, many of the challenges the poor face could be avoided or resolved if they had more money at their disposal. This includes having enough money to avoid food insecurity.

There are always exceptions. Perry, for example, could earn more money than he chooses given the various options available to him and likely be healthier as well. But exceptions like Perry do not support stereotypes of the poor, as the other guests at TWBD illustrate. Instead, Perry reifies existing stereotypical beliefs based less on fact, more on assertion or limited contact with those below the poverty line.

Guests at TWBD who work full- or part-time sometimes also face food insecurity. This includes individuals such as Peggy and many others who may have worked much of their lives but frequently earned only the minimum wage or slightly above it. Even Mike, who has a strong work ethic along with his skill set, must sometimes rely on TWBD. Ahmed, his wife, and his children, all Iraqi immigrants in search of a better life in our country, have fallen through bureaucratic cracks at a state university.

For many years economists have studied the impact of a low minimum wage upon poverty rates. The federal minimum wage, the minimum wage standard in Oklahoma since 2014, has been $7.25 per hour. A minimum wage of $7.25 does not eliminate poverty; rather, it at best sustains it. Those who must work full-time at this wage remain poor.[14]

The poor in Oklahoma know that the minimum wage is a poverty wage. It is why they sometimes decide it is not in their own best interests or their family's to work a minimum wage job. Minimum wage can, in fact, force workers to work multiple jobs.[15]

Cheap and reliable public transportation in Hereford is another key factor disadvantaging the poor in Hereford. It keeps those who cannot afford a car not only from getting to their job but taking advantage of stores with the best prices. The high cost of renting in Hereford is yet another.

An abusive marriage can be the start of poverty for some. Marci's Native husband left her for another woman when Marci was diagnosed with breast cancer. Her husband was abusive, but Marci stayed in the marriage because of their four children and her fear of moving from her hometown. When she made the move to Hereford, she was able to return to school, find a better job that provided for her family, and get support from a nearby tribal nation.

Overweight and obesity plague those in poverty. But overweight and obesity are not the direct result of laziness, no more so than for the nonpoor. Jed, along with Joe and Kathy, who also appear obese, unfortunately may face the possibility of serious health issues in the future with no health insurance.

Poor Oklahomans frequently face multiple challenges. Mary Ann and her sister Heather, by way of illustration, must confront several generations of her family burdened by being poor. There seems no end to the problems she and others in this three-generation family face. Mary Ann and Heather are not alone in confronting the challenges of multigenerational poverty.[16]

Many guests at TWBD may face a variety of impediments that keep them below the poverty line. These challenges can be temporary or lasting. An additional list of stumbling blocks for those in poverty is plentiful: They sometimes are not permitted to work at all because of perceived stigma. They are full-time caregivers for others in their household. If no longer able to work, they have no other income than Social Security or very limited retirement and pension funds. They are attempting to live off of federal or state programs specifically targeting the poor. They are disabled. They are homeless. They are single parents with no or limited day care. Multiple health issues keep them from working. They lack the money to pay for health care. They are not familiar enough with the work culture to understand what conditions of work and benefits should be provided to them by their employer. They are stuck with an education that provided them job skills unnecessary in today's labor market.

There remain many guests at TWBD whose full stories have not been told. Joe, who cuts the lawns of fifty customers every year, cannot find any other work for four or five months each year because of what appears to be a mental disability. Lacking the capital to purchase and maintain a vehicle to transport his equipment, he pushes his lawnmower through the Hereford streets from one job to the next. George and son Scott, who, because they also lack reliable transportation, frequently must confront the harsh Oklahoma weather after their visit to TWBD. Taking turns in the afternoon heat of 102 degrees one day in 2022, they have to maneuver their rusty grocery cart filled with TWBD plastic bags two miles to their apartment. Since there are few sidewalks along the way, they stay on the shoulder of the busy road when there is one. When there is no shoulder, they must carefully maneuver through the traffic in the far-right lane to avoid serious injury.

In general, helping TWBD guests seems to lead directly to volunteers demystifying many preconceived misconceptions about those in poverty. The challenges faced by guests like Peggy, Elizabeth and Fred, Nancy and Sid, Marci, Mary Ann and Hank, James, Ahmed, Jed and Lula, Perry, all their close and extended family members, and hundreds and hundreds of guests just like them at TWBD are impossible to ignore. This sea of humanity may be a wake-up call to some volunteers, who then decide to spend more and more time volunteering at TWBD or helping those in need in additional ways outside of the food pantry.

The only groups of volunteers at TWBD who may continue to harbor negative stereotypes about those with food insecurity are relatively easy to identify. They consist of those who are specifically assigned to work as TWBD volunteers to fulfill a community service requirement for a school class, church, or sorority. These individuals for various reasons do not want to be at TWBD and often find ways not to participate fully, including leaving early.

In a state ranking sixth from the top in food insecurity, these brief descriptions of the perspectives of the poor and their households at Thy Will Be Done in Hereford are but a few of many stories yet untold. Joey and Kathy, for instance, are residents of a small community in rural Wells County outside Hereford's city limits. What about those who face poverty in rural Oklahoma?

3

Macon

Poverty is not a big problem in Macon.
—Pastor David Alfred Meyers, First Church of Macon

By the time Rowdy reaches the western outskirts of Hereford, a light rain begins to fall. Slamming his foot on the gas pedal, he careens Thy Will Be Done's freezer truck past sprawling fields of cotton and grazing cattle. In no time at all he reaches the small town of Macon.

Three days each week Rowdy directs the stocking and shelving of grocery goods. Thanks to his supervision, along with other volunteers of similar dedication, TWBD grocery shelves are always filled with food. When one item runs out, volunteers under Rowdy's supervision restock the frozen chicken, fresh squash, gallon jugs of apple juice, and canned vegetable soup. Even when Rowdy, a retired accountant with the Hereford school district and self-taught forklift operator, is not at TWBD in person, he might as well be, because his tutored disciples mimic his detailed instructions.

When Rowdy learned that TWBD was starting to serve small communities throughout Wells County, he quickly volunteered to oversee the operation. Macon, population 1,200, was at the top of the list because of its poverty rate of 38 percent, noticeably higher than Hereford's and almost triple the state average.[1]

Janice, the director of TWBD, is very aware of food insecurity issues in Macon because she has talked with Macon residents who are guests at the pantry in Hereford. She has also discussed Macon's poverty issues with several Macon and Hereford community leaders. As a result, in 2021 TWBD began sending a freezer truck once a month to Macon filled with boxes of food. Recently several other rural communities in Wells County with high poverty rates have been added to TWBD's list.

This March afternoon is, according to the weather forecast, not the best time to be driving to Macon. The television meteorologists, who uniformly hold a position of high respect among the public throughout the state, predict winds of thirty miles per hour or more along with heavy rain in and around the Macon area. Wells County lies squarely in the middle of Oklahoma's Tornado Alley. Fortunately, the expertise of the Weather Forecast Office of the National Weather Service in Norman generates detailed and reliable state forecasts—forecasts Oklahomans have, over the years, come to trust.

Forecasters have warned Macon residents that within the next twenty-four hours increased atmospheric turbulence is likely to culminate in tornadic winds. Rowdy, seemingly oblivious, barely takes his foot off the gas as he makes a sharp right turn off of the state highway and directly onto an empty Macon street. A brief glimpse of downtown Macon discloses next to nothing but a handful of people walking the downtown streets. At one thirty on a weekday afternoon, there are a total of four cars on Main Street. Just a few blocks farther on, Rowdy pulls up in front of his destination.

With its peaked roof line and impressive steeple, the stone-and-brick First Church of Macon sits on a slight rise on Logan Avenue just south of where it crosses D Street. The church's exterior appears to have been painted recently and the spring grass, bushes, and trees neatly trimmed. In contrast, it is surrounded by several houses with boarded windows, crumbling rain gutters, and other signs of disrepair.

Light rain beginning to fall, Rowdy directs a handful of volunteers to unload the freezer truck. He is a man of few words who prefers to lead by example. He is also strong for his size. With his own two hands he unloads the big tents—about six by twelve feet when erected—then starts stacking the boxes five high. Three volunteers soon share in carrying the bulky tents to the edge of the church's property facing Logan Avenue, then begin to unpack them. Another group of volunteers who just arrived carry the food boxes to where the tents will soon be erected.

After the Macon residents in their vehicles show their TWBD cards or are otherwise vetted by a staff member standing under the shelter of the newly erected tents, guests form a line of cars and trucks on Logan Avenue. Each patiently waits their turn to pick up their prepackaged food. It takes an additional five minutes before volunteers from both Macon and Hereford fill the two tables under the tents with last-minute food items not included in the boxes packed in Hereford. These new items include fresh vegetables and cookies.

The light rain slows to a drizzle, but it is quickly followed by a brisk western wind. Spring weather in Oklahoma is a volatile stew of colder, dry western air from Colorado stirred into a much warmer, wetter jet stream blowing in from the Gulf of Mexico. When these opposites collide under the right conditions, Oklahoma has a dark history of becoming ground zero for severe thunderstorms and deadly tornadoes. In 2013 an EF5 tornado with winds peaking at 210 miles an hour killed twenty-four residents of Moore, just south of the Oklahoma City metroplex. Another 212 were injured.[2]

Volunteers, concerned the tents might be blown over by the afternoon winds yet to come, attach additional ropes from the tent corners to large metal trash cans. The trash cans have been filled halfway to the top with quick-dry cement. Jerry-rigged but effective contraptions, it takes at least two volunteers to roll each trash can into place.

Just before the first Macon residents pick up their boxes, a man walks up and tells the volunteers he wants to make a donation. He keeps chickens. Then, without any further explanation, he carefully unloads twelve cartons of eggs from two plastic bags. He is immediately thanked for his thoughtfulness, but with his right hand he dismisses any suggestion that his kindness is special. He leaves quickly before telling anyone his name, although one of the Macon volunteers recognizes him.

Several Macon drivers, newcomers to the TWBD food truck, now pass by on Logan Avenue to ask when and how the food will be dispensed. Each time they do, honks of greeting fill the air. Only a few minutes pass before the wind picks up several notches, this time bringing with it a driving spring rain. The frontline winds of this afternoon storm hit with enough bravado to drive most of the volunteers to the shelter of the church. The hardiest two volunteers, who soon will be completely soaked, stand their ground and keep a watchful eye on the boxes of food. They are not worried about Macon residents taking more than their fair share. That is unheard of. They are worried the boxes will get soaked.

At the doors of the First Church of Macon, Pastor David Alfred Meyers, dressed in jeans and a polo shirt, welcomes volunteers seeking shelter from the rain. He also graciously offers any newcomers a quick tour of his church. Meanwhile, Rowdy once again settles back in the driver's seat of the freezer truck, one wary eye glued on his tents. The lines remain firmly anchored to the concrete-filled garbage cans as the raindrops pelt the stretched canvas with thuds as loud as hail. But the forecast is once again right on target. No hail, which is often a precursor to tornadoes, falls on the First Church of Macon. At least not this afternoon.

All the volunteers who sought shelter inside the church remain cheerful as they wait out the bad weather. After the worst of the wind and rain have subsided, they seem more determined than ever to distribute the food boxes. Ever vigilant, Rowdy keeps the motor running in the freezer truck so the food packages he holds in reserve remain as fresh as when they left TWBD's walk-in freezer.

Only minutes after the rain and wind have subsided, a handful of Macon residents make their presence known. They are on foot and look untouched by the downpour. The small group of five or six must have been waiting patiently in one of the houses directly across Logan Avenue from the church. Soon qualified by the staff member from Hereford, these are the first visitors to receive their food boxes. After a few words of thanks to the volunteers, their arms carefully wrapped around the cardboard boxes, they disappear down Logan Avenue.

The skies over Macon remain ominous but then clear up a little. At this point in the afternoon, a van from the Oklahoma State Department of Health pulls up to the curb in front of the church. With little fuss, a middle-aged man and two women emerge. The three state health workers tell everyone assembled under the tents that they are in town to provide information about COVID-19.

Since the first days of COVID, all across Oklahoma vaccination and booster rates have remained very low when compared to national averages. The residents of Macon, according to these state health workers, are no exception. Not surprisingly, unvaccinated and unboosted Oklahomans suffer from a relatively high percentage of COVID-19 cases. As well, there are correspondingly high percentages of hospitalizations and deaths in Oklahoma related to COVID compared to most other states (see chapters 4 and 7).

Based in nearby Guthrie, these health workers tell everyone within earshot that misinformation about COVID-19 is rampant throughout the state. If any Macon residents have questions, the health workers have answers based upon the scientific information they receive directly from the U.S. Centers for Disease Control and Prevention.

In spite of many uninformed or misinformed Oklahomans, this afternoon there is not a single resident of Macon who takes the time to speak with these three health workers. After about forty-five minutes, all three wave goodbye to the volunteers, climb back into their state van, and drive back to Guthrie.

During this interlude, a stream from the run-off caused by the downpour forms less than twenty-five yards down Logan Avenue. The drivers who are beginning to line up in their vehicles for the free food boxes must slow down before sloshing through the fast-moving, rising water. A man on a Harley motorcycle, wearing no helmet, approaches the line of cars and trucks waiting on Logan for the distribution of food to begin. Evidently taken by surprise by the newly formed stream, he brakes too quickly. Losing control, he and the motorcycle do a slow-motion tumble into the reddish-tinged storm waters. But before those who rush to help can reach him, the motorcyclist jumps to his feet and motions to onlookers that he is unhurt.

The motorcyclist tries to reclaim his partially submerged motorcycle, but with no success. A bystander finally helps him right the heavy machine, then between them they push it to the safety of higher ground. The motorcyclist, drenched to the bone, walks aways from the accident without any apparent injuries, except perhaps to his pride. Presumably he leaves his motorcycle behind to retrieve some dry clothes before returning for both his ride and his TWBD food box.

One of the volunteers who sees the submerged motorcycle in the pop-up stream shakes her head. "He doesn't know how to ride through water. Hit his brakes too hard." There is not much sympathy shown. The motorcyclist who took a dive into the stream, now nothing but a shallow puddle, does not return. No one talks about making sure he gets his box of TWBD food.

It takes less than an hour to dispense the boxes of food to all those who line up in front of the church. A total of eighteen drivers receive food boxes for their households, not counting those who come on foot. Last of all, the four Macon volunteers, all members of First Church of Macon, also receive food. The minister, Pastor Meyers, personally hands the boxes to them.

While the residents of Macon pick up their food, two different men share their stories about food issues in Macon. One says he pays for a deer hunting license every year so he can have enough meat to see him through hard times. The other says that he used to trap animals for his meat but gave it up several years ago. The streams and ponds nearby, he tells me, are too polluted to stock fish.

This afternoon the majority of those in Macon who receive TWBD food boxes are, according to one of the local volunteers, first timers. Local volunteers placed signs in downtown Macon and at all the churches to announce the event at First Church of Macon.

The Macon recipients genuinely seem grateful to receive their packages of food. Several admit they would prefer to pick up their food in

Hereford, but their work schedules keep them from making the drive. Macon employers, they also say, will not allow them to take time off from work, even if unpaid, to drive to Hereford and back. Without their employers' permission, these Macon-based employees fear they will lose their jobs if they drive to Hereford for free food.

While the packages of food are distributed, Pastor Meyers goes from one car to another greeting those lined up in front of his church. He asks after their families and other loved ones, frequently sprinkling community news into his conversations. As it turns out, Pastor Meyers is a strong supporter of TWBD and a major facilitator in the delivery of its food packages to Macon.

After Pastor Meyers greets everyone who lines up for a food box, he ambles back to his church. Seeing there is no immediate need for our help, my research assistant and I follow him into his basement office just one door down a long hall from the sacristy. The pastor graciously asks us to sit in two comfortable chairs in front of his expansive wooden desk. It is covered by various stacks of papers and framed color photographs of his family.

He gives a quick overview of the many congregations he has served in Oklahoma. He also mentions his ten years' work in the development office at Hereford State. Development offices at colleges and universities are most often where various fundraising projects originate, targeting alumni, special friends of the institution, and supporters throughout the community. It turns out that Pastor Meyers also taught college and university classes at several different public and private institutions in Oklahoma. He has an undergraduate degree and a master's. In addition, he is only short a few course hours from qualifying for a Ph.D. After qualifying and passing his comprehensive exams, he would be allowed to research and write his dissertation, then successfully defend it to earn his degree.

"I know you are aware of the high poverty rate here in Macon. How as pastor of this church do you find solutions to the problems that usually result from such a high poverty rate?"

Pastor Meyers seems a little surprised, even taken aback. "Poverty is not a big problem in Macon," he replies in a steady voice. "We have a ministerial alliance made up of the major churches in Macon. We take care of any problems that develop. But really, food is not a problem here. Any kids who need it get free breakfasts from federal programs. And lunches, too. Of course, they have to qualify. Since President Biden, things have gotten better than they were before. Almost everyone in town has big gardens. Food around here is pretty cheap."

"Food insecurity has got to be a real problem."

"Not really," he responds. "This is a small town. I would hear from members of my congregation or one of the other ministers if anyone doesn't have what they need. Let me give you an example of what I'm talking about. Several months ago, a young woman moved here from Tulsa along with her mother and her daughter. First thing, we got together to find this woman steady work at the restaurant out on the highway. You probably passed it when you came in from Hereford. We found her a place to live and paid her rent and other costs for her and her family, until she got back on her feet again. Unfortunately, she moved on after a few months, but we saw to it that she and her family got what they needed."

"You've got to remember that the statistics about Macon are never going to be that accurate," he continues. In the case of Macon, the numbers can exaggerate the real situation. Take my congregation. I've got about eighty some families altogether. I'd have to say they are all in good shape or I would know about it. Now, granted, many of them are older or retired, but they can be counted on to help each other out if needed or help others who are not part of my church. It's the same with the other big churches in town."

"But what about the downtown area? It looks like a ghost town."

"That is an unfortunate situation," Pastor Meyers admits. "We've got some local storeowners who for whatever reason—and it's complicated—don't want to rent their buildings to outsiders. The owners are mostly well off and don't really need the money. You see, Macon has plenty of jobs and we're not that far from Hereford. I even know some people who live here but work in Tulsa. Macon is doing okay. We look out for each other. This is a good place to live, to raise a family. It's a safe place."

But before returning to Hereford, we have a brief conversation with a community volunteer. He is one of the Macon locals who handed out boxes of food. As it turns out, he is not from Macon but an Israeli student who has been living in Macon for the past four months. In general, he is puzzled by what he has experienced.

The Israeli student says, "I've enjoyed my time here. Everyone is very friendly. But I am confused about what I've seen. There are people trying to help the situation and there is a real need for it. But I don't see how things are changing for the better because the need seems greater than most people are willing to admit."

Meanwhile, Rowdy has been listening to the weather report from the front seat of the freezer truck. There is a good chance the storm is not over. He and the other Hereford volunteers soon set off for the return trip to Hereford to avoid the bad weather. Late that night an EF1 hits Macon. An EF1 tornado has winds between 86 and 115 miles per hour. Thankfully, no one in Macon dies or requires hospitalization. According to media reports, the EF1 damaged several Macon houses.

A few weeks later I return to Macon to talk with more residents. Just entering the town, I encounter a blockade by Oklahoma state troopers that reroutes all traffic around the central part of the community. Then the blockade directs drivers east onto the state highway in the direction of Tulsa. Determined to reach my original destination, there is no choice but to take side streets circling back to downtown Macon. Along the way a state trooper tells me that this is not a practice drill, it is a real emergency.

That same evening three different Oklahoma television news teams track the hostage situation in Macon. An older man took a family member hostage. But first he dragged his aging mother into the front yard by her hair. Then he barricaded himself inside his house and threatened to commit suicide. When he brandished a gun at law enforcers, local police at the scene called in a SWAT team. The authorities soon placed Macon High School, a few blocks away from the site of the hostage-taking, on full lockdown.

For whatever reasons, after six hours of negotiation between the suspect and the SWAT team, no progress was made. Since the older man, a well-known resident of Macon, was still threatening his mother and himself with harm, the SWAT team finally fired tear gas into their house. Then, when the suspect again came out his front door with his gun in his hand and refused to drop it, an unnamed member of the SWAT team shot him. Fortunately, after undergoing surgery, the hostage taker survived.[3]

Pastor Meyer's exact words from behind his expansive desk now resonate: "We look out for each other. This is a good place to live, to raise a family. It's a safe place to live."

Macon Revisited

Like many nonmetro Oklahoma communities, Macon was founded before statehood in 1907. The community was platted out in 1895 to be adjacent to a railroad junction. At the time, cotton was the main money crop and a local entrepreneur had already built a successful cotton press to handle the abundant harvest.

Then oil was discovered, not only in Macon but soon after in the nearby community of Wellington. In 1913 these two oil fields, the Macon field and the Wellington field, together produced 220,000 barrels of oil per day, or 80,300,000 barrels per year.[4] By comparison, the European Union at one point in 2022 announced it would significantly cut back its reliance on Russian oil by 100,000 barrels a day in response to the Russian invasion of Ukraine.[5]

At the town's peak, the 1920 U.S. Census counted about 2,600 residents. But ever since the inevitable oil bust that follows a boom, the population has been in steady decline. Macon and several other rural Wells County communities all experienced similar oil booms and busts. After reliance on oil, their local economies most often shifted back to agriculture and ranching. Hereford was one of the only exceptions in Wells County, snagging a public state college that eventually proved capable of providing long-term economic growth and stability to many residents. One well-known cattleman in Wells County, who preferred to remain anonymous, detailed his personal experiences. Over several cups of coffee at one of Hereford's six Starbucks, Jacob, now in his early seventies, described the working cattle ranch a few miles outside of Hereford where he was born and raised.

This area cattle rancher graduated with a degree in agriculture from Hereford State in the early 1970s. At that time the enrollment barely exceeded three thousand. While still a student, however, he says he learned the nuts and bolts of the ranching business by buying and selling the cattle he raised on his family's ranch. He got so good at it, while still a student at Hereford State, that he began buying, raising, and selling cattle for friends who knew and trusted him.

When this same respondent entered the workforce full time after graduation, he and his growing family could "live decent" with a herd of two hundred cattle. One cow required on the average eight acres of grazing land to support it. This required, according to his math, a minimum of 1,600 acres of land to support his family. These acres did not need to be all in one place, but at least nearby enough so he did not have to waste time driving from one location to another to tend his herd. The young cattle rancher bought three additional plots of land to increase his own total property, separate from his parents' land, to the desired 1,600 acres. He paid one of the Hereford banks "short-term interest money" to purchase these three plots. Then the unexpected occurred.

Long-term interest rates increased to as high as 18 percent in the 1980s.[6] Simultaneously, there was a big downturn in cattle prices. Seeing future financial ruin ahead unless he acted in his own best interests, this young cattle rancher paid off his short-term debt to his Hereford lender. Then, free and clear, he walked away from the cattle business, albeit with the hope that the industry as he knew it would soon reappear. The simple fact was, he says, he could no longer support his family by raising and selling cattle. At the time it never occurred to him that small-scale cattle ranching as he knew it was finished for good.

Other ranchers in Wells County were not so well capitalized or savvy. As a result, many ranchers around Hereford and throughout Wells County paid a heavy financial and emotional price as the industry changed. Suicides and other kinds of self-destructive behavior were common during these years. This was especially the case when ranchers realized they might lose ownership of their land.[7] This was land many inherited from their parents or grandparents, land their families had worked to develop over multiple generations. As such, their ranches were an essential part of their self-identity, a part of who they were and who their children would eventually become.

While our respondent rancher was smart enough to avoid 18 percent long-term bank interest rates, both national and international agricultural corporations were gobbling up enormous parcels of ranching and farmlands from struggling family operators throughout the United States. Using economies of scale and state tax incentives, Seaboard Corporation, for example, built a massive facility in the panhandle of Oklahoma. Seaboard is one of the largest producer of hogs in the world.[8]

Small-scale Oklahoma producers of hogs, cattle, and chicken were virtually driven out of the marketplace by national and international businesses like Seaboard. A small-scale rancher in Hereford could not take advantage of corporate economies of scale even though corn and cotton prices were, at least in more recent years, coming back a little. For example, most of the wheat Wells County cattle ranchers used to grow for themselves or bought locally from other growers is now trucked in from Texas and Kansas.

Wells County small-scale ranchers have become proverbial business dinosaurs. Moreover, ranch land in Wells County, while relatively inexpensive compared to some other parts of the country, is not appreciating at the same rates it did in the past. The selling price in 2023 averaged $3,937 an acre.[9]

"Use to be," my rancher respondent stated. "Like the saying goes, 'ranchers live poor but die rich.'" Ranchers grazed their cattle on land with no debt, land they owned free and clear of the banks. They butchered cattle for their own use, and frequently their wives, who also may have helped with all of the ranching chores, grew big gardens and kept chickens. Their land appreciated over time. Upon the death or retirement of the family landowners, land would be transferred to other family members or to nonfamily small-scale farmers. The profit from the sale of land assured a debt-free retirement. Those days, this respondent recognizes, are long since passed.[10]

He continued, "You can't make it on ranching alone! You don't see ranchers hauling cattle to sale in their trailers anymore. Driving like they did right through downtown Hereford."

For many local Hereford ranchers, raising cattle was something they continued to work at because it was what they best knew how to do. But they could not make a real living at it. Now small-scale ranching is more a time-consuming hobby than a family business paying the major bills and providing a dependable economic future. Ranchers still can make a small profit off their home-grown cattle, but the majority need at least one spouse with another full-time job.

Subsequently, Wells County communities dependent on the needs of ranching and farming families who did not live in town lost valued customers upon which so many Oklahoma small towns, now post-oil bust, relied. The residents of these very modest communities, like Macon, have few real options. Residents seeking viable jobs must vote with their feet.

The business leaders of these same communities, often edged on by state economic experts, dream and bet on big, new industries or development projects to relocate to their area and return their towns to their oil-boom glory days. All have met with mixed records of success.[11]

Diversification of production on the family ranch and farm, despite what many academic agricultural economists have been preaching for years, is more difficult than it sounds. To expect ranchers and farmers to pivot to new businesses like raising llamas, or to rake in profits from a mix of Halloween mazes, wedding venues, bed and breakfasts, or a slew of other proposed alternatives is unrealistic. Oklahoma ranchers and farmers have little control or responsibility for macroeconomic forces that may be global in reach.

One result of this trend is that a majority of rural communities throughout Wells County have downtowns that resemble ghost towns. Streets once boasting locally owned businesses lie empty, and the buildings still standing are in dilapidated condition. The same is true of the houses and apartments of residents throughout these same communities, like Macon.

There are some remarkable exceptions to this economic trend throughout Oklahoma. One frequently touted is Pryor, Oklahoma, now home to a Google data center. The town has increased in population from 8,327 in 1990 to 9,444 in 2020, a population gain of 12 percent. Google states that it has invested $4.4 billion in its business operations at Pryor and created eight hundred full-time jobs at a variety of different pay levels.[12] But for every success story like Pryor, there are fifty Macons.

Two weeks after the hostage taking and shooting in Macon, residents again complained to the elected members of their town council about the stench coming from the creek directly adjacent to the only low-income housing project in town. Residents both at the housing project and those living nearby have been complaining about the putrid smell for months. The creek flows directly under the state highway connecting Macon to Hereford. A recent study by state highway engineers indicated that a town-owned drainage pipe had been pouring raw sewage directly into the creek for an undetermined amount of time. Macon residents had been complaining for a very long time.[13]

As reported in a local newspaper, the Macon mayor acknowledged problems with an eight-inch pipe that carried raw sewage from the Macon low-income housing project to the creek. The mayor's acknowledgment of the problem, however, came only after irate Macon citizens had apparently complained about the stench for years. After an emergency meeting, Macon officials finally allocated $70,000 to the cleanup and repair project. The money, in fact, was taken from federal COVID-19 relief funds Macon received through the American Rescue Plan Act of 2021.

When the mayor was asked if the money had been originally budgeted for other needs, he said, "We damn sure did. But there's nothing else we can do." Originally this same COVID-19 money had been allocated to make improvements to the town's water system because the system was "disintegrating." The money was reported to also go for "work on a water lift station and the town's water tower." The mayor is straightforward about not having the funds to bring his community's public services up to code. "The whole city has a crumbling infrastructure," he writes in the local paper.

Macon is, in fact, one of the poorest communities in Wells County, with a poverty rate of 38 percent—roughly three times the state rate. In Macon, Whites compose 78 percent of all residents. However, though White residents in Macon have the largest number of poor, they do not have the highest poverty rate in Macon. Hispanics number about 9 percent of the population but their poverty rate is 50 percent. No Blacks live in Macon. The Native American population is 2 percent. While there are a very small number of Native Americans who attend Macon public schools, according to school officials, they do not live in Macon.[14]

In 2022 median household income in Macon was $38,462, compared to the state average of $67,330. Said another way, Macon's average per-capita income is about 56 percent of that for all of Oklahoma, one of America's poorest states. At the same time, about 20 percent of all Macon citizens in poverty are employed. These residents constitute Macon's working poor, those who work but at $7.25 an hour, or slightly more. They still fall below the poverty line.[15]

The strong opinions of Pastor Meyers to the contrary, poverty is in fact a very serious problem in Macon. The pastor's reluctance to accept the truth about poverty in his own hometown does not negate relevant facts. For whatever reasons, he and a handful of the major religious leaders in Macon have convinced themselves that Macon families, including children, have enough food to eat. Nevertheless, Pastor Meyers has arranged for Hereford's TWBD food pantry to truck in free boxes of food. This free food is dispensed in front of his own church. Sometimes the free food is handed out by Pastor Meyers to residents he knows by name.

On our fourth visit to Macon, Pastor Meyers spends more than an hour discussing a variety of topics about his town from behind his church office desk. He first describes in detail his lifelong role as a religious leader in a variety of towns throughout Oklahoma. While it turns out that he soon plans to retire formally from his present church, a position for which he receives a modest salary, he intends to continue to serve as its unpaid pastor. Pastor Meyers undoubtedly has a strong commitment to the spiritual well-being of his congregation.

Pastor Meyers also talks openly about his views on poverty in Macon and throughout Oklahoma: "Since the 1980s, philanthropy has become an industry in Oklahoma," he says. Nonprofits like TWBD have replaced the traditional role of churches, according to Pastor Meyers, and provide more than adequate help to the poor.

He continues: "Free food is really not necessary for Oklahomans. Especially kids. I have been in the homes of the poor in Macon and most of them are comfortable with their poverty. They do not need food because it is available to them. Food is not an issue in Macon." He reiterates that the belief that kids go to sleep hungry in Macon or anywhere else in Oklahoma is for the most part a myth. Proof of this, he argues illogically, is that the Hereford food bank now makes regular visits to Macon.

As far as access to health care, Pastor Meyers knows that the only on-site health care available in Macon is provided by a trained nurse at a clinic called Hereford Medical Care. She spends two mornings a week seeing patients from her office in downtown Macon.

Again, thinking there must be some data completely overlooked that would support Pastor Meyer's assertions, we examined additional resources and documents. Besides agriculture, there are no other major industries in Macon and the surrounding area. However, small farmers and ranchers in Wells County continue to face, as discussed, a history of falling prices, which had peaked in the 1980s.[16]

Our review of an unpublished "Macon Oklahoma Business Directory" yields a total of seventy-seven businesses, although some are listed more than once. Along with the single, part-time medical clinic, it has one branch bank, one night club, one liquor store, one machine shop, one industrial equipment and supplies store, and one funeral home. The *Macon News*, a weekly and the only newspaper covering Macon along with two other communities, is based twenty miles away in Wellington.

Macon also has two gas stations, two beauty shops, two insurance companies, two used car dealers, three restaurants, and five churches including the First Church of Macon. Although the town once had a grocery store, it has been many years since that business closed its doors. Two convenience stores provide a very limited selection of foods that can be reheated in on-site microwaves. Frozen pizza, according to residents, is one of the most popular foods available in town.[17]

For every downtown business open to customers, there are at least four or more closed or abandoned. Several downtown buildings are literally crumbling to the ground, piles of used bricks from their walls stacked in front of them on the sidewalk. According to a crumbled-up piece of cardboard on the sidewalk, the bricks are for sale.

The largest single employer in Macon is the public school district. The Macon school district, according to its website, employs forty-five teachers, bus drivers, custodians, and cooks. Its total enrollment is 408 students.[18] The school district's stated goal, as expected of all public school systems, is to provide an adequate education to the children of the town and surrounding district. After they graduate from high school, the children of Macon should be able to apply those learned skills to find work or continue their education at other public and private institutions of learning. To that end, the school district provides a wealth of online data suggesting that the quality of education provided children attending Macon schools is more than satisfactory. This repeated online insistence by representatives of the school system that it is achieving its stated goals is suspect.

The quality of Macon's public school system can best be objectively judged by examining scores on standardized tests that all public school students in Oklahoma are required to take. These state test scores reflect an unbiased overview of the quality of education each Oklahoma public school system provides. Standardized test scores interpreted in an objective fashion are, in short, a better evaluation tool than assertions or interpretations of the data provided by local stakeholders, which may be self-serving.

According to the test score data provided by the Macon school district in 2022, test scores for its students have actually declined since 2017. State tests administered in Macon's public schools ranked Macon students 243rd from the top when compared to a total of 540 Oklahoma school districts. Further, according to this same data, only 33 percent of all Macon students enrolled in the Macon district schools scored at "proficient" levels in math, and only 34 percent were "proficient" in reading/language arts. At best these test scores place Macon students in the forty-fifth percentile compared to all other Oklahoma public school students.

What must be considered when judging the test scores of Macon students is that Oklahoma public school students score among the lowest of all students in the nation. Based upon standardized test scores for the entire state, for example, 71 percent of all fourth grade Oklahoma children are not proficient in reading skills. As well, 74 percent of all Oklahoma children are not proficient in math. Further, 15 percent of all Oklahoma children do not graduate from high school on time. Recently, Oklahoma public school students were ranked second-worst in the nation with regard to overall quality of public education. Math test scores, for example, were forty-seventh in the nation, as were reading test scores, compared to all other states.[19]

Standardized test scores of Macon students strongly suggest, in contrast to the misleading interpretation offered by Macon school administrators, that the majority of Macon students lack adequate proficiency in basic educational skills. This lack of adequate proficiency holds, not only when Macon students are compared to other Oklahoma students throughout the state, but also when they are compared to the majority of other public school students throughout the nation.

Other Communities in Wells County

Besides Macon, which has one of the highest poverty rates in Wells County, other small towns dot the landscape surrounding Hereford. They include the largest, Wellington with 8,000 residents, along with the much smaller communities of Likens, Roncow, Hiply, Evers, and Lone Pony. These rural communities share the common burden of contending with persistent and pervasive poverty, though some have relatively unusual histories.

Wellington is the largest of the rural towns in Wells County. Although it had shared with Macon and other communities throughout the state a cycle of oil boom and bust, it enjoys a comparatively resilient economic base because of a happenstance of geography. Unlike Macon, Wellington is located at the nexus of one of the three interstate highways that cut through Oklahoma. In addition, a major rail line links Wellington to Texas and the petroleum-rich coast of the Gulf of Mexico. Early on, Wellington's location attracted the eye of independent oil and gas companies. Jobs at this tank farm, and the jobs they create, keep Wellington from being as poor as other Hereford County communities.

At first sight, Wellington appears not to resemble any of the other Wells County communities. Six blocks of retail stores line the main avenue running through this town. But the facts about poverty tell a different story. Of the 8,000 residents, 71 percent are White, 8 percent Native, 6 percent Hispanic, and 5 percent Black. Wellington is, like Hereford and Macon, another town in Wells County with a White majority of residents. Although the poverty rate of around 20 percent, one in five residents of Wellington, is among the lowest in Wells County, Wellington's poverty rate is well above the state average.[20]

A closer inspection of the rest of Wellington, including the downtown area, quickly squelches the idea that poverty is not a serious issue. Five blocks from the main major thoroughfare with its relatively prosperous businesses sits a large abandoned and deteriorating town center. Derelict buildings reflect the former grandeur of the past oil boom years. As in Macon, many of the buildings are crumbling to the ground. But in Wellington the buildings are much grander in scale than in Macon, and the downtown area is roughly four times the size. Wellington is home to one of the most formidable ghost downtowns in rural Oklahoma.

That said, there is a small section of Wellington, one square block of downtown real estate, that has been substantially recapitalized. Two upscale restaurants anchor the block, along with a movie theater transformed into an entertainment venue. There are also a locally owned coffee shop and three other retail stores catering to shoppers.

Likens, with about 3,200 residents, is a suburb of Hereford and contiguous with Wells County. Until the late 1990s it was a community in its own right, although a rural community in decline. Since the 2010 U.S. Census, elected officials brag, the population has increased by almost 25 percent. Because Likens is close enough to Hereford, an increasing number of employees with jobs in Herford have chosen to live in Likens. As well, Likens has a less expensive housing market along with a growing reputation for the quality of its public school system. Likens nevertheless has a poverty rate of 37 percent, one that matches Hereford's and far exceeds Wellington's. Almost 86 percent of Likens residents are White. Hispanics and Natives are about 2 percent each. By the numbers, most in poverty are Whites.[21]

Likens's public schools have increasingly hired spouses of faculty employed by Hereford State College. They may be graduates of Hereford State with teaching credentials and advanced graduate degrees in education or related fields. Choosing to remain in the area because of their partners' employment at Hereford State, these men and women contribute to the positive reputation of Likens's public schools. This group of teaching professionals have found it desirable to work in a smaller school system than Hereford's even though salaries are lower in Likens.

Roncow and Hiply are two separate, very small communities less than eight miles from each other. Roncow is has a population of over 400—about double that of Hiply. Residents of Roncow are 74 percent White, while Rowcow's White population is 85 percent. If the two very small communities were combined, the total population still would be less than that of Macon.[22]

The difference between Roncow and Hiply, on the one hand, and Macon on the other, is their respective poverty rates. Roncow's poverty rate is 31 percent and Hiply's is 15 percent, in comparison to Macon's 38 percent. A major reason for lower poverty rates is that both Roncow and Hiply are within a short driving distance to relatively high-paying jobs in Hereford. At the same time, the cost of living including housing is lower in these two rural communities than in Hereford.

More than one Hiply resident depends on TWBD on a regular basis. In her forties, Sheena has two children, one a teenager with a permanent disability. At one time Sheena, a single mother, commuted to Hereford daily, where she worked at a job paying her about $13 dollars an hour because of her job experience. But now she works in Hiply at the only convenience store in town. There she earns $7.25 an hour, the minimum wage, for her labor.

This TWBD guest left her Hereford employment because she felt she had no other choice. Sheena could not afford to hire someone to watch her son while she worked in Hereford. In contrast, the convenience store in Hiply that employs her is within walking distance of her modest home. During her lunch hour Sheena checks on her son and feeds him lunch. Since he is only a minute's walk away, she can be there for her son immediately should he require attention. Paid child care in Hiply is not an option, even if Sheena could afford it.

Evers, another community contiguous with Wells County, is one of thirteen surviving Black towns in Oklahoma originally settled by African Americans between the end of the Civil War and 1920. Originally there were fifty such communities in Oklahoma, but many of these nonmetro communities, predominantly relying on farming and ranching, have since died out.[23] One might expect the community surrounding Evers State University to be a mirror image of the Hereford State community. Instead, the Historically Black College, though a land-grant institution just like Hereford State, has an annual budget of less than 10 percent of its neighboring educational institution.

The town of Evers has been unable to benefit from the presence of an economic engine like Hereford State College. Faculty and staff in general, along with many others employed at Evers State, do not choose to live in this community. Instead, they commute from other towns and cities including Oklahoma City. Despite being the home of an HBC, Evers is and always has been a community in which poverty is pervasive and persistent.

In 2021, Evers had a population of 1,600 residents, 75 percent of whom were Black. Evers's poverty rate is 36 percent, higher than Hereford's and comparable to Macon's. As with Hereford, the presence of some students living in Evers may overstate the poverty rate. In any case, Evers has among the highest poverty rates in Wells County—almost three times higher than the state rate. Given that the vast majority of Evers residents are Black, Blacks also form the largest number of those who are poor in Evers.[24]

Less than twenty miles from the Wells County line is Lone Pony, a rural community of about 1,900 residents that impacts Wells in significant ways. Lone Pony is adjacent to the Pawnee Nation. Some members of the Pawnee Nation live in Wells County and attend public school systems. They and other tribes also have a growing presence at Hereford State College. The poverty rate in Lone Pony is much lower than that of almost all other Wells communities.

In 1874 this Native tribe, once numbering about 60,000, but now with less than 4,000 on the tribal role, was removed to Indian Territory. In 1893 lands surrounding their reservation were opened to White settlers. Lone Pony was founded in 1894, like so many other communities adjacent to a rail line. However, there was never an oil boom in Lone Pony, as was the case with so many Oklahoma towns. Agriculture always formed the basis of this community's economy, along with its location adjacent to the Pawnee Nation.

Lone Pony's poverty rate is 14 percent, a significant decline since the U.S. Census first collected poverty data in 1959. The majority of Lone Pony residents are White, about 65 percent, or Native, about 22 percent. There are various indicators that the poverty rate for Natives in Lone Pony has markedly declined, as is true for the White population. First and foremost, a modest tribal-owned casino has funneled increasing employment, revenue, and social services to tribal members. Other residents of the community who are not Native have also benefited. It is also possible, but not certain at this point, that Natives in Lone Pony received one-time COVID-19 federal funds passed on to them by their tribe.[25]

Casino profits in Lone Pony helped build a new health facility for members of this tribe. This new facility also serves members of other Oklahoma tribal nations who have medical issues. Local casino profits now provide for increased medical resources to Pawnee tribal members by way of general social services available through the statewide medical system funded by Native Oklahomans.

Increased tribal resources among Natives in Lone Pony also mean increased job opportunities in tribal businesses. In turn, the overall town economy has improved. This increase in economic activity has directly improved the economic status of the majority White population. An observational appraisal of Lone Pony suggests that the downtown square, the heart of this small town, is on the upswing, as is the campus of the Lone Pony public school system. Several tribes around the state, as early as 2014, raised their entry-level wage at tribal casinos and other businesses to $9 or more an hour, with future raises anticipated.[26]

One of thirty-eight federally recognized tribes in Oklahoma, the Pawnee tribe in Lone Pony has not experienced the same scale of economic development as the Cherokee Nation, the largest tribe in Oklahoma. Tribal nations in 2019 employed 54,000 Natives and non-Natives at annual wages approaching $2.5 billion. In that same year, tribal investment in Oklahoma had a total economic impact of $15.6 billion dollars. Data collected since 2011 show a massive positive impact on the Oklahoma economy.[27]

The poverty rate in Lone Pony is still 14 percent, about the same as the state poverty rate. But the very good news in Lone Pony is that this rate is in significant decline. That decline appears closely tied to the revenues produced by the casino and the positive impact of casino revenues upon both Natives and Whites. When *Forbes* magazine released its 2024 best employers in Oklahoma, two Oklahoma tribes topped the list. The Chickasaw Nation was number one, with CEO Bill Anoatubby at the head of 13,500 workers in the state. Second was the Choctaw Nation, 12,000 Oklahoma employees, led by CEO Gary Baton.[28]

This brief examination focusing on the rural communities in Wells County suggests, not only that poverty is pervasive and persistent, but that the rural poor continue to have unmet basic needs. While rural residents who are minorities in general have markedly higher poverty rates than Whites, the majority White populations in towns like Macon vastly outnumber minority poor. In rural Wells County the faces of the poor are most frequently White faces.

This is never truer than in Macon, in spite of what some religious and community leaders may contend. Although rural communities in Wells County have different histories, these histories are germane to their present economic status. Nearby Lone Pony has witnessed marked improvement in the economic status of its residents, primarily driven by casino revenues and related Pawnee Nation business efforts.

In rural Wells County, assumptions about alleged flaws in the personalities of the poor restraining upward mobility are often misguided. Those who are poor simply do not have enough money for the basic requirements of life, which include food. As a result, like the majority of Hereford guests at TWBD, they can face multiple challenges to succeed. Not having enough money limits their options to decisions they are forced to make, just like in Hereford.

The rural residents of Wells County come to the doors of TWBD for the very same reasons as Hereford residents who have a poverty rate of almost 30 percent. They line up in good weather and bad, although in the past three years the pantry has sent their freezer truck to their small towns. But clearly the rural residents of Wells County need much more than TWBD can provide. TWBD's major purpose always has been to provide enough food to those who face food insecurity. It offers a temporary remedy to guests, not a cure for poverty. What other services do the guests, both those who live in Hereford and those who live throughout the county, lack at TWBD?

Luke embodies a partial answer to this question, although certainly he is, as are all guests, a unique individual with his own personal history. Luke is forty-five but looks much older. He shows up one afternoon at TWBD dressed in his own particular way. He appears overweight but not obese. In spite of his size, his stained pants are much too large for him. In contrast, he has managed to squeeze into a new T-shirt several sizes too small. A brand new gimme cap rides atop his head.

Luke also wears a distinctive belt that looks homemade. It is at least nine inches wide. Between his belt and his pants, Luke has randomly placed an assortment of tattered bird feathers of various sizes, some as long as twelve inches or more. Sticking out from beneath his belt, between the bird feathers, are two pencils and other useful items including a toothbrush.

When Luke turns his back to reach for a food item on the pantry shelves, a large coffee cup, completely hidden by his girth, protrudes from this same belt. At one point he mentions the address where he and his nephew live. But by his appearance alone it seems that he likely spends much of his time on the streets of Hereford. Luke is one of Hereford's invisible homeless who, according to many in town, do not even exist.

Luke says, "I have adult diabetes. I've been here before. I have adult diabetes and have to have insulin two times a day. After three years they still can't seem to get me regular. I got a nephew depending on me now. Gotta see how it turns out. He's a teenager."

"How old is he?"

"Seventeen." He picks out several desserts from a shelf and a big box of doughnuts Luke says are for his nephew. If Luke is homeless, so is his nephew.

"Luke, how is it working out living with your nephew?"

"Okay. He likes to eat a lot."

On the way to his wreck of a car, Luke repeats that the Hereford doctors still have not got his diabetes "regulated."

"Why not?"

"They kicked me out of the diabetic clinic."

"How come?"

"They said I was not keeping my appointments, so they had to kick me out. Same with my old doctor."

"So, what are you going to do now?"

"I got a new doctor. He's telling me I got adult diabetes and I gotta get it regulated."

TWBD is providing Luke and his nephew enough food to meet their temporary needs. But this food pantry cannot provide Luke with the proper medical care required to get his adult diabetes "regulated." The medical consequences of diabetes can be dire. At best the TWBD staff can only urge him to see other public or private providers of health services. But giving Luke the contact number of a social worker who might be able to help him is a stab in the dark. Since he and his nephew are also likely to be homeless, the two of them may need additional help as yet undefined.

I ask Luke, "So, what are you going to do now?" It turns out Luke's only choice at managing his adult diabetes is to return to this "new doctor." But even if his new doctor can achieve what Luke's old doctor and a clinic could not, Luke has other problems. So too does his nephew.

The solutions to the challenges both Luke and his nephew confront are much larger than receiving three or four more days of food. Exactly what are the chances of resolving their nexus of problems, including not just food insecurity but Luke's Type 2 diabetes and their probable homelessness? What are their real chances of Luke and his nephew escaping poverty in Hereford, Wells County, Oklahoma?

4

Missions of Care?

A homeless man froze to death in downtown Hereford
about ten years ago. That got their attention.
—Hereford social worker

Food security is a basic necessity of life. Thy Will Be Done is not the only provider in Hereford and Wells County offering food to those who need it. A brief examination of other private and public food providers to the poor, some of which offer additional services, establishes a foundation for TWBD's relevancy. This includes a closer look at why and how five local churches became involved in supporting a food pantry like TWBD.

At the same time, food security is not the only basic necessity of those in poverty. A dive into Hereford's largest emergency home shelter from the perspective of those who seek a safe and secure roof over their heads can shed light on the efficacy of the entire provider system for the poor.

Both public and private providers strive to meet the food needs of the poor in Hereford, Wells County, and around the state. Some of these needs may be more or less than they might at first appear. One of the most highly visible but misleading segments of this network of public and private providers in Hereford is a Greek fraternity at Hereford State College. In the good name of community service, this private attempt by the brothers produces what appears to be a sumptuous annual donation to feed the hungry.

As measured only by the annual number of cans of food collected, over the years this fraternity has been increasingly successful. The fundamental problem with their accounting system, however, is that it may unintentionally mislead many in Hereford into believing that food insecurity for the poor has been eliminated by just one annual donation. Unfortunately, even if well-intended, a glimpse at this private effort sheds doubt upon these annual endeavors to provide food security for all in Hereford who require it.

With fanfare once a year this fraternity collects thousands of pounds of canned food. Fraternity brothers put up posters throughout the city advertising the annual event and identifying collection points. Stories in the town and campus newspapers detail the fraternity's community service.

Hereford residents may quite easily imagine, because of the attendant self-publicity, that food insecurity after the frat has helped collect a mountain of canned food is no longer a pressing problem. In fact, those organizations whose task is to provide food year-round to those facing food insecurity do much of the work involved. This includes storing the canned food, then distributing it to those who require it on a timely basis. The fact is that the amount of food collected by the frat is a drop in the bucket. By no means does the canned food come close to meeting the real needs of all those facing food insecurity. The annual Greek food drive in Hereford arguably is better than no food drive at all. But one result is that some in the Hereford public walk away from the canned food campaign with the misbelief that they have substantially benefited those far less fortunate than themselves in the birth lottery. In effect, those in poverty can once again be ignored until next year's can campaign.

It is noteworthy to consider that area grocery stores and restaurants donate food to TWBD and other food providers on a regular basis. These retail businesses, unlike the frat, rarely publicize their charitable work.

If the fraternities and sororities, along with a majority of numerous other college campus clubs and organizations, were in tune with the needs of the hungry in Hereford, they would realize that those with not enough food may be sitting next to them in class.

On a sunny weekday in late April 2022, Rowdy loads up the TWBD freezer truck with an assortment of basic food items. But this time Rowdy is not driving the two-lane rural highway to Macon or other Wells County communities. He does not leave the Hereford city limits. It takes him less than five minutes to drive to married student housing dorms on the campus of Hereford State College. Students along with TWBD staff and volunteers have already set up three tables.

From 11:00 a.m. to 1:30 p.m., Hereford State students and family members, the majority of whom live in campus housing, select free food items from the three tables. Some are on their way to classes, some on errands. They stop at the tables when they realize, if they did not already know, that all the food is free.

Student volunteers tack up notices announcing TWBD's regular campus visits, but a majority of students say they read the announcements online. Students and other household members chat up the volunteers, also students, while they mill around the tables. Some students who drop by for the first time are hesitant, even shy. They act as if they do not know why they came. Except, yes, this month they could use some free food.

By their body language there are also others who seem interested in the food but instead keep walking. They pass up the free food, we surmise, because they are embarrassed other students might see them.

When students from Hereford State come as guests to TWBD, they are much more open about their food needs. That is because they are less worried about being judged by the volunteers at TWBD. At the food pantry, students are more open to expressing their frustrations with not having enough food on their table.

In addition to graduate student Ahmed, who is unable to feed his family during the summer months, along with several undergraduate student guests including Sid and Nancy, there are others at Hereford

State College who are anxious when they first enter TWBD. They do not want anyone to know that, although they are students, they do not have enough money to buy all the food they require. These students, as evidenced by Mr. Lee and Stella, offer insights into some of the challenges with which college students must contend.

Mr. Lee, as he prefers to be called, is twenty-seven years old and lives in one of the campus student dorms next to married student housing. He has a roommate who is also his best friend. Between the two of them they share cooking almost all their meals; according to Mr. Lee, the price of food on campus is much too expensive. Mr. Lee and his roommate, whom he prefers not to identify by name, cook the majority of their food in their campus apartment. Since they do not have a kitchen, this is against the dorm rules. Far from perfect, it is the only solution they can think of.

Mr. Lee has been a guest three different times at TWBD. Unlike some other international students at the college who have come to TWBD, he is not a vegetarian. Nor does he or his roommate, like Ahmed, refuse to choose food items at TWBD past their expiration date. Their stumbling block is more basic: they just do not have enough money to buy all the food they need.

Like Mr. Lee, Stella, who also is twenty-seven, is single and has a very tight budget. She just received a master's degree in information technology from Hereford State. She still has a few more weeks in student housing but is not certain where she will live after that. She mentions that she visits TWBD as a guest because she does not like going to the TWBD food tables on campus. She worries other students will recognize her and is embarrassed that they might find out about how pressed she is for money.

To her credit, Stella has already had several job interviews in Oklahoma City. More are scheduled. As yet, however, she has no concrete job offers. Oklahoma City is not her first choice to live in, but she sees it as a stepping-stone to future out-of-state jobs, which she counts on paying better.

Stella used to work full-time in a marketing job in Oklahoma City. She hated the work and saw little room for advancement. Knowing she was taking a risk, she saved what money she could before she quit her marketing job to return to school. A job in IT, she says with confidence, gives her a chance of a better future. It also provides the opportunity to move to Dallas or Houston eventually. Those big cities pay much better, she believes, than anywhere in Oklahoma. In Dallas or Houston she also can begin to save money to start paying down her student debt.

After eighteen months in graduate school, Stella has no savings left. She feels she made the right decision to change careers, but she is only beginning to come to terms with her student debt. She borrowed to the hilt to return to graduate school. She was also forced to sell her car to help pay her bills. To save money when she visits TWBD, Stella takes the bus with a friend. She says that alternatives like local taxis and Uber are too expensive.

After Stella chooses her food items at TWBD, it takes her another twenty minutes to pack, then repack, the food into her backpack. Even then all her food does not fit. Janice, the TWBD director, notices her dilemma and finds her two large cloth bags. Now Stella can carry her free food on the bus ride back to campus more easily.

Wynette Grubner, currently an administrator serving the health and well-being of children in Hereford, offers a very different perspective to food insecurity than a fraternity or Hereford College students. She has been working hands-on with Hereford children for eighteen years. Since the young frequently do not have a voice, she tries to represent their best interests based upon her knowledge of their needs. For the past seven years she has been in a leadership position in the state system of social service providers.

From her second-floor office two blocks off Hereford's Main Street, Ms. Grubner is the first to describe a tragic death—a death that directly resulted in the mobilization of congregants and their leaders in the five major downtown churches to create TWBD. She says simply, "A homeless man froze to death in downtown Hereford about ten years ago. That got their attention."

At the time of this death, Hereford services to the poor were provided by a public and private network which, at the time, from Ms. Grubner's perspective, was problematic. These providers included, among others, the Greeks, Hereford State College, the Salvation Army, the public school system, and local offices of state social service providers.

Congregants of the five downtown churches were shocked by the needless death of a homeless man just blocks from the doors of their sanctuaries. In response, they began organizing a coordinated effort to help those in poverty based upon their Christian values and beliefs. Under the guidance of their religious leaders and the knowledge of experienced congregants who had lived in cities outside of Oklahoma, Thy Will Be Done was created.

It took two full years. One contentious problem emerged when congregants decided a food pantry was badly needed. Some of the existing food providers in Hereford did not want their help.

The Hereford chapter of the Salvation Army is a key part of the provider network serving those who do not have enough food. Ms. Grubner is quick to praise the overall intentions of the local Salvation Army. At the same time, she recites a list of problems faced by the local branch of this international association that curtail its effectiveness. Food, of course, is just one of the services offered by the Salvation Army to the poor.

She believes that, when it comes to providing food for those in need, Hereford's Salvation Army was hampered by its own leadership. Infighting between existing providers prevailed when the food pantry was first proposed, then escalated as planning for it came to fruition. Providers to the poor, including the Salvation Army, were disgruntled because they felt they were not given enough credit for the good work they had long been doing in Hereford. The Salvation Army leadership saw no real need for a food pantry, least of all one directed by newcomers who lacked expertise. The local Salvation Army leaders took an active part in this squabble. They felt, according to Ms. Grubner, that TWBD was infringing upon its longtime goals and objectives, a history of more than 150 years of service around the world.[1]

Ms. Grubner describes a disagreement between the new kid on the block, TWBD, and other providers such as the Salvation Army as a "turf war." The Salvation Army, with its international scope and presumed knowledge of poverty from years of service, can, she believes, vary in effectiveness depending on the stability of its local leadership, and she questions the consistency of the local leadership in Hereford. She observes that it has been burdened by frequent turnover in recent years and staffed by those with limited experience and commitment.

She is, at the same time, quick to acknowledge the expertise and resources of the Red Cross. She praises it, on the one hand, for its ultimate professionalism, yet emphasizes that the Red Cross can be utilized only in times of natural disasters such as tornadoes and flooding. Unless there is a natural disaster, the poor in Hereford and Wells County do not qualify for its services. Most important to those without enough food in Hereford, she emphasizes, are free or discounted school food programs including breakfasts and lunches. She, like Pastor Meyers in Macon, sees these kinds of programs as crucial to the health and well-being of children of those who are poor.

Both private and public food providers at the local and state level offer a wide variety of services to those facing food insecurity. Regrettably, Oklahoma public schools, one vital part of the statewide provider network, are severely understaffed and underfinanced. Oklahoma per-student public funding in 2024 was fifth from the bottom of all states, at $9,200.[2]

The problems faced by the Macon public school system, in other words, are found throughout all of Oklahoma. This leaves administrators, classroom teachers, school counselors, and other staff less time to address the specific needs of students who fall below or near poverty. Students who have problems connected to poverty status, such as food and housing, cannot always get the attention and support they deserve. Adding to the problem is the fact that Oklahoma public school teachers have a long history of being inadequately compensated for their classroom duties (see chapter 8).

There are several federal and state programs that acknowledge the special needs of hungry children. During the Oklahoma school year, qualified children receive free or reduced breakfasts and lunches at their schools. These meal programs make good sense. Children do not have a reasonable opportunity to learn at school or at home if they do not have enough food to eat. Programs that provide these children with food during the summer months, even though they are not in school, are also crucial to both their well-being and their educational progress.[3]

Since 2010 more than 60 percent of all school-age children in Oklahoma qualify for free or discounted meals.[4] During COVID-19 the federal government made available to all students, poor and nonpoor, free or reduced-price breakfasts and lunches. After June 2022, however, about half of all Oklahoma school districts opted out of receiving resources to operate summer food programs. The governor of Oklahoma opted out of summer food programs for school-age children in 2024. In direct contrast, some states support free lunches for all students using state funds.[5]

As reported in local media, public school systems like the one in Marlow, in Stephens County in the southern part of the state, encountered problems when requiring families of school-age children who did not speak English as their first language to fill out the necessary forms to get free or discounted school meals.[6] This school system, and others throughout the state like the Midwest City and Del City public schools, both in metro Oklahoma City, also faced pushback from the public about required bureaucratic forms. As reported in state media, spokespersons for public school administrators as well as politically active groups of parents intentionally shifted the need for the food program to other issues—immigration, rights of privacy, and competency in English. Regardless of political perspective in this ongoing debate, it is all school-age children of those in poverty who have the most to lose.

There is a list of other federal and state programs on the website of the Oklahoma Department of Human Services (OKDHS) designed to serve adults and children who do not have enough food to eat or issues related to food insecurity. An emergency hotline puts those who call in contact with the Supplemental Nutrition Assistance Program (SNAP). In SNAP, 67 percent of the enrollees are children, the elderly, the disabled, women, and infants. As well, there is the Children's Supplemental Nutrition Program (WIC), which was particularly relevant when public schools closed during COVID-19. There is also the Senior Farmers Market Nutrition Program. Finally, the Oklahoma Nutrition Information and

Education (ONIE) Project offers an informative overview to recipients who are unhoused.

Additional relevant federal and state programs fall under the purvey of OKDHS. In general, OKDHS seeks to provide "help to individuals and families in need through public assistance programs and management services for seniors and people with disabilities." In turn, OKDHS falls under the supervision of the Oklahoma secretary of health and human services.

Of all Oklahoma government agencies, OKDHS has the largest number of workers; as of 2017, it employed 7,300. This same agency is also the third-largest recipient of public allocations in Oklahoma.[7] Other services those in need might receive not directly under OKDHS include the Oklahoma Health Care Authority, the Department of Mental Health, Substance Abuse Services, the Department of Health, the Department of Veterans Affairs, and the Department of Rehabilitation Services.

There is an OKDHS branch in every one of the state's seventy-seven counties. Regardless of this extensive network of public providers and their available resources for the poor, there are those critical of this department's access and quality of care.

Ms. Grubner succinctly sums up this bureaucratic structure, whose major purpose is to provide basic social services to those who require them. She personally witnessed and experienced much over her many years of working inside this network, including working from a state office for those in need that is two blocks from where the homeless man froze to death. "All these agencies have so many potential resources, but they do so little," she says.

Hereford High School is one example of Ms. Grubner's observation, particularly when she questions the quality of information and care available for those in poverty. Several other informants, all of whom wished to remain anonymous for fear of losing their jobs, supported her comments. Hereford High School, they say, has no concrete estimate of the number of homeless students in their school system.

According to the U.S. Department of Housing and Urban Development, Oklahoma ranks among the top seven states for percentage of youth homelessness. More than 20,000 Oklahoma youth less than eighteen years of age are homeless.[8]

In Macon, children of both the poor and the nonpoor have a variety of problems that professional therapy, if available, can address. These mental health issues range in severity, but psychological problems among Macon youth can benefit from services not offered in Macon. The same may be assumed for other rural communities throughout the state.

Although available in Hereford, there are a limited number of private professional providers serving the children of the poor. Adolescents, especially those in poverty, may confront combinations of issues including suicidal thoughts, drug problems, and sexual assault. Or, as suggested by informants, there may be adolescents who are runaways, homeless, victims of child abuse, or other circumstances requiring professional psychological counseling. These children do not have the same access to the services as the nonpoor. Even in Hereford, not to mention the more rural parts of Wells County, the lack of health insurance, as evidenced by guests at TWBD, is a barrier to adequate services.

Time and again, however, the preferred choice of treatment for youth is some form of medication. One informant in the Hereford school system observes, "I am not against medicating students. I am against over-medicating them. I believe [professional] therapy should be part of the equation."

The director of community and systems initiatives at the privately funded Healthy Minds Policy Initiative, stated, "Fortunately we're at a place in the mental health field that we happen to know a lot about what works in preventing and treating mental health problems. And so, it's less of an issue of knowing what to do, and it's more of an issue at this point of quickly organizing and creating these plans and putting them in place." Only 130,000 of the estimated 700,000 Oklahoma public school students currently benefit from a school counseling system. This counseling system, the Multi-Tiered System of Support, has been demonstrated to benefit school-age children.[9]

The children of the poor, especially minorities, may end up being adjudicated rather than going to classes in Oklahoma public schools. The

Oklahoma Office of Juvenile Affairs (OJA) contracts to specific county commissioners the responsibility for county juvenile detention centers. There are eleven detention centers in the state that hold male and female juveniles after their arrest and during the court process, then supervises the placement of convicted juveniles in the Oklahoma detention system.[10]

Oklahoma's network of juvenile detention centers has a prevailing history involving the mistreatment of adjudicated juveniles in custody, especially those who are poor and minorities. Over the past five years scandals involving elected officials and employees have declined but continue to rock some county-run detention centers. These scandals include the abuse of children under the supervision of OJA. The misuse of public funds for personal gain is also a troubling problem.[11] The general consensus is that OJA has, nevertheless, improved in recent years. This improvement comes at least in part as a direct result of increased public oversight.[12]

Mission of Care

The public providers of food and related services to the poor in Hereford, Wells County, and across the state require applicants to navigate a relatively complex institutional network. It is appropriate now to pivot to a deeper understanding of homelessness in Hereford and Wells County from multiple perspectives, including those in need and providers. Guests at TWBD may lack not only food but reasonable housing, like Norma and her mother, who had just been evicted, or Luke and his nephew.

Having enough food to eat from one day to the next is essential. So too is adequate housing a fundamental necessity of life for everyone. Without a safe and secure place from one day to the next, there is very limited sense of well-being and inadequate opportunities to flourish.

It takes several drive-bys for us to finally identify the Mission of Care (MOC) in Hereford. This is the primary emergency shelter in Hereford and Wells County, with a total of six bedrooms designated for homeless women and their children and fourteen bedrooms for unhoused men. The shelter is identified by a small sign that is impossible to read from a passing car. There is no street address visible on the building. To one side of the nondescript, one-story MOC building is a small parking lot with numerous warnings to drivers. In bright red lettering drivers are told that if they do not have the correct MOC sticker they will be immediately towed. Each parking space at MOC is numbered in letters twice the size of the small sign out front.

MOC is funded by the U.S. Department of Housing and Urban Development (HUD). Located across the street from a car parts store, MOC is not more than a mile from the front doors of Thy Will Be Done. Painted on the green tile in the small entrance lobby are bright black outlines of footprints where one must stand while waiting in line. But there is no line. Someone looms behind a thick plastic shield mounted on a high countertop, but their face is indistinct even under the bright lights. The atmosphere of this constructed space immediately feels unfriendly. The first impression suggests that within these walls one has been demoted to the status of MOC's choosing. At MOC one is never a guest, as they are at TWBD. What is communicated although not spoken is that one should enthusiastically appreciate whatever may be offered.

After taking a close look at the business card that must be slid through a small opening in the plastic barrier, Assistant Director Sally Dumont slowly emerges from behind her siloed counter. By rote she lists the rules and regulations that always must be followed by every applicant. Words matter. The assistant director specifically refers to each person entering the MOC lobby seeking emergency housing as an "applicant." Everyone is an applicant until they have successfully filled out several HUD and MOC forms. If and when the applicant meets all the requirements for entrance into MOC, he or she is given permission to sign all the forms presented to them—at which time MOC calls them a "resident."

Every resident must follow all HUD and local MOC rules and regulations. If residents do not follow the rules and regulations 24/7, they will be terminated and must immediately leave MOC regardless of the circumstances or any explanations they might offer. At best, if terminated from the status of resident, they are allowed by MOC to reapply after three months. There are, in short, no excuses allowed for not following the rules and regulations applicants have signed off on.

HUD has a reputation among other local service providers for being, at worst, an entrenched bureaucracy with a tedious mountain of rules and regulations. A part of President Johnson's War on Poverty, HUD was created in 1965. According to this sixty-five-year-old institution, what exactly is their definition of a homeless person? The answer to this rudimentary question, as offered by Dumont, is, "It depends." According to HUD, for example, an individual is not considered homeless until they have doubled up for fourteen days. If they are living in a motel, they also are not considered homeless. In fact, HUD's definition of adult homelessness on its website, including the documentation required, stretches on and on and on. There is also a separate five-page HUD-based definition to determine when young people are officially homeless.[13]

At a later date we meet with MOC director Clara Newton. Dressed in professional attire markedly different from that of those she is meant to serve, she talks in an animated voice about the weather and the demands of her job. After a few more minutes in which she lists all the services MOC provides to the homeless, she pauses in mid-sentence and abruptly changes her tune. "What do you need?"

I ask Director Newton for her latest MOC annual report. It will provide the facts about the services MOC provides as well as further insight into its rules and regulations. The annual report should, in short, clearly demonstrate what services MOC provides, to whom, at what cost, and what degree of success as defined by HUD. While MOC's annual report will, of course, demonstrate to the public and other audiences how it meets all the standards and duties it is required to meet, it should not be expected to provide the perspective of those in crisis seeking emergency shelter.

"No problem," the director says in a friendly voice. Immediately she herself goes about the process of printing a special copy of her agency report for 2022, then hands me a stapled fourteen-page document filled with charts and numbers.

"Do you have enough resources to meet your needs?" I ask as I look through some of the data.

"No," she says.

Director Newton seems to know exactly what she wants to give her residents. But she also seems to realize that MOC, for whatever reasons, does not now provide them. She would like to offer classes that instill the practical work skills most of her residents lack. That way they could find a job and, most important, afford to pay rent. If they earn enough money for rent, the residents can then transition out of MOC.

When Director Newton is asked, based upon her ten years of experience at MOC, what kinds of skills would help her residents find a job, she does not hesitate: "Almost all skills."

Does she have any contact with or receive support from Hereford State College?

"No."

Then I ask the director about her relationship with law enforcement in Hereford. Her response seems enthusiastic: "They get here in less than two minutes. I have a great relationship with them. They get special training. They don't come in here like gangbusters. They calm the situation down and do their job. They don't bust heads. They listen to their problems and figure out what they can do about it."

Has the COVID-19 pandemic been a special problem at MOC?

"Yes. During 2022 our case load fell," she says. Silent alarm bells resound. Common sense suggests that the case load at MOC should have risen during COVID-19 because of the increased needs of the poor for housing.

Director Newton says she does not know how many people in Wells County were homeless in the year 2022, the year covered in her last annual report. She reiterates that there is no official count available or even an estimate by any agency in Hereford or Wells County of the number of homeless in her area.

I ask her if she ever has to turn anyone away from Hereford's only emergency shelter.

"There are many more people who apply than meet HUD requirements," she says.

"How many?"

"Hundreds," says Director Newton.

MOC's annual report lists the HUD programs it can provide: "Emergency Shelter, Homelessness Prevention, Permanent Housing-Rapid Re-Housing, Hereford Permanent Housing, Transitional Housing, Veterans Permanent Housing, and Permanent Housing-Permanent Supportive Housing." Some of these programs have their own special requirements for applicants, including documented disability and veteran status.[14]

The data in MOC's annual report for 2022 also provide insights about the quality of services to the homeless seeking emergency shelter. It is important to remember that, although MOC is not the sole provider of emergency shelter for the homeless in Wells County, historically Wells County has one of the highest poverty rates in poor state.

According to the 2022 U.S. Census, the White population of Wells County has a poverty rate of 24 percent. The population of Whites, contrasted to the much smaller number of all minorities in Wells County, is 57,754 of a total population of 81,989. Although Wells County Whites have a lower poverty rate, at 24 percent, than all other Wells County minorities, they compose by far the largest portion of those who fall below the poverty line.[15]

In Wells County there are a total of 14,023 Whites who are poor. The face of poverty in Wells County, as is the case for Oklahoma as a state, is a White face. Nevertheless, minorities are fewer in number throughout Wells County than Whites but have much higher poverty rates. My estimated number of poor minorities in Wells County is 2,878. Blacks, for example, are 1.4 times more likely to be poor in Wells County than Whites. Black residents alone in Wells County number 2,272. Asians in Wells County are also more likely to be poor than Whites in Wells County, 1.5 times more likely. Native Americans are 1.4 times more likely to be poor than Whites, the same poverty ratio as Blacks according to the census data.[16]

HUD programs at MOC are divided into three categories. One is Emergency Housing, Supportive Housing, and Outreach. In 2021, MOC admitted 175 individuals into this category of programs. Another thirty-five people were served by MOC in the Transitional Housing Program. In the third category, eighteen homeless people were eventually provided

Permanent Housing. In short, there were a total of 228 individuals served by MOC, assuming no one simultaneously fit in more than one of these three categories. This number, at its largest possibility, 228, still seems remarkably small given the prevalence of poverty in Wells County. At the same time, the MOC facilities, a total of twenty bedrooms, also seems grossly inadequate considering the poverty demographics.

With a poverty population of almost 17,000 in Wells County, the fact that MOC provided emergency shelter services in 2021 to at most 228 appears problematic, all the more since in this year many of the poor nationwide and in Oklahoma lost their jobs or could not afford to pay their rents or mortgages because of COVID. As mentioned, Director Newton stated in our first meeting that "hundreds" of applicants were turned away from MOC. The number of homeless poor in Wells County served by MOC, the major provider to those requiring emergency shelter, was a paltry 1.3 percent of the total county poverty population.

Additional information from informants inside Hereford's health care system, along with Hereford and Wells County residents, public officials, and others familiar with the network of social providers in this area, suggests a deep concern with the adequacy of services provided by MOC. These different perspectives suggest a context in which to better understand MOC's efficacy as a major provider to the unhoused than does strictly relying on its annual report.

Wendelle Towles, a longtime resident of Hereford, provides another viewpoint of MOC's annual report and the part MOC plays in the local social service network. When Ms. Towles graduated from Hereford High School, she could not afford the skyrocketing tuition of Hereford State College or any of the other nearby institutions of public education. Married and a mother by her mid-twenties, she worked a variety of jobs before stumbling into the field of social work. She now, because of job experience, degrees, and certifications, holds a mid-management position in a local public provider of social services to the Hereford poor.

From Ms. Towles's position, she sees MOC as failing to meet the needs of those who are homeless. She readily admits that MOC "checks all the boxes," referring to HUD's strict admission requirements, which must be met by all applicants, and rules and regulations for continuing as a resident once admitted. If they do not keep a low profile, they risk being summarily ejected into the streets. At the same time, she describes meeting all HUD qualifications plus MOC's as a serious disservice to those in need.

The result, she contends, is that some homeless individuals and their families find themselves with nowhere safe to spend the night. Based on her experience, she observes that there are many who seek shelter at MOC but few who actually receive it. This results, she claims, not only because of HUD regulations but also because of additional regulations and decisions concocted by the MOC director and staff. Barriers to admitting applicants to MOC services, aside from HUD regulations and MOC requirements, include these: any applicant must not have any outstanding arrest warrants, must not use any illegal drugs or have a record of illegal drug use, and must not be from a household in which there is domestic abuse.

The first MOC requirement is legitimate. In contrast, the domestic abuse requirement, according to Towles, can cause harm to an applicant desperately seeking a safe and secure place. The partner, always female, is left with an impossible dilemma. Does she stay with her partner to face additional abuse possibly, directed at both her and her children, or does she leave? If she leaves her partner and their home, only to find that MOC's rules automatically exclude her, she may face a far worse set of circumstances.

Finally, if a resident, male or female, misses staying at MOC for one night, as defined by MOC, they automatically are terminated. Failure to follow this rule means, according to Towles, they "are kicked out." Other informants with knowledge of MOC have supported these same concerns.

The MOC board of directors, composed primarily of Hereford medical professionals and other members of the local business community, appear to not question their director about the impact of HUD and MOC rules upon Hereford and Wells County homeless applicants. Regardless of the board's possible intent, the MOC rules prevail.

Interviews with past and present Hereford law enforcement suggest that they have received a clear message from community leaders, one that the MOC board has not chosen to contradict. The director is quick to admire the effective techniques used by law enforcement officers to diffuse various situations arising after desperate people are denied a safe place to stay. Given nothing but a list of bad choices, it is understandable why desperate MOC applicants or residents may act desperately.

The Hereford police say they sometimes provide bus fares to the homeless. The money comes out of their own pocket or an unofficial office fund to pay for a night's stay for the homeless at a local motel. As necessary, they tell the homeless they will be arrested if they do not leave town. At the very least, they are told to not draw attention to themselves if they remain in Hereford. They must become invisible. Above all else, they should stay out of the downtown area and other places where there are shoppers or those attending athletic events. If the unhoused do not leave town, they may be arrested. A record of misdemeanors keeps them from admittance to MOC, as suggested, but it also adds to police leverage when they insist they leave the Hereford city limits.

Addiction to drugs is common among the homeless, as is the case with the general population. This general population includes students at Hereford State College who may use both legal and illegal drugs to excess. Students may be asked to leave restaurants, bars, and stores before the police are notified. There is a double standard in place: Hereford State students are treated with much more tolerance by local businesses and law enforcement than those who are homeless. In sharp contrast, according to Ms. Towles, community leaders view the Hereford homeless as a detriment to their businesses. This message has been clearly conveyed to the Hereford police. The last thing residents and visitors to Hereford want to see on the streets of Hereford are the homeless or any others who look like they may be poor.

As evidenced by the guests at TWBD, the poor and the homeless are not always distinguishable from the general population of nonpoor. They can and do look like many other Hereford residents, especially in a community where university students, faculty, and staff intentionally dress in alternative styles. Says Ms. Towles, based upon her experience, "They [the homeless] could be just someone riding on a bike with a backpack."

About MOC, she concludes, "Hereford has a homeless shelter," but "it functions as if it is trying to keep them [the homeless] out unless they fit certain standards."

Up until the death of a homeless man on the Hereford downtown streets, the needs of the homeless were seen by most residents as an embarrassing nuisance that was bad for the local economy. Law enforcement, following the message conveyed to them by community leaders, did their best to make sure the poor and homeless stayed out of the sight of the general public. One of the only public spaces they could gather was an underpass not far from MOC. From the street directly above, no one could see them.

One of Hereford's two low-income housing projects constructed in the early 1990s was situated on the southern fringe of the city far from the sight of most citizens. This housing project was also far from Hereford's shops and stores, making private transportation a necessity for residents because public transportation was, and still is, expensive and undependable.[17]

The only other public housing in this city of 50,000 was recently built on the far western fringe of the city.[18] The placement of the low-income housing projects in Hereford involved a decision-making process sanctioned by the mayor and the city council. It also required buy-in from the business community and the general public, all of whom had the opportunity to express their viewpoints at public forums and in the media. Residents of one of the planned housing projects, a majority of whom are Blacks, had minimal input into final decisions regarding location.

Informants within Hereford State, including faculty, students, and staff, admit that homelessness among the student population is a problem. It is seen by these individuals as a small but crucial problem. There are no public reports by the college that describe the problem, although the institution has experts who might be called upon.

It is also difficult to find any Hereford State administrator who is willing to talk about unhoused students or, for that matter, university students who have food insecurity. One university employee tells me she is very concerned about the LGBTQI student population because she knows friends and other students who have been disowned by their families and, as a result, have nowhere to live. Runaways are not unusual in the LGBTQI student population, she says, and sometimes they become homeless.

There are also stories of Hereford State students who may be staying with friends, living temporarily out of their cars or trucks, or camping long-term at nearby public parks—all because they cannot afford to pay the high rents and other fees. But no one to date has put numbers to these accounts or been tasked to study the "nonexistent" problem further. At this point, it is only verifiable that there are university students who face food insecurity and also students who are homeless.

Thy Will Be Done in its present form sustains thousands in Hereford and surrounding Wells County each year who do not have enough food to eat. A major question still remains, however. Is TWBD, in conjunction with a network of other private and public food providers, doing enough for those who face food insecurity?

Swarming around the poor at TWBD, Hereford, and throughout other Wells County communities are a variety of cultural myths about the poor and poverty that are not based on evidence. At a minimum, the evidence suggests numerous other interpretations: The poor are not lazy but frequently hard workers. The poor are not living high on the hog from public largesse. The poor frequently are compelled to take care of members of their household, which then precludes certain family members from working. The poor often have disability and health issues that can limit the kinds of job they can work and hold. When forced to quit working, the poor have little savings upon which to rely. Child care is often unavailable and can limit parents from working. Poverty for some can be a generational issue from which it is difficult to escape. Obesity and overweight are not unique to the poor and do not denote laziness. The working poor and even the middle class can find themselves in situations in which they require temporary help to get back on their feet. A constant overriding theme is that those seeking food, housing, or both find it very difficult to live off the minimum wage.

The network of providers, though vast and complex, is far from perfect. Those who make the big decisions in Hereford and Wells County—elected officials, business leaders, and others—are not always enthusiastic about serving those with food insecurity or providing housing or other services for the homeless. Community leaders would prefer that both the hungry and the homeless be invisible or, at the very least, take their problems to another town. To that end, the unofficial message they send to Hereford law enforcement is to kick the problematic poor down the road.

In general, the poor in Hereford and Wells County, whether facing food insecurity, homelessness, or both, are seldom asked to engage in decisions directly impacting their own well-being. Poverty, the voices of the poor strongly suggest, is less about their alleged personality inadequacies than it is about confronting a series of bad choices. The consequences of not having enough money can leave the poor with nothing but bad choices to make. A working wage of $7.25 an hour in Hereford and Wells County creates, sustains, and reproduces persistent poverty.

The needs of those in poverty in rural areas in Wells County may be somewhat different than in Hereford, but the similarities outweigh most differences. Challenges in transportation, access to service providers, and quality of care appear more evident in the rural communities in Wells County than in Hereford.

TWBD is but one example of Oklahomans attempting to take care of other Oklahomans. This tradition of caring for those in need is based upon a group of faith-based Oklahomans in five Hereford churches sticking to their bedrock Christian values and leanings as expressed at Matthew 22:39: to "love thy neighbor as thyself."

Only in my third year of research at TWBD did I begin to learn about a much larger food pantry network throughout the state that receives relatively little public attention. This network appears, at first glance, to be supported by a variety of different churches throughout the state as well as other volunteer organizations and government entities. The existence of this statewide pantry network suggests a history of caring in Oklahoma that is largely undocumented.

Nevertheless, words from one Hereford informant who witnessed MOC at its worst still ring in my ears. He describes an incident that took place there during one of the coldest winters on record. His first-person observation of this incident epitomizes the powerlessness and fragility of those facing the consequences of poverty:

"There was a 21-year-old mother with an 18-month-old child who shows up at MOC. It is right in the middle of the cold spell in 2021. It's fourteen degrees out. MOC added an additional twenty-five beds for extras on account of the cold. The mother of the baby calls the woman behind the counter a bitch and the woman behind the counter kicks her out of MOC. That night a mediator attempts to talk to the staff at MOC but is told MOC policy is the mother and her child can reapply for admission in ninety days. But because of the cold, they have decided the mother and her baby can reapply in thirty days."

5

More Than Sixty Years of Persistent and Pervasive Oklahoma Poverty

Robert Lee Maril and Sarah Watson

> I don't think any Okie governor or the Oklahoma State Legislature has ever used the "poverty word."
>
> —State economic expert

From the perspectives voiced by the guests at Thy Will Be Done, along with other state experts, it is evident that many Oklahomans often have a variety of misconceptions about poor Oklahomans and poverty. Many continue to believe or act, for example, as if poverty in their state is not a significant problem. Since that belief is strongly held, the problems the poor face are by definition assumed to be trivial. Many Oklahomans may also firmly believe that, even if poverty is a significant issue, it is a minority issue rather than a White issue.[1]

These and other misbeliefs about the poor and poverty circle like turkey vultures around a cluster of accepted, taken-for-granted notions with little basis in fact. These falsehoods about who is poor and why they may be poor also neglect the consequences those below the poverty line confront on a daily basis.

We turn now to a brief analysis of poverty based upon U.S. Census data. These more than sixty years of data present facts about poverty in Oklahoma and, at the same time, shed light upon poverty and its direct consequences. They also facilitate a comparison between the consequences of poverty in Oklahoma and that in all other states.

The U.S. Census is the best primary source of poverty data over time. First and foremost, its information on poverty in Oklahoma covers more than sixty years. Although poverty thrived long before statehood in 1907, the census bureau began to collect statistics systematically measuring the economic status of its residents in 1959. Since that time it has provided a fact-based, comprehensive picture of Oklahoma poverty that has for the most part been ignored.

Some of the specific ways poverty impacts the guests at Hereford's TWBD, Mission of Care, and the residents of Macon and other communities throughout Wells County are described in the previous chapters through the perspectives and voices of the poor and professionals working with them. In contrast, the census's poverty statistics of Oklahoma document consequences the poor may face in all seventy-seven Oklahoma counties. These poverty rates over time also provide a more complete understanding of the challenges faced by those who are poor statewide.

When considering the poverty statistics the census collects for Oklahoma and the nation, remember that these numbers reflect the well-being of real people—like the guests and their families at TWBD, the residents of MOC, or those who face poverty in the small towns throughout Hereford County. Hunger and homelessness are two of the immediate needs the poor frequently grapple with. But there are other consequences of poverty, in part suggested by the guests at TWBD, that require scrutiny given the census findings.

The definition of poverty used by the decennial U.S. Census focuses upon income thresholds varying by family size and composition. If the family's total income is below a certain threshold, then all individuals in the family are defined as being in poverty. Before-tax income is used to establish the family's poverty status, but not capital gains or noncash benefits including, for instance, Medicaid and food stamps. Poverty thresholds are updated for inflation on the basis of the Consumer Price Index.[2]

First, how many Oklahomans are poor? In 1959 the U.S. Census counted 679,517 individual Oklahomans who fell below the poverty line. This statistic was almost one-third of all individuals in a state population numbering 2,274,988. The number of Oklahomans in poverty from 1959 to 1979 then substantially declined. Nevertheless, the Oklahoma poverty rate for individuals in Oklahoma remained high compared to most other states.[3]

During this twenty-year span from 1959 to 1979, poverty decreased from about 30 percent of the Oklahoma population to about 13 percent. In part this was the positive result of President Lyndon Johnson's War on Poverty, which became law in 1965. Even so, because of population growth in our state, by 1979 there were still almost 400,000 Oklahomans who were poor.[4]

Although there was a real decline in both the percentage and number of the Oklahoma poverty population in the 1960s and 1970s, the poverty rate of poor Oklahomans remained significantly higher than the national average. Since 1979, Oklahoma poverty rates, already high in Oklahoma compared to most other states, have risen higher. From 1979 to the most recent decennial census, taken in 2019, the Oklahoma poverty population increased by approximately 20 percent. Nearly 600,000 Oklahomans were then in poverty, a number approaching the Oklahoma poverty population in 1959.[5]

Oklahoma's poverty rate for the past six decades has always been markedly higher than the national average. From 1959 to the present, in fact, Oklahoma poverty has outdistanced the national poverty rate. In 2019, Oklahoma's poverty rate was about 15 percent, while the national average was at about 12 percent. And some Oklahoma counties have twice the poverty rate or more of the state average.[6]

The good news about the poverty rate in Oklahoma and the nation is that poverty rates are no longer at the all-time highs of 1959. However, the bad news is that Oklahoma still trends, after more than sixty years, very high when compared to all other states. The most recent decennial census identifies Oklahoma as the eighth-poorest state in the nation. The number of Oklahomans in poverty, as suggested, is about the same as it was in 1979. Relative to other states, Oklahoma poverty is both persistent and pervasive.

Poverty data for 2019 demonstrate a rise in the rate among Oklahoma families, a surge similar to upticks in 1990 and 2000. In 2019, about 105,000 families in poverty were counted by the census. The number of Oklahoma families in poverty was actually greater in 2019 than in 1979: 105,000 families versus about 102,000. These same data also show both Oklahoma family poverty rates and individual poverty rates being consistently higher than those in other states. When the number of Oklahoma families in poverty is compared over the past sixty years to the number of American families in poverty, Oklahoma's rate is consistently higher than the national average. The gap actually increased between the percentages of those families in poverty in Oklahoma and the national percentages for families in poverty.[7] There is one exception to this sixty-year trend: in 1980, Oklahoma the individual and family poverty rates were approximately the same as the national averages.[8]

As of 2019, only Mississippi, Louisiana, New Mexico, Kentucky, Arkansas, West Virginia, and Alabama have higher poverty rates than Oklahoma. Mississippi, Louisiana, and New Mexico clearly rank among the first tier of the poorest states in the nation, with respective poverty rates of 20.3 percent, 19 percent, and 18.2 percent. In the second tier of poorest states fall Kentucky (16.3 percent), Arkansas (16.2 percent), and West Virginia (16 percent). Alabama, followed closely by Oklahoma, make up the third tier of states with the highest poverty rates. Oklahoma's rate is just 0.3 percent lower than Alabama's and only 0.8 percent lower than West Virginia's.[9]

Said another way, Oklahoma, the eighth-poorest state in terms of poverty rates based upon the U.S. Census, is only by a relatively slim margin not a member of the second tier of states with the highest rates of poverty. This second tier of poverty states, like those in the first tier, have long been recognized for their persistent and pervasive poverty populations.

What is outstandingly clear is that Oklahoma's poverty rate in comparison to all other states has always been unusually high. This is important to remember because of what sometimes passes for common sense in Oklahoma. There is the proverbial explanation by Oklahomans that the state is somehow unique because it has boom-and-bust economic cycles based upon the oil and gas industries. Allegedly, according to this common chorus, a rising tide lifts all boats. All Oklahomans in persistent and pervasive poverty must do is be patient. All they have to do is wait, because soon they will be able to enjoy the benefits of a forthcoming boom. These U.S. Census numbers suggest, in contrast, that even in the midst of so-called boom cycles Oklahomans have experienced more than their share of poverty for more than sixty years.

Without doubt, the state economy is to a great degree influenced by the oil and gas industries. According to those industries, they "support more than 351,000 jobs, provide over $32 billion in wages and contribute more than $57 billion to the state's economy." These two industries account for a whopping 22 percent of the gross domestic product (GDP) of Oklahoma. As well, they account for 3 percent of the total U.S. GDP, not including offshore sites.[10] The gas and oil industries in Oklahoma are followed in importance to the economy by trade, transportation, and utilities at 18 percent of the Oklahoma GDP, state government at 14 percent, and finance at 11 percent.[11]

The largest single state employer in Oklahoma is the U.S. Department of Defense. Oklahoma military bases employ a total of 69,000. The largest of these bases, Tinker Air Force Base in Oklahoma City, employs 26,000 military and civilians. The next-largest single employer is Walmart, at 32,200. The University of Oklahoma is third at about 18,000. The fourth- and fifth-largest state employers are two Native tribes, the Chickasaw Nation and the Choctaw Nation, at 11,300 and 10,000, respectively.[12]

In spite of the gas and oil industries, over more than six decades the Oklahoma poverty rankings have been getting worse over time, not better. Oklahoma's poverty ranking average from 1959 to 1989 tied for fourteenth from the top compared to all other states. In 1999 it was rated the sixth-poorest of all states, and in 2019 the eighth-poorest. Even in eighth position, as noted, Oklahoma is very close to the second tier of poorest states.

Poverty in Oklahoma, historically one of the poorest of all states, is not decreasing, nor is it staying the same. Poverty in Oklahoma, based upon the best data available, is continuing to make this state one of the poorest in the nation. Yet persistent and pervasive poverty throughout Oklahoma is rarely a topic voters or their elected representatives regularly discuss.

The U.S. Census data show that Oklahoma poverty is primarily a White problem in terms of numbers of poor, not only in Wells County but throughout the majority of the state. This is because Oklahoma is, as a result of its history, predominantly a White state, with exceptions like the eventual recognition of the thirty-nine tribal nations and the history of black communities.

Oklahoma poverty also is not equally distributed throughout its population. One of eight White Oklahomans is poor. Since 1959, when economic data were first gathered, however, Oklahoma minorities continue to be disproportionately represented compared to Whites among the poor. Oklahoma poverty rates are still much higher for minorities than for Whites. One of four Blacks fall below the poverty line in Oklahoma, almost double the poverty rate for Whites, and slightly less than one of four Hispanics are poor. The poverty ratios of Native Oklahomans and those reporting as two or more races are one of five, again compared to one of eight for Whites.[13]

Whites who are poor are a far larger group than minorities. A total of 361,088 Oklahoma Whites in poverty were counted by the most recent U.S. Census. The state poverty rate for Oklahoma Whites is 12.6 percent. Far fewer African Americans are poor in Oklahoma, 75,015, but their poverty rate is 26.1 percent. Oklahoma Latinos have the second-largest minority poverty rate at 23.4 percent but the largest number of minority poor, 102,516. Those who identify as two or more races have a 18.9 percent poverty rate and number 56,731. Native Americans in poverty in Oklahoma number 57,364, with a poverty rate of 18.1 percent.[14]

These data emphasize that over more than six decades there have been two significant changes in the Oklahoma minority population with regard to poverty rates. One is that Native American poverty in Oklahoma in the past two decades has declined to 18.1 percent—still disproportionately much higher than for Whites but substantially lower than at any time in the past than sixty years.

One explanation of a falling poverty rate among Natives is that the largest tribe in Oklahoma, the Cherokee Nation, along with much smaller tribes like the Chickasaw and Choctaw Nations, are benefiting from their investments in the casino industry. We see this in Wells County with the relatively recent economic vitality of Lone Pony (see chapter 3). Although Natives in Lone Pony are a minority percentage of the population, their economic status had improved, as has that of the White majority there.

The federal government passed legislation in 1988, the Indian Gaming Regulatory Act, intended to improve the general welfare of tribes by creating a new source of income. Three classes of games were established, each with its own regulatory structure as well as a federal compact required. Class I focuses upon social games centered upon tribal celebrations with small sums of money as prizes. Class II games include bingo and similar games in which players bet against each other. All other gaming, including casino games such as slot machines, blackjack, and poker, are Class III.[15]

Oklahoma voters approved Class III games in 2004. At the same time, all Native tribes within the state were legally mandated to apply to the Department of Interior for permission to operate Class III gambling, and all tribes had to accept and follow a binding compact model. By 2021, thirty-three of the thirty-eight Oklahoma tribes operated 133 casinos throughout the state.[16]

In addition to employing more than 113,442 workers in Oklahoma, in 2019 licensed Oklahoma tribes paid workers wages and benefits of $5.4 billion. Their total impact on the Oklahoma economy was $15.6 billion. Tribes in 2019 spent huge sums, $228.4 million, upon tribal education and human capital development. By providing health care for tribal members, they reduced state matching funds for Medicaid by $234.7 million. According to the same report, $84 million went to Oklahoma school districts, cities, and counties.[17]

In 1999 the poverty rate of Oklahoma Natives was 28.1 percent. By 2019 the poverty rate among Oklahoma Natives had declined to 18.1 percent. This sharp decline in the rate of about one-third over two decades demonstrates the importance of employment opportunities. An Oklahoma Native who is poor can be explained more by the wage she or he receives than by presumed personality flaws perpetuated in the dominant White culture. It is also possible during this period that COVID-19 public funds provided additional income for Natives and other Oklahomans.

It should be noted that, although Natives by law do not pay a state tax, they currently pay a fee to local and state government based upon their revenue from casinos. That fee is on the average, according to the Oklahoma Council of Public Affairs, about 2 percent in 2022.[18]

A second major change described by the U.S. Census data in poverty rates among minorities is the growth of the Latino population in Oklahoma over the past two and one-half decades. Latinos have a relatively high rate of poverty among Oklahoma minorities, second only to African Americans. Latinos in poverty in Oklahoma numbered 438,106 according to the 2019 U.S. Census.[19] Latinos live throughout the state, but the highest concentrations of this growing population are in Oklahoma City and Tulsa, the two major metro areas.[20] There are a total of 101 legislators in the Oklahoma House of Representatives and forty-eight senators. As of 2022, this growing Oklahoma Latino population is represented by only four legislators.

U.S. Census data describe the relationship between poverty and gender in Oklahoma. While female adults number almost the same as males in a state approaching a total of four million inhabitants, they have a poverty rate of 16.9 percent compared to 14.3 percent for their male counterparts. Minority women in this state have much higher poverty rates than do White women. About 13 percent of White Oklahoma women are below the poverty line compared to 29.2 percent of all Black women. Similarly, 28.6 percent of Oklahoma women who identify as "some other race" are poor. Hispanic women in Oklahoma have a poverty rate of 26 percent, while about 16 percent of Asian women are poor. Native American women in poverty in Oklahoma are at about 22 percent. Although the poverty rate among Native women is still very high compared to White women, it has substantially declined.[21]

It is notable that, although women are better educated in general than men in Oklahoma, they work at jobs that pay salaries lower than for men. These jobs include sales and office industries, education, food services, and personal care services. From 2015 to 2019, according to economist Laura J. Ahlstorm, "Oklahoma women earned 74.5 cents for every dollar earned by a man." Given these discrepancies in pay, she observes that "women will not reach earnings equality with men in the state until 2076."[22]

The experience of TWBD guests with the high cost of child care in Hereford and throughout the county (see chapter 3) are also common throughout the state. Evidence-based statistics for the costs of child care in Oklahoma are worth citing verbatim: "The annual cost of childcare for an infant in Oklahoma in 2020 was $8,940, or $745 a month." The typical single parent in Oklahoma, much more likely to be female than male, can spend 40 percent of their income on child care alone. Summing up, Ahlstorm remarks that "lack of affordable childcare may prevent parents from working. The costs of childcare may also be more of a hardship for single parents, especially single mothers, who have to spend a larger percentage of their income on childcare."[23]

Poverty based upon age is particularly challenging in Oklahoma. Children and the elderly are particularly vulnerable. The impact of hunger on poor children, through no fault of their own, cannot be overstated. As suggested earlier, more than one in every five children in Oklahoma below eighteen falls below the poverty line. According to the U.S. Census, Oklahoma's poverty rate for children is 21.5 percent, compared to the national average of 17 percent. Said another way, Oklahoma children are more than 20 percent more likely to fall into poverty than children nationally. The number of Oklahoma children in poverty, keeping in mind that Oklahoma has a relatively small population, is 186,000.[24]

Poverty statistics from the U.S. Census Bureau's Household Pulse Survey and other relevant census data provide an additional perspective of poor Oklahoma children. Using economic well-being indicators, the Casey Foundation ranks Oklahoma the eighteenth-worst state regarding the economic status of children. When "Family and Community Indicators" are considered, Oklahoma's children, compared to all other states, rank tenth-worst.[25]

Oklahoma children in poverty face many more obstacles than the nonpoor. Oklahoma Child Welfare Services confronts serious problems among Oklahoma youth. In spite of their attempts to serve the needs of children in poor families, Oklahoma ranks fortieth in overall child well-being.[26] The purpose of Child Welfare Services in Oklahoma is "to improve the safety, permanence and well-being of children and families involved in the Child Welfare system through collaboration with the families and their community." Unfortunately, the history of Oklahoma Child Welfare Services is burdened by systemic problems that cannot seem to be rectified. In 2008 a federal lawsuit was filed against Child Welfare Services, then called the Oklahoma Department of Human Services. Child advocacy plaintiffs alleged that the Department of Human Services, the defendant in the federal lawsuit, failed to protect children in the state's care from neglect and abuse. These allegations found support in newspaper accounts of abused and neglected children as far back as the 1980s.[27]

The settlement of the 2008 lawsuit, not reached until 2012, required that three independent experts monitor a federal court-approved plan (the Pinnacle Plan) to improve the way Oklahoma's Child Welfare Services provided services and protection for children in its custody. After five years of supervision and monitoring, three outside experts did not believe measurable improvement had been made in good faith in seven areas. Improvements were expected to be observed in the areas of "maltreatment of children, development of foster homes, regular and consistent visitation of caseworkers, reduction of the number of children in shelters, placement stability, child permanency through reunification adoption or guardianship, and manageable caseloads for child welfare staff."[28]

From 2012 until 2017, the state government failed to make any substantive changes to the provision of welfare services to children. In 2017 the three independent experts selected by the federal court stated that Oklahoma had not made a good faith effort. Instead of arguing the merits of their case yet again in federal court, as expected, the State of Oklahoma agreed to leave the monitoring of its welfare services in the hands of the three independent experts for an undefined period of time.[29]

Also of special concern are the consequences of being a poor older adult in Oklahoma. Eleven percent of older persons in Oklahoma do not have enough food to eat.[30] The elderly in Oklahoma, including the poor, have the seventh-worst ranking in the nation when it comes to housing. Equally concerning is the percentage of geriatric providers per thousand adults in Oklahoma: Oklahoma seniors rank fourth-worst in the nation, emphasizing that access to health care is highly problematic.[31]

Individuals like Norma's mom at TWBD, as well as other guests, appear to have severe dental problems. These observations are strongly supported by statistical data. Older Oklahomans have bad teeth in part because they have inadequate access to dentists. Senior Oklahomans place forty-fifth in the nation in the percentage of teeth extractions required because of lifetimes of inadequate dental care.

Smoking tobacco is one way TWBD guests, including older males, pass the time before the doors officially open. After they push their carts across the parking lot to their car or truck, men and women often light up their cigarettes. Some males chew tobacco while seated in the waiting room or, more rarely, while selecting food from the pantry shelves. Oklahoma older adults, including poor seniors, frequently use tobacco products, ranking fourth among all states.

In terms of the consumption of health foods, older Oklahomans rank forty-seventh, at the bottom compared to all states. Oklahoma older adults are also among the least likely to engage in physical exercise, again ranking forty-seventh.

The suicide rate among all older Oklahomans has been substantially higher than the national average for more than ten years.” The rate of drug overdose of older Oklahomans is also reported higher than the national average. Finally, the quality of Oklahoma nursing homes for senior Oklahomans is cause for serious concern (see chapter 6). Given these statistics, it is not surprising that elderly Oklahomans rank third-worst in the nation in percentage of early deaths between the ages of sixty-five and seventy-four.[32]

Perhaps not surprisingly, given the data cited above, the disabled who are poor in Oklahoma also must confront the consequences of poverty at alarming rates. About 28 percent of all disabled Oklahomans are poor. The disability rate for Oklahomans is 17.2 percent of the total population, 671,748 people including all adults and children. This figure does not count those disabled who are institutionalized. Of this total disability population, according to the U.S. Census, those with hearing problems are 5.3 percent. Vision problems included 3.7 percent of all disabled. Oklahomans with cognitive disabilities include 7.3 percent of the disability population. Those who have ambulatory problems are 8.7 percent of the total disabled, and 6.9 percent have problems associated with independent living. Finally, self-care issues impact 2.9 percent of all disabled Oklahomans who are not institutionalized. A special subpopulation with an even higher poverty rate is disabled civilian veterans: 35.8 percent. More than one of every three civilian veterans in Oklahoma are disabled.[33]

U.S. Census data that assess the relevant status of impoverished Oklahoma disabled over time by other demographic characteristics, including race, appear to be unavailable. According to the ILR Yang Tan Institute, data from 2001 to 2013 in Oklahoma conclusively show that the number of disabled men and women age eighteen to sixty-five, with or without a work limitation and living in households below the poverty line, has steadily increased. In 2001 there were 265,000 disabled individuals, but by 2013 their number had increased to 317,000.[34]

Oklahomans in general, and the poor in particular, lack adequate medical insurance. Medical services available to pregnant women who are poor, including prenatal care, can determine the health and well-being of the child as well as the mother. Access to a system of professional medical care is a primary determiner of whether a mother can get the best prenatal care available. Mothers in poverty are also much less likely to have access to general medical care, including prenatal care, because of the cost.[35]

Before 2021, Oklahomans without health insurance were 14.3 percent of the total population. By comparison, only 3.0 percent the Massachusetts population lacked medical insurance. The health and well-being of adults in a poverty household directly carry over to the well-being of their children. As we have seen with many guests at TWBD, health issues can be a major reason parents in poor households cannot work full- or part-time. Caring for adults in the household who are sick, disabled, or elderly also explains why many adults in poverty households cannot work.

Oklahoma in fact ranks as the second-worst state in the country in terms of medical insurance coverage. To the detriment of those who are poor and without medical insurance, the state government chose not to spend federal dollars during the first two years of the COVID-19 pandemic to provide medical insurance to all Oklahoma residents in need. Nevertheless, when finally given the opportunity to vote on the issue in 2021, a majority of Oklahomans voted for Medicaid expansion to the non-insured. Comprehensive health insurance for all, called Wellcare in Oklahoma, was provided for the first time to adults age eighteen to sixty-four.[36] After the thumbs-up by the voting public for the expansion of medical insurance, a new program was offered by the Oklahoma Health and Mental Health Department in March 2023. For the first time, health services for Oklahoma women during pregnancy and postpartum were provided. These services, if continued, will help to reduce a relatively high infant mortality rate in Oklahoma as well as health risks to new mothers. When adults in a household have an opportunity to receive health services, children in these same poor families directly benefit.

During 2022, Wellcare was expanded to the 14 percent of the population who were not covered by the federal COVID-19 supplemental Medicare insurance, SoonerCare. The data show that after those uninsured were covered by Wellcare, health indicators for this population immediately began to improve. Nevertheless, the one-time federal funds approved in 2021 by a majority vote of Oklahoma voters have ceased. Oklahomans in need of insurance coverage during the COVID-19 pandemic will again be without medical insurance. It is not clear at this point if and how this public health policy issue will be resolved, since the federal government recently discontinued SoonerCare.[37]

Another aspect of health care for Oklahomans and the poor is that Oklahoma, prior to Wellcare in 2020, was one of the three lowest-performing states with regard to "56 measures of health care access and quality, service use and cost, health disparities, and health outcomes." The other two low performers were Mississippi and West Virginia.[38]

Given these findings, it is not surprising that Oklahomans suffered greatly when the pandemic hit. "The findings are stark," stated Dale Bratzler about the results of a study in every state of the number of preventable COVID-19 deaths. Bratzler was at the time the chief COVID officer for the University of Oklahoma.[39] A report by Brown University and Microsoft AI for Health stated, "If 100 percent of eligible adults in Oklahoma had been fully vaccinated . . . 5,833 of the 14,380 Oklahomans known to have been killed by the virus might still be alive today."[40] Oklahomans of all ages who were fully vaccinated in 2021 were just 38.3 percent of the total population. Those who received boosters to the vaccine were 24 percent of all residents.[41] Concluded Bratzler, "And even if you looked at if we hit 85 percent [fully vaccinated]—which we haven't yet; we're only at about two-thirds of people 18 and over who've been vaccinated—it would have been 3,600 fewer deaths in Oklahoma."

Education in Oklahoma schools, according to the U.S. Census, is highly correlated with poverty. Keeping in mind the importance of the quality of education in Oklahoma, the best data available demonstrate a direct relationship between educational attainment in Oklahoma and poverty. The census bureau reported in 2021 that those twenty-five years without a high school degree had the highest poverty rate, 26.1 percent. Oklahomans who graduated from high school had the next-highest poverty rate, 15.9 percent. Those with some college or an associate degree had an 11.2 percent poverty rate. Oklahomans with a bachelor's or higher degree had a 4.8 percent poverty rate, the lowest poverty rate in the state based on educational attainment.[42]

In general, residents of Oklahoma do not spend enough time in school to achieve all the benefits they might otherwise accrue. Nor does the measurable quality of public education in Oklahoma compare favorably to the national average. About 90 percent of all school-age children in Oklahoma attend public schools. The current system of public education can leave those already in poverty with few good choices in the labor market. Dropouts may be working so their families can thrive, helping their families care for household members, or for any of many reasons suggested by guests at TWBD.

A primary cause of the inadequacy of many Oklahoma public schools is insufficient fiscal resources. Macon and other communities in Wells County, as previously discussed, find it very difficult to provide adequate public education via their own taxing districts. Money alone, of course, cannot solve all educational problems. Public schools at a minimum also require excellent leadership, parental engagement, qualified and dedicated teachers, and broad community support.

Problems in public education across the state, granted there are exceptions, begin when the legislature and state leadership earmark funds to public schools. Public high schools, vocational schools, community colleges, and state colleges and universities must not just promote and graduate Oklahomans; the diplomas granted must reflect that their graduates meet or exceed national academic standards. Adequate financial support of public education does not guarantee excellence in Oklahoma, but without it excellence remains a dream.

Educational attainment statistics, the number and percentage of Oklahomans by age group who stay in school and each year accumulate additional educational skills, are not encouraging. The U.S. Census divides the population into two groups, those age eighteen to twenty-four and those twenty-five years and older. The educational attainment in 2022 of the younger group, 388,812 in number, suggests trends that can lead to serious educational inadequacies. In this age group only 40 percent are high school graduates, 37 percent have some college or an associate degree, and 8 percent have a bachelor's degree.

The statistics are even more concerning for Oklahomans over twenty-five years old. Numbering 2,636,889 of the Oklahoma population of about four million, again only 40 percent have a high school degree. About 20 percent have attended college but have no college degree, and another 10 percent have earned an associate degree.

In some ways even more concerning are the educational attainment statistics of this older group in terms of success in middle school and high school. Of this much larger population of Oklahomans, 4 percent have less than a ninth-grade education, 7 percent may have attended ninth through twelfth grade but have no high school diploma and did not graduate, and 22 percent attended college but have no degree. In this same group, 8 percent have an associate degree as their highest degree.

In sharp contrast to a majority of Oklahomans with limited educational attainment, another group of Oklahomans are relatively well educated. About 18 percent of those above twenty-five years have a college or university degree, and 9.6 percent have a graduate or professional degree.

There is, then, a great disparity in educational attainment among Oklahomans. On the one hand, about a third of those twenty-five years or older have graduated from college and may have a higher degree. At the other end of the continuum are a significant number of Oklahomans who did not graduate from high school. Between these two groups are a third group who have attended college but have either no college degree or an associate degree as their highest degree. These educational attainment trends are even more extreme for those between the ages of eighteen to twenty-four.

Standardized test scores are one measure of the actual knowledge and skills learned in Oklahoma public schools as compared to years of educational attainment. These same standardized Oklahoma scores can be compared to national averages. The Macon public school system, as discussed earlier, touted its standardized test scores. A closer examination, nevertheless, revealed that Macon student test scores were, when compared to those of the rest of public school students in the state, only at best approaching the fiftieth percentile.

A still more revealing way to measure the efficacy of Oklahoma public schools, not just the Macon public school district, is to compare standardized tests scores in Oklahoma to national averages. According to 2022 U.S. Census data, 71 percent of all Oklahoma fourth graders were not proficient in reading in Oklahoma, and 74 percent of all Oklahoma eighth graders were not proficient in math. In comparison with all other states, according to the Casey Foundation, Oklahomans hold the forty-fifth position from the top. Only Nevada, Arizona, Louisiana, Alaska, and New Mexico have lower standardized scores. The overall quality of public school education in Oklahoma, based upon these standardized test scores, is inferior.[43]

U.S. Census figures also record that 57 percent of all children in Oklahoma age three and four years are not in school. Research on preschools, including the Head Start program, has repeatedly shown that enrollment at this age improves basic skill levels in younger children when entering kindergarten. If children are not then offered high-quality educational opportunities in subsequent years, their standardized test scores decline precipitously.[44]

This brief analysis of the relationship between education and poverty must also consider individuals who, in spite of a lack of formal education, exceed in their jobs and accumulate wealth. There are also those who receive an education, but one that does not prepare them for the job market, yet still excel. In short, there are those who succeed despite the restrictions imposed by a limited education—but they are not the average, they are the exception.

There are also those children, as discussed earlier, who win the birth lottery. Education may not be an impediment to financial success for these individuals. They may, for example, birth their way into executive positions in family businesses in which they cannot fail to earn unearned salaries and other perks. There are those, too, who choose not to work at all or only very little while living off family largesse. These individuals are rarely labeled lazy or slothful by either their own social groups or society in general.[45]

The impact of state financial support to public schools, nevertheless, cannot be overemphasized. This is certainly true of districts with significant percentages of children in poverty. Stable funding of public school districts and public institutions of higher learning are not, of course, the only answer to maintaining and improving public education. The Macon school district, like several other school districts in Wells County, must make every tax dollar count, since it covers an area with a poverty rate of 37.3 percent.

In the past two decades, indications among the majority of Oklahoma public school districts, especially those with high poverty rates, are that local and state funding is in general insufficient. There have been numerous years when the state economy was strong, as reflected in significant public tax surpluses, but allocations to public education did not reflect these fiscal resources.

Salaries of Oklahoma teachers are a major indication of state fiscal resources appropriated to public education being out of step with the needs of public schools. In 2016, salaries for Oklahoma teachers in public primary and secondary schools averaged the fourth lowest in the country. Only Mississippi, South Dakota, and Arizona paid their teachers less than Oklahoma. As reported by the Poynter Institute, the average salary in 2016 for the three different teacher pay grade levels in Oklahoma was $41,834, compared to a national average of $59,978.[46] As demonstrated in *Waltzing with the Ghost of Tom Joad*, the rhetorical contention that the cost of living in Oklahoma is so low that it makes up for the difference in teacher salary does not stand up to rigorous economic analysis.[47]

There is a long history reflecting elected politicians' lack of interest in funding public education in Oklahoma. After a teachers strike in 1990, the Republican majority in state government, aided by some Democrats, employed tax surpluses to reduce taxes for Oklahoma businesses and industries and to support infrastructure projects around the state.

The public narrative from the state legislature for continuing to ignore the real needs of public school education has not been apologetic. Lower taxes, this narrative asserts, will benefit the economy and, at the same time, attract more business outside the state to move their operations to Oklahoma. A rising economy spurred by the direct effect of legislative distributions of tax surpluses to businesses and industries, so the narrative goes, will lift all boats—even the boats on which the poor remain unwilling passengers. As reported in 2016 by the Poynter Institute, two years before a second statewide teacher's strike, the Oklahoma legislature gave $493 million to state energy companies.[48]

This rather consistent political strategy by the Republican majority has failed to support the quality of education offered by the Oklahoma public schools adequately. Teachers have not and will not, in the long run, choose to work in an underfunded public educational system. Instead, they will vote with their feet, choosing to move to other states where salaries are much higher.

Since educational attainment is strongly related to poverty, in Oklahoma the poor are especially victims because of those elected officials in charge of distributing tax surpluses. Private schools in general in Oklahoma are not affordable to the poor. The 1990 teacher's strike temporarily benefited public school teachers, giving them smaller class sizes and resources, thereby improving the quality of public school education. By 2017, however, two more decades of neglect by state leadership left public school teachers weary of state legislative priorities. The most recent estimate of Oklahoma public school teacher salaries in 2023 is that the average Oklahoma salary is about 30 percent below the national standard. Class size again grew unrealistic as school systems were forced to make choices from a list of bad options, including the availability of adequate class materials, building maintenance, and other educational essentials.[49]

Before the strike of 2018, there were teachers in Oklahoma who were forced to take second and even third jobs to make family ends meet. One Tulsa teacher, Teresa Dank, made headlines. She took to the streets, as reported in the summer of 2017, to panhandle for money to purchase the necessary teaching materials for her students that her school could not provide. Bargaining between teachers and elected officials broke down in early April 2018. For only the second time in history, public school teachers went on strike statewide—this in spite of some reluctance upon the part of their own union, the Oklahoma Education Association.[50]

The Republican Oklahoma governor at the time compared teacher demands for decent salaries to "teenagers wanting a better car." In return, normally complacent Oklahoma teachers, along with some of their students, jammed the halls of the state capitol in Oklahoma City to protest against decades of stingy allocations from their state legislators. During these protests, teachers turned the governor's words into popular chants to the sound of their jiggling car keys. Students from Tulsa's Edison High School carried signs reading, "Roses are Red, Edison is Green, Disrespecting Teachers is Mean."[51]

The pay raises reluctantly agreed to in 2018 by many state legislators brought teachers' salaries from near the bottom for all states to thirty-fourth from the top. Still lower after their salary boosts than in neighboring Texas, some Oklahoma teachers left the profession altogether or, like others before them, moved to significantly higher teacher salaries in Dallas and Houston.[52]

In 2022, 24 percent of all public school teachers in Oklahoma quit their jobs. To its credit, the Oklahoma legislature finally passed legislation in 2023 that was expected to benefit underpaid public school teachers across the state. The new legislation provides $625 million targeted at raising teacher salaries. An additional $150 million was allocated to school resource officers, "$10 million across three years to hire reading instructors and $12 million for teacher maternity leave." Some 50,000 Oklahoma educators were expected on the average to receive raises of $4,766 for the 2023–24 school year, increasing the average teacher salary, according to the Oklahoma School Board Association, to $60,307.[53]

Data from the U.S. Census and other related fact-based research paint a stark picture of poverty in Oklahoma. The poor have suffered the abhorrent consequences of pervasive and persistent poverty since statistics were first systematically collected in 1959. It is vital to remember that these statistics describe and affect real people, like the women, men, and children who come to Thy Will Be Done because they do not have enough food to eat.

Over more than sixty years, the poverty rate has declined but the actual number of poor Oklahomans continued to increase. The majority of those who are poor are White, as has been the case since 1959. At the same time, minorities have a poverty rate two to three times that of White Oklahomans.

The only good news about the Oklahoma poverty rate in the past twenty years is the decline among Natives, although at this point in time it remains markedly higher than for Whites. The decline appears to be primarily the result of casino revenue owned by the tribal nations.

In addition to all minorities, there remain those who regrettably suffer disproportionately from poverty. These include women, children, the elderly, and the disabled. Military veterans with disabilities are also one of subpopulations especially vulnerable to poverty in Oklahoma.

The COVID-19 pandemic revealed specific inequities facing health care in Oklahoma with consequences. This includes the misinformation made available to the general population, including those in poverty, a topic that remains under-researched.

Public education in Oklahoma plays a huge role in determining who is poor and who is not. U.S. Census data, in fact, demonstrate a significant relationship between those who are poor and the number of their years of schooling. There is, at the same time, a long history of the underfunding of Oklahoma public schools, including not paying teacher salaries at rates comparable to other states.

Legal suits brought against taxpayer institutions designed to protect the welfare of citizens, like the Pinnacle Plan to reform Oklahoma Child Welfare Services, sadly reveal a history of systemic neglect by state bureaucracies. In other states these same kinds of services ameliorate the consequences of poverty upon children.

There is a direct relationship between the Oklahoma economy and poverty. There appear to be real reasons the state economy over time is relatively stagnate when compared to the business climate in other states with far lower poverty rates than Oklahoma.

Stereotypes of the poor and poverty can dominate political discourse and public decision-making. A reframing of Oklahoma history focusing upon the role of political corruption and its subsequent impact upon the poor may offer additional insights into both causes and solutions of impoverishment in a state rich in natural resources.

6

A Culture of Political Corruption

Robert Lee Maril and Jayme Hall Johnson

First thing he says to me, you know, sometimes I get money for the commissioners. He called it walking around money. I can get you $300 or $400 walking around money.
—Bob Anthony, Oklahoma Corporation commissioner

Politics in Oklahoma manifests itself in various aspects of the lives of all those who reside in its shadow. Political corruption, however, always betrays itself by inevitably subverting basic democratic rights. Regardless of party affiliation, political corruption can create and support various forms of individual and institutionalized violence frequently aimed at the least powerful. These forms of violence, in an attempt to exert control in the best interests of those who hold both legitimate and illegitimate power, may be both overt and covert.[1]

The consequences of Oklahoma poverty leave guests at Thy Will Be Done in precarious positions, often with only bad choices. This is also true for applicants to Mission of Care and other providers in Hereford, Macon, and all of Wells County. Moreover, longitudinal U.S. Census data and other research further describe and explain at the local and state levels some of the dire consequences of being poor (see chapter 5).

Although political corruption erodes our democracy, it is the Oklahoma poor, because of the marginality of their lives, who may suffer the most.[2] It is useful, therefore, to briefly reframe Oklahoma politics from the perspective of its historical impact upon the poor and, in addition, upon other private and public institutions and industries.

Political corruption after statehood in 1907 was by no means a stranger to Oklahoma's smaller cities like Lawton. With about the same population as Hereford, Lawton is in southwestern Oklahoma directly adjacent to Fort Sill military base. Fort Sill employs the largest number of military and civilians, more than 34,000, of the five military installations in the state, including Tinker Air Force Base in Oklahoma City.[3] Nevertheless, this Comanche County city has a high poverty rate, currently at 19 percent, compared to the state average.

Jake Hamon is typical of some individuals who came to Oklahoma when it was Indian Territory.[4] In a flash he became a rich and influential politician in the new state. By the time Hamon was appointed to his first official position, he was a successful oil man who had joined with John Ringling of circus fame to build a railroad. His first political appointment in Oklahoma was as the first district attorney of Lawton.

Hamon, a Democrat, staked his claim on the position of district attorney even though prior to his appointment he had been accused of rousting gamblers. A few years later he was denounced by Thomas Gore, who eventually became a U.S. senator, for Hamon's attempt to bribe him. Gore stated that Hamon's failed bribery was "over sale contracts with the Choctaw and Chickasaw nations." As a result of these charges, Hamon was fired from his position as Lawton's district attorney.

This scandal involving Hamon was, however, more portentous than it seemed at the time, both for Oklahoma and for Hamon's expectations of power at the national level. The recently elected Harding administration in 1920 admired Hamon's political style. President Harding seriously considered him for a cabinet position in his administration. "The Harding administration wanted Hamon to reunite with his family and to leave his secretary back in Oklahoma." Instead, before he could be officially appointed by the Harding administration to a national position of influence, he ended up drunk and shot dead. The scene of the crime was in the same hotel at which he and his secretary had previously dined. After Hamon's death, the shots that killed him were described in the murder trial of this same secretary: "Those bullets ended decades of [Hamon's] bribery and king-making" in Oklahoma.

Political corruption in the new state of Oklahoma involved individuals such as Jake Hamon but also elaborate community and statewide networks of conspirators. Prior to statehood, much of the violence initiated by a culture of political corruption was directed toward Natives, Blacks, and impoverished Whites. The Osage tribe, as depicted in the recent book and film *Killers of the Flower Moon*, experience another way Oklahoma's culture of political corruption worked and usually prevailed after statehood. Osage County is the northeastern part of the state bordering Kansas. Pawhuska is its county seat.[5]

A vast conspiracy to steal oil rights from the Osage tribe was the goal of a long list of prominent Osage residents, the majority of them White. The Osage, a small tribe, had been allocated a large amount of land in the north-central part of the state. The land was largely considered worthless until vast oil resources were discovered beneath it. Almost overnight members of the tribe became immensely wealthy. Politicians, judges, lawyers, and other officers of the law, along with bankers and other prominent businessmen in Osage County, fomented a decades-long conspiracy to intimidate and murder selected Natives. Their goal was always to obtain control of their oil rights. This conspiracy thrived from 1910 to 1930, a conspiracy far larger than depicted in the film.

The modus operandi of this conspiracy was to poison, bomb, shoot, maim, intimidate, and kill Osage individuals who held rights of ownership to oil royalties. Often the conspirators claimed legal guardianship of Indian children to steal their wealth from them and other family members. Osage County as of 2022, despite the once incredible wealth of the Osage tribe, has a poverty rate of 13.5 percent, slightly higher than the state average.[6]

A similar but much larger political culture of political corruption, one that existed for decades throughout the state, violated the legal rights of other Oklahoma tribes with oil wealth. Angie Debo shows in her many books how the Bureau of Indian Affairs was complicit in these systematic crimes against Natives.[7] The details of the decades of political corruption throughout the state are documented in her research. In turn, Debo was blacklisted from ever teaching in public schools and universities in Oklahoma, despite her impressive academic credentials and remarkable scholarship. By the 1930s less than 5 percent of the oil rights once legally owned by Oklahoma Natives remained in their control.

The Tulsa race massacre in 1921 also exemplifies how minorities, many impoverished, have been treated in Oklahoma when they escaped poverty by pulling themselves up by their own proverbial bootstraps. White mobs, urged on by the Ku Klux Klan, murdered up to an estimated three hundred residents of Black-owned businesses and residences in Tulsa's Black Wall Street. Bodies of Black men, women, and children were summarily dumped into the nearby Arkansas River by the White mob or haphazardly thrown into mass graves. More than a century later, the exact number of those murdered has still not been established.[8]

Political corruption played an active role in the Tulsa race massacre during and after the White rampage. The White mob was given a free pass for all its murders, beatings, and total destruction of the Black business and residential district. City and state leaders not only allowed this mayhem to continue but also made certain no White rioters and racist killers ever were judged for the vicious murders and other crimes committed during the riots.

During the massacre, the Oklahoma KKK was active in organizing and directing the murders, beatings, and other assaults of Black victims. The accounts of these events were then systematically expurgated from public libraries and schools in Tulsa and other parts of the state.[9] The explicit message to the KKK was transparent. These violent racist crimes were explicitly sanctioned by powerful White politicians and community leaders. Black Oklahomans, if they were able to, fled for their lives to the relative safety of other states.

Jack C. Walton, a Democrat like Hamon, also exemplifies the individual brazen level of corrupt Oklahoma politics in the early 1920s. His form of violence was more covert, but nonetheless a subversion of the democratic process. Walton was the fifth governor of Oklahoma and the first to be removed from office.[10]

As he was running for the office of governor, Walton publicly criticized the Oklahoma KKK while actively seeking their advice and counsel. But his duplicity stopped once elected, after which he quickly placed himself at the center of a statewide patronage system. This corrupt government bureaucracy included appointing his personal favorites, despite their lack of qualifications, to a wide variety of state positions including at state colleges and universities.[11]

Public higher education, from Governor Walton's perspective, was just one more state agency he could use to pay off his friends and supporters by giving them jobs. In return, of course, Walton expected both adulation and compensation. When his critics complained and sought legal action against him, he placed the entire state under martial law.[12]

The ninth governor of Oklahoma (1931–35), William H. Murray was an experienced state politician who served as the head of state government during the early years of the Great Depression. During his four years as the elected leader of the state, Governor Murray, a Democrat, regularly employed the state national guard to control what he viewed as unrest by unpatriotic workers and those too lazy to appreciate what his state had to offer. Part of this unrest included organized labor protests against starvation wages and brutal working conditions. At the time, these protests and demonstrations were labeled un-American.[13] The governor's reliance on force and violence by the national guard affected not only the working poor but increasing numbers of the poor who simply did not have enough food to eat. Desperate enough to protest, in return they were vilified.[14] Oklahomans with the least political power and economic status suffered greatly. Those who resisted—especially miners, small farmers, the urban poor, and other blue-collar workers including union organizers and their members—were regularly beaten and jailed.

Some of the victims of these brutal excesses by the state's chief executive voted with their feet. Like the fictional Tom Joad and his family, they set out for the greener pastures of California. In California, of course, those lucky to have made it there were frequently isolated in camps, exploited for their labor, and, all the while, blamed for economic and political conditions over which they had no control.

Throughout his long political career, Governor Murray was a unique and increasingly ruthless politician. In the early years he relied on his real roots in Texas as a small farmer. In fact, he openly advocated for those who were taken advantage of by the wealthy. Eventually tagging himself "Alfalfa Bill," he hid behind his role as the Oklahoma version of an idiot savant. As Alfalfa Bill, Murray dressed for public appearances in long underwear reaching below the cuffs of his pants.

In the 1920s, Alfalfa Bill increasingly found the ideas of the Oklahoma KKK appealing. By the time of the Great Depression, he was strongly opposed to President Roosevelt's New Deal agenda. This included Roosevelt's intention to protect the best interests of the less fortunate and needy who were staggered by a failing national economy. Alfalfa Bill deserted those he early on had staunchly championed, remapping his politics to conform to a White supremacist agenda.

Growing numbers of starving and homeless poor, including immigrant blue-color workers, needed the governor's help in curbing the worst economic disaster the state had ever endured. Instead, they got Alfalfa Bill. In his KKK scheme of things, the victims including immigrants and White union members were, along with the other minorities in Oklahoma, themselves to blame for all the problems they confronted.

Governor Alfalfa Bill should be remembered, according to one source, for the number of times he called out the national guard at times of unrest.[15] After the Great Depression ended, the former governor turned to writing books that further displayed his far-right political leanings.

Democratic governor J. Howard Edmonson, who served from 1959 to 1963, was one of the first elected officials to acknowledge publicly the overwhelming depth of the Oklahoma culture of political corruption in his own party and, at the same time, attempt to reform it. Winning the governorship by a landslide, Edmonson believed he had a mandate from his party to finally bring reform to an out-of-control, entrenched political system that also included the Republican minority. Edmonson first advocated specific reforms, eventually targeting both houses of the state legislature and all levels of state government.

Governor Edmonson attempted to pass a set of new state laws including, in addition to the repeal of Prohibition and the creation of liquor control measures, a merit system for legislators, control of their purchasing powers, and a tax plan incorporating public accountability. His reforms aimed at reining in the state legislature's financial largesse as well as its reach into county and city governments. Among these reforms was an attempt to reform extensive corruption among county commissioners.[16] In addition to the statewide reforms, Edmonson dared to take on traditional Oklahoma powerbrokers, including three-term senator Robert S. Kerr and his family. Senator Kerr was a major owner of Kerr-McGee Oil Industries, an Oklahoma drilling company that became a global conglomerate in offshore fossil fuels and minerals.[17]

Edmonson had the support of his own party when he first took office, but soon elected Democrats, their appointees, and others who were part of the massive misuse of public funds recognized that his proposals affected their own illicit incomes. In less than two years' time, Edmonson's own political party turned on him. His exit from Democratic state leadership was a clear signal that an elected official who rocked the political boat, even a governor who won by a landslide, was not tolerated.

Under the ruling Democratic Party, systemic misuse of public funds had endured for decades. This system efficiently channeled public funds to those who were politically powerful but in many cases then quickly also became wealthy. This infrastructure of graft stretched throughout the state and included the county legal system of sheriffs and district attorneys. Funding for public schools, the construction and maintenance of public buildings, parks, roads, bridges, and the jobs that accompanied them were part and parcel of the dominant system in place.

Eight years after Edmonson's political fall, in 1971 David Hall, also a Democrat, became the twentieth governor of the state. By that time, the traditional political hold of the Democrats over county, state, and nationally elected representatives showed signs of slipping. Hall, a Tulsa lawyer and professor, faced the standing governor, Republican Dewey Bartlett, in the general election. Republicans made political corruption a mainstay of their election strategy. They already had found some success in gaining the support of Oklahoma voters tired of the way their tax money lined the pockets of Democrats.

Democrat Hall prevailed in this election, but he angered the publisher of the family-owned *Daily Oklahoman*.[18] The *Oklahoman* long viewed itself as the state's newspaper. In such a capacity it held considerable power. Three days after Hall left the governor's office in 1975, he was charged with two federal felonies, bribery and extortion.

Hall was found guilty of conspiring with his secretary of state. Specifically, he was convicted of directing state retirement employee funds to W. W. "Doc" Taylor, a businessman in Dallas. Serving nineteen months of a three-year prison sentence at a federal prison in Arizona, Hall became the first Oklahoma governor to be convicted of any crime while serving as the head of the Oklahoma state government. After his release from prison, he was disbarred in Oklahoma.[19]

For the first seventy years of statehood the Democratic Party, the majority party, was also the political party of graft and corruption in this state. The Republicans gradually won the voter's overwhelming confidence, first at the national level, then at state and local elections. But not before additional charges of corruption rocked the Democrats at other levels of state government, including the judiciary.

Rumors and allegations swirled for years around Oklahoma judges receiving bribes from special-interest groups to render sympathetic verdicts. In the early 1960s these charges were finally verified against Oklahoma Supreme Court justices. Charges were brought against three justices. They were eventually found to have accepted bribes in return for overturning cases adjudicated before them for twenty-five years. First, Justice N. S. Corn was charged with income tax evasion and convicted. While serving his prison term Corn provided evidence leading to the impeachment or resignation of two additional justices, Earl Welch and

Napoleon Bonaparte Johnson. Because of this case, the selection process of Oklahoma Supreme Court justices was amended.[20]

Former justice Corn eventually admitted that in his twenty-five years on the court there was never a year he did not take a bribe to change his decision in a case. Shortly after finding out about his fellow justice, William A. Berry said, "Described here were the actions of three justices, impugning the integrity of the whole court, and violating the very canons of truth and fairness."[21] Blatant corruption in the Oklahoma Supreme Court undermined the entire system of justice and further allowed political corruption to flourish. Why should any Oklahoman follow the rule of law when the most powerful and wealthy paid judges off as if their offenses were mere traffic tickets?

Given this dominant culture of corruption since statehood, which included all branches of government at all levels, it is surprising in some respects that county officials managed to escape public oversight.[22] Outlandish as it may sound to those who are not Oklahomans, until the 1980s only one county commissioner in all of the seventy-seven counties had ever been charged with corruption while in office. This errant county commissioner was tried by a jury of his peers and found guilty. However, in spite of his jury conviction, he received a suspended sentence.[23]

Coordinated multiple investigations by federal prosecutors into political corruption by Oklahoma county commissioners began in 1980 and lasted four years. Along the way a systematic examination of the daily machinations of elected officials throughout the majority of Oklahoma counties uncovered a dominant, self-assured, and omnipresent culture of political corruption.[24] For as long as several generations of Oklahomans could remember, the majority of elected county officials, Democrats, felt free to plunder tax money allocated to their districts for projects only partially completed or never seeing the light of day. In the rhetoric of the day, a solid county infrastructure was supposed to guarantee growth and sustain local economies. The vast majority of all these elected officials and appointees at the county level were Democrats, although some county Republicans, as was the case in Wells County, also joined in the feast upon public funds.

Widely recognized by constituents whose complaints about the misuse of their tax dollars were legion, county officials rarely received the oversight of state legislators at the capital in Oklahoma City. But county commissioners were frequently supported by a blatant system of corruption that could include county judges and local law enforcement. Since statehood, corruption at the county level was supposed to be all smoke and no fire, both to the general public and to potential whistleblowers.

Misuse of public funds throughout the seventy-seven counties along with favoritism to certain constituents was the norm, not the exception. Buoyed by signs of disgruntled Democratic voters as early as the 1960s, the minority Republican Party recognized a genuine opportunity in the taken-for-granted reelection of the longtime Democratic speaker of the house. In 1966, Democrat J. D. McCarty confidently sought his fourth consecutive term.

McCarty represented a very poor district in southeastern Oklahoma where, not surprisingly, voting turnout year after year was far less than the dismal state average. Those holding power were so formidable that many voters, both Republicans and Democrats, no longer participated in the political process. But when given an alternative, disaffected county voters swung in line behind a Republican unknown. The unknown candidate, Vondel L. Smith, was a local funeral director with no political experience.[25]

House speaker McCarty experienced one of the most notorious upsets in Oklahoma history at the hands of his relatively obscure Republican opponent. Now politically defrocked, McCarty was soon convicted of tax evasion and on his way to a federal prison. Nevertheless, the majority party in the state legislature, where the Democrats had prevailed for so many years, was not about to change because of one election. Upon release from an Arkansas prison after six months' imprisonment, McCarty soon became a lobbyist and local television election pundit after rejoining his insurance firm.[26]

In 1980, when the first earnest effort to clean up political corruption at the county level systematically throughout Oklahoma was announced, not surprisingly it was met by public skepticism. One among several of the federal prosecutors was William S. Price, who served as the assistant U.S. attorney in the Western District of Oklahoma from 1975 to 1982 and then as the U.S. attorney for the Western District from 1982 to 1989. His investigations with his team of attorneys soon grew into hundreds of cases against elected county politicians and their cronies. The weight of evidence they amassed was impressive.[27]

Very early in the process, several county commissioners realized that it would be in their own best interests to flip. Turning against fellow commissioners and longtime business partners in crooked schemes, they provided unflattering descriptions of the massive misuse of public funds. In the end, criminal cases were brought against Oklahoma county commissioners in sixty-six of the seventy-seven counties. Federal attorneys provided limited immunity in some counties in return for testimony against co-conspirators. It took Price and his colleagues almost five years to prosecute all the cases. Although there were exceptions, the vast majority of these commissioners were Democrats.

The prosecution of this statewide Democratic political corruption was called Okscam. Discovery and prosecution of elected county commissioners uncovered a deep culture of political corruption that undermined basic democratic values and processes in every corner of the state. When the legal dust settled from Okscam, Price and his colleagues had brought to justice a total of 224 defendants. Of this, 162 (72 percent) were county commissioners. Elected officials, appointees, and those who bribed them were given the chance to admit guilt when confronted by the evidence or go to trial. Their longtime cronies were contractors, suppliers, and others living well off taxpayer money.

When convicted, most of these corrupt county commissioners and their cronies were sent to prison. Most served relatively short sentences, but several diehard officials who believed they were above the rule of law ended up serving longer terms. A handful who had their day in court in the final days of prosecution spent ten years or more in federal prisons.

If added together, the bribes given by contractors and suppliers to county commissioners in the Okscam cases litigated were estimated to syphon off more than $200 million from county budgets. In current dollars, this totals more than $700 million per year.[28] Scholars consider Okscam to be one of the largest cases in the history of corruption in state government.

Examined further, these federal investigations led by the office of the attorney general of Oklahoma most often involved kickbacks from state allocations to Oklahoma county commissioners. These kickbacks were so ingrained in the political culture that the bribes were considered by a majority of elected county officials a normal part of conducting county affairs. County corruption had been going on for so long that most commissioners literally assumed it was their right to receive at least a 10 percent kickback. So also did contractors and suppliers for all projects funded by appropriations to maintain or improve county infrastructure such as roads and bridges. This county system of conducting business was, according to many, the only way they ever knew.[29]

Investigators discovered two basic kinds of illegal deals. In one, an elected county commissioner purchased supplies for road or bridge construction or improvements. His guaranteed share was 10 percent of the total cost of materials from the local vendor of the materials. In the second crooked scheme, a county commissioner purchased the materials to build or improve some part of the infrastructure of his county, but, although the purchases appeared on invoices as legal documents of the use of state money, in fact the improvement project was never initiated. The materials documented were never actually delivered. Nevertheless, the county commissioner split the legislative appropriation between his own bank account and his cronies. In these kinds of criminal arrangements, it was not unusual for bribes to the elected official to exceed 20 percent or more of the legislative allotment for the project.

County commissioners and their cronies were not the only ones affected by this political corruption. Under Oklahoma law, county commissioners legally owned and supervised all county courthouses and offices. In addition, they had the legal heft to sign off on budgets for other elected county officials including district attorneys and sheriffs. Since the district attorneys and sheriffs were dependent on the commissioners for both their budgets and their office space, as a group they were prone to ignore the kickbacks in order to keep in the good graces of the Democratic political machine. County district attorneys and sheriffs also chose to ignore the continual complaints from residents in their county about the bad roads, unsafe bridges, and all the other public projects, including school facilities, never completed.

Over the years, county commissioners grew more and more entitled and emboldened. When arrested by federal prosecutors, their reaction was frequently to claim they were only doing what other elected officials had always done before them. How, therefore, could they be guilty of any crime?

Okscam, which exposed one of the worst cases of political corruption of state officials in any state at any time, emphatically suggests that other branches and levels of Oklahoma government including state agencies had the same taint of privileged malfeasance. In the end, it was only federal intervention in the shape of a team of diligent attorneys that finally revealed this charade covering up absolute hubris—hubris that was a disservice to all residents of Oklahoma counties, but particularly those in poverty. It was the poor who could least afford the misuse of public tax dollars that otherwise could have been directed toward their interests. These interests included, among others, new jobs, county infrastructure spurring economic growth, and a fair legal system for all constituents.

Wells County did not escape Okscam. In 1982 two Wells County commissioners were forced to resign after signing plea agreements with the attorney general. Prosecutors found more than enough evidence to convict these two commissioners, both Republicans. Evidence collected in the investigations proved that they accepted kickbacks from at least one local construction company. From January 1975 to April 1981, at least one supplier paid kickbacks of about $55,000 to each of them.[30]

One major consequence of the corruption Okscam uncovered was that Wells County residents became even more skeptical of their elected officials. In principle, elected politicians are supposed to conduct themselves honestly and with decorum while promoting the interests of their constituencies. Skepticism in Wells County with regard to Okscam corruption did not diminish over time, nor did the corruption end. In 1996, the district attorney of Hereford pleaded guilty to embezzling almost $85,000 of public funds while serving his constituency. He used these stolen public funds to pay off his own loans and credit cards.[31]

By the start of 2000, the majority of Oklahoma voters, including independents, had shifted their party allegiance to the Republicans. Up until 1948, Oklahoma had strongly supported Democratic presidential candidates, and Democrats had maintained a tight grip on state government. But since that time, except for the election of Lyndon Johnson to the presidency in 1964, Oklahomans have chosen Republican presidential candidates. Soon they were voting for Republican candidates by a consistent margin of at least two to one. Since 2003, a Democratic presidential candidate has failed to win even one county of Oklahoma's seventy-seven.[32]

After Okscam, Democrats temporarily lost the governorship. Since then, Republicans have won the governorship six of nine times, and all of them in the past sixteen years. Republican supermajorities currently control both the state house and senate. At this writing, almost all state-level departments and agencies in Oklahoma represent the best interests of elected Republicans and their appointees. Oklahoma is one of the reddest states in our nation.

Turning the Democratic Party into the minority party in Oklahoma did not, however, erase the blatant culture of political corruption. A lobbyist of one county recently called for the Oklahoma legislature to relax its oversight of county public funds. He reasoned that a plethora of laws enacted after Okscam to curtail excesses of county commissioners were no longer necessary. The legislature, he suggested, should pay more attention to statewide issues.[33]

Penn Square Mall in Oklahoma City was first opened in 1960. I remember it as a unique retail space offering a new kind of shopping experience to northside residents. My family moved to the northwest suburbs. At the time, the new mall, where my mother shopped, included a very small bank, Penn Square Bank.[34] By the time of the newest oil boom in Oklahoma and Texas in the late 1970s and early 1980s, a handful of aggressive bankers at Penn Square Bank were handing out loans to oilmen and pretend oilmen like cotton candy at the Oklahoma State Fair. Offering them financial backing, regardless of their experience in the oil and gas markets, rapidly changed an insignificant mall bank in Oklahoma City into a reckless financial institution threatening the entire American banking system.

In the process of becoming a major player in the oil boom, Penn Square Bank cast aside traditional banking practices in favor of graft and corruption. From all around the country reputable financial institutions soon funneled enormous fiscal resources into this bank. Relatively naïve investors both desired and were urged to get in on the ground floor of an oil boom that would, unlike other booms before it, never go bust. Penn Square Bank had so much oil business, million-dollar deals were being made in every bank space available, including closets.

The oil boom, notwithstanding the advice of financial advisors, was followed in the early 1980s by the oil glut. Prices for crude crashed. So many bad loans were handed out in such an unfathomable fashion by Penn Square Bank that the Federal Deposit Insurance Corporation (FDIC) finally closed it down. In 1982, long lines of anxious customers formed outside the bank to grab their money while it was still available. And Penn Square Bank hurt not only local customers but big money from other national banks around the country. Some critics suggested that the magnitude of the problem portrayed a national banking system on the brink of insolvency. The Continental Illinois National Bank and Trust Company, for example, alone held $326 million of Penn Square Bank's bad paper of well over $1 billion. Other major banks far from Oklahoma borders suffered staggering losses because of Penn Square Bank's dubious loan practices. All investors not fully insured by the FDIC lost their shirts.

Eventually the FDIC and other investigators focused upon two men who were alleged to be responsible for the Penn Square banking debacle. One was Bill P. Jennings, chairman and CEO of Penn Square Bank. The other was a newbie banking star, William G. Patterson. Patterson had been picked by Jennings to head the oil-and-gas lending department at Penn Square Bank. After being convicted of defrauding Chicago investors, Patterson spent two years in prison. Jennings, however, never saw the inside of a cell. After Patterson's trial and conviction in Illinois, Jennings returned to Oklahoma City, where he spent the rest of his days running his own commercial nursery. He died in 2003.[35]

Penn Square Bank is an example of a predatory business enterprise ineffectively regulated by the federal government. Most of the local bankers feigned surprise when Penn Square went under, but the rumors had been rife about the criminal excesses at the bank for quite some time. Penn Square Bank created widespread economic damage in Oklahoma and throughout the country, not only in dollars lost. The American banking system was not as infallible as the public imagined. Within state boundaries, 139 Oklahoma banks soon collapsed. The majority were small-town Oklahoma banks, an economic blow to the rural poor.[36]

At the same time, of course, Penn Square Bank created distrust of honest operators and investors in the oil and gas industries. But banks and their investors were not the only ones to suffer from these questionable business practices. Oklahomans at the other end of the economic spectrum, those already poor, also suffered as a result the scandal. This included the loss of jobs, growing personal debt, lack of access to adequate medical care, and a number of other immediate consequences resolved only by having money to pay the bills. Those in poverty, or falling into poverty, suffered far greater consequences than the crooked business community.[37]

Many both in Oklahoma banking and the oil and gas business were shocked by the illegal and unethical practices of banking officers at Penn Square Bank. That said, the majority of those who financially fed at the trough, excluding only Patterson, were never adjudicated.[38]

The county government corruption exposed by Okscam in the 1980s and the decades-long malfeasance of the state supreme court are not the end of it. Oklahoma commissions, departments, and agencies have by no means been immune to systemic corruption that places the interests of the few before those of the public. The Penn Square Bank scandal was a harbinger of the corruption embedded in the Oklahoma Corporation Commission.

The OCC is a key regulatory commission assigned by the Oklahoma constitution to keep a close eye upon a significant part of the business sector in Oklahoma. Under Article IX of the constitution, the OCC regulates the oil and gas industries, for more than a century at the core of the state economy. The OCC also oversees the regulation of all public utilities, including transportation and communications.

The OCC's legal responsibility is to protect the public from the excesses of the businesses they oversee. It regulates these industries so that the public's best interests, including those of the poor, are not neglected in favor of unreasonable charges or rates for fundamental services provided by these for-profit businesses. Voters statewide elect three OCC commissioners for staggered terms of six years each. Today the OCC's interests also cover the enforcement of "federal regulations for underground injection of water and chemicals."[39]

The OCC is housed in the Jim Thorpe Office Building adjacent to the State Capitol Complex in Oklahoma City. It is also just a few blocks from the house on Culbertson Drive where I was born and raised. The statue of Jim Thorpe, who grew up on the Sac and Fox reservation in Oklahoma, sits outside the doors of the multistoried building and was a common sight for me. Day in and day out, the OCC addresses issues that directly impact the pocketbooks of all state rate payers, including those below the poverty line. To accomplish these tasks, the three commissioners direct 450 state employees. The OCC's annual budget is $60 million.

Decisions at the OCC directly influence the daily cost of living of those who are poor. This includes, among others, utility bills and public transportation upon which many in poverty must depend to reach their employment. What may to the nonpoor seem like small monthly augmentations to utility bills to the poor can mean not being able to buy enough food for their households, pay off growing medical debt, or meet their rents.[40]

In January 1988, at a time when the Democratic Party had been replaced by the Republicans as the majority party in state and local government, Bob Anthony, a Republican, was elected to one of the three positions at the OCC, joining two others of his political party. Soon after Anthony was sworn into public office, he visited attorney William L. Anderson. He did so because "Tater," as the lawyer was called by those who knew him, was one of the most experienced representatives of the big utilities with which Anthony and the OCC worked daily. Tater, in fact, had served for more than five years as the OCC general counsel before he became what he now was, one of the most influential lobbyists for private businesses regulated by Oklahoma government agencies and departments.

When interviewed on PBS's *Frontline*, Commissioner Anthony said, "I can remember the first time I stopped off to see Bill Anderson (Tater) in his office. I was told he was a popular lobbyist for some of the big utilities and he was very well informed about the issues, some of which are pretty complex. . . . First thing he says to me, 'you know, sometimes I get money for the commissioners.' He called it walking around money. 'I can get you $300 or $400 walking around money. I do that for the commissioners.' That was kind of a shocking thing."[41]

Anthony took the money soon offered to him by Tater, all of it in bills Tater stuffed into a brown paper bag. Then without hesitation the brand-new commissioner called one of his former high school classmates in Oklahoma City. That acquaintance was U.S. District Attorney William S. Price, the same individual who had led a team of federal litigators in Okscam. Soon after, Anthony and Price met with two agents of the Federal Bureau of Investigation.

Subsequently, over the course of more than two years, the OCC's Anthony recorded conversations of elected officials and lobbyists like Tater. Many of these officials were Republicans, like Anthony, or lobbyists who courted Republican politicians and their appointees for their clients with cases before the OCC. According to Anthony in the *Frontline* interview, Tater "comes off as a good ol' boy. Everybody calls him Tater. You know, just a country boy going about his business. He's short, overweight. His friends kid him that he walks like a duck. And he does. He's got a soft, raspy voice."

But Tater, if looked at through the reframing of Oklahoma history, falls well within the tradition of former governor Bill Murray and his pals. Murray's intentional dumbing down before the public in order to persuade and control his followers, personified in his alter ego Alfalfa Bill, was both pure political theater and political sleight of hand. What you saw is not what you got. The same thing for Tater, a shrewd, well-educated individual who knew the inner workings of a state bureaucracy whose major role was regulatory watchdog for certain large industries influencing multistate areas.

In a series of unpublished interviews in the late 1990s, I asked Commissioner Anthony why he agreed to wear a wire for the FBI. "It wasn't a wire. I would never wear a wire. See, they tape it to the small of your back and run the mike down your sleeves or your front and tape it to your chest. I agreed to use the Nagra. It's a German-make tape recorder. Supposed to be the best there is. It's what the FBI always uses. The FBI installed the Nagra in a briefcase I had on my desk. With lots of stacks of papers and files. It would be maybe 18 inches from Bill Anderson's [Tater's] mouth, and he never knew it. I'd turn it on when he came in. Sometimes I'd have two Nagras going, especially when the FBI thought there was going to be an exchange of money. We wanted to get every word he said, not miss a thing."

Anthony gave the FBI more than two hundred tapes he recorded, including numerous conversations in which Tater offered him bribes.[42]

"But why did you do it?"

There is a long pause after my question. Then Anthony finally says, "It never occurred to me not to do it."

In Anthony's telling and as verified by FBI tapes of the conversations, Tater soon again ambles into his office in the Jim Thorpe Office Building.[43] Anthony is still sorting out boxes in his office from his previous position as the CEO of C. R. Anthony Department Stores, a regional department store chain. The OCC commissioner has the Nagra the FBI gave him set up in his briefcase inconspicuously lying on the corner of his desk. From the transcripts of the FBI tapes verbatim given to me by Anthony:

TATER: (Unclear). (Sound of door). (Unclear).

MR. ANTHONY: Here it is. Uh now this . . . this thing we were talking about the other day. Uh you know I need to be just awful careful.

TATER: Alright . . . it'll be cash and I'll have names of people that (unclear) . . . list of contributions.

MR. ANTHONY: Okay, so it will all be in cash.

TATER: Cash and no damn strings attached and then all I want from you or anybody is a fair shake.

MR. ANTHONY: Okay.

TATER: If I can't see my client gets a reasonable amount, if I get a fair shake, then I oughta be fired anyway.

MR. ANTHONY: Yeah.

TATER: Be cash. I'll give you names of people who are not connected to the Commission.

MR. ANTHONY: Okay.

TATER: (Unclear).

MR. ANTHONY: Okay.

TATER: I (Unclear) anybody in my life expect anything except a fair shake.

MR. ANTHONY: So that's (Unclear) . . .

TATER: (Unclear) . . . you've got to shave every morning and look yourself in the mirror . . . by doing what's right.

MR. ANTHONY: Right. Now that's uh a lot of names but there's lots of people . . ."

The first bribe Tater offers Commissioner Anthony is $10,000. He also gives him a list of fifty names, each masked as a $200 contribution for Anthony's political campaign. Contributions less than $200 do not require a name to be reported. The list of names is intended to protect Anthony from violating any campaign laws.

Since stepping down from his job as the general counsel for the OCC, Tater knows all about the campaign laws. For several years he has represented large utility companies and other private businesses that the OCC regulates. Lawyer Tater's intent is never to give the money to Anthony's campaign but directly to Anthony, so that his illegal contributions do not show up on documents Anthony must file. Soon Anthony receives another bribe from Tater, this one for $15,000 for a new car.

In return for the total sum of $25,000, Anthony is expected to represent the best interests of Southwestern Bell Corporation, which currently has a case before the OCC. This multistate corporation is alleged to have overcharged Oklahoma rate payers by tens of millions of dollars. This includes poor Oklahomans who, like everyone else, require a phone to navigate the challenges they confront in their daily lives.

Because of the overwhelming evidence Anthony collects for the FBI, as well as the evidence from co-conspirators involved in this criminal case, a judge eventually sentences Tater to thirty-three months in prison. David H. Miller, an employee of Southwestern Bell, is also found guilty in this same bribery case.

As it eventually emerges, Tater attempted to bribe Anthony along with at least one of the two other OCC commissioners. A majority vote by Anthony and one other commissioner would guarantee that Southwestern Bell's proposed rate hikes would become law. As well, Southwestern Bell's alleged multi-million-dollar overcharges to customers would be ignored. As it turned out, contrary to Tater's best efforts, in August 1995 the OCC eventually required Southwestern Bell to cut its phone rates to customers by $92.8 million and to return to its Oklahoma customers overcharges of $148.4 million."[44]

Tater and Southwestern Bell's Miller also tried to bribe OCC commissioner Robert E. Hopkins, also a Republican. Hopkins, unlike Anthony, never reported the money he received to law enforcement or the county district attorney. Commissioner Hopkins was tried alongside Tater and Miller. All three were found guilty in 1997. Hopkins received the same sentence as his two co-conspirators, Tater and Miller, of thirty-three months in prison.

Documented corruption of Republican OCC commissioners instigated by large utilities such as Southwestern Bell goes far beyond the framing of these events as just another unfortunate political scandal in Oklahoma history. Tater was following in the tradition of a long line of lobbyists representing business interests with deep pockets who bribed Oklahoma politicians, their appointees, and friends throughout all levels of state government. This included not just the new minority party, the Democrats, but the new Republican majority party. In Oklahoma, political corruption is endemic.

The nursing home industry is another locus of longtime graft and corruption within all levels of Oklahoma government, regardless of the state's constitution or the legal and moral expectations of the public who put their trust in the hands of those they elect. The Oklahoma Department of Health for many years failed to provide oversight for the standard of care provided to nursing home residents, many of whom were elderly. Instead, individuals within the highest levels of the Department of Health turned their constitutional and ethical obligations into personal revenue streams.

Twenty-year-old rumors about corruption in the nursing home industry were finally investigated not by state officials but by the FBI in the late 1990s. The FBI's findings emerged in the spring of 2000 when the acting director of the Department of Health, among others, was indicted. Frank Keating, the Republican governor at the time, called the series of criminal offenses uncovered by the FBI and eventually other investigations to follow "an issue of raw, unadulterated corruption."[45]

"It's obscene to me and it's absolutely without question true that people died in facilities because of that corruption," stated one longtime observer of Oklahoma nursing homes. Said another, whose grandmother died a week after the corruption scandal first broke, "I think one of the toughest things was knowing my grandmother was—what happened to her? Why is my grandmother dying of gangrene in a nursing home?" According to this same report by *CBS News*, the family whose grandmother died of gangrene while in the care of a nursing home had a doctor who regularly signed off on her well-being. But the doctor was not a physician. "Dr. Susan Byrd is in fact a nurse with a doctorate in education."[46]

In addition to the acting director of the Department of Health and eventually one owner of a nursing home, nine other "ghost employees" of the department were discovered, including a former Oklahoma senate majority leader. Records show that Jim E. Lane, a Democrat from Idabel, received $17,178.60 in mileage, lodging, meals, and other travel expenses claimed to be related to "technical assistance to administrators."[47]

Before these investigated revelations, some nursing home operators were given advanced warning of when and where inspections by the Department of Health might occur. These warnings allowed corrupt nursing home owners to fix temporarily or completely hide their failure to meet state regulations governing nursing homes.

Brent VanMeter was the acting director of the Department of Health when he took bribes that directly affected the well-being of nursing home residents. He financially profited at the expense of the health, well-being, and lives of nursing home residents. Those who are poor in nursing homes have far less clout than others to call attention to their problems, let alone to attempt to change this system of abuse and neglect for profit.

In early May 2000, according to the FBI, VanMeter called up an owner of a nursing home to say he would be dropping by to collect an envelope. According to the FBI, which was following VanMeter, he drove directly from his state office to the nursing home to collect his bribe, then went to a local casino and spent all of his bribe money gambling.[48]

VanMeter also regularly solicited kickbacks from nursing home owners in return for information about Department of Health nursing home inspections. "Hundreds of patients daily are at 'serious risk of harm' from falls, broken bones, bedsores and 'lying for hours in their own waste,'" according to Esther Houser of the Oklahoma Department of Human Services. At least forty Oklahoma nursing homes were identified in the investigation.[49]

Upon his conviction, VanMeter stated, "I deeply regret the things that I did. I'm sorry for the problems and the misery it brought to many people." Regardless of this admission of guilt after the fact, he was accused of creating "a culture of corruption: homes tipped off before inspections, inspector's reports altered, serious violations simply ignored." The Department of Health at that time had about two thousand employees supervised by VanMeter, who was sentenced by a judge to two years in prison and a fine and subsequently received an additional two years in prison for bribing nursing home operators.[50]

One of the nursing home owners at the time, Robert Smart, was also convicted of bribing VanMeter. Smart owned eleven nursing homes throughout Oklahoma. At the time of his conviction, it was reported that he lived "in an 8,000-square-foot mansion with white columns, a flag, metal gates and a well-manicured yard. Horses and a buffalo herd roam nearby." Health department commissioner Jerry Nida eventually remarked, "We've had a contaminated batch of apples at the health department. Brent VanMeter couldn't have done all this by himself. Brent was like a fox guarding the chicken house."[51]

Oklahoma is the fifth-largest producer of natural gas and the sixth-largest producer of crude oil in the United States. Some of the nation's largest natural gas and oil fields lie within the state's boundaries. When it comes to natural gas reserves, Oklahoma also has the fifth-largest proven reserves, superseded only by Texas, Pennsylvania, West Virginia, and Louisiana. Oklahoma is also home to one of the most strategic pipelines crossing the country and is also the site of one of the nation's largest tank farms.[52]

Production of Oklahoma shale gas markedly began to increase in 2010 as new drilling technologies were fine-tuned and increasingly utilized, including horizontal drilling. Oklahoma, in addition to the oil and gas reserves, has 6 percent of the nation's shale reserves. Using new and existing hydraulic fracturing technologies, shale gas production in Oklahoma increased dramatically.

It is also within this period that earthquakes, previously a rarity in the state, abruptly escalated. Critics pointed the finger at injection wells, which force large amounts of fluids into the earth under high pressure. This wastewater disposal, which is separate from the fracking process, may also contain toxic chemicals. The number of Oklahoma earthquakes of 3.0 Richter or greater leaped from twenty in 2009 to 103 in 2013. In 2014, Oklahoma earthquakes of 3.0 or greater skyrocketed to 595, then in 2015 to 887. Then, beginning in 2016, earthquakes of 3.0 or greater dramatically declined. In June 2023, the number of earthquakes at that magnitude numbered just six.[53]

In the days following a policy pivot in 2015, Governor Mary Fallin channeled an additional $1.4 million to the OCC. This funding was to hire new staff and other resources to oversee the regulation of injection wells. Further research is required to document the earthquake property damage suffered by those in poverty along with the total costs to all Oklahomans adversely affected.[54]

While experts disagree on how to define and rank political corruption on a state-by-state basis, the methodology utilized by the Corruption in America Survey at Illinois State University is among the best. In the most recent ranking, researchers rated Oklahoma among the top eleven states in illegal political corruption. The study defines illegal corruption as "the private gains in the form of cash or gifts by a government official, in exchange for providing specific benefits to private individuals or groups." When all states are ranked by legal political corruption, Oklahoma again ranks in the top eleven states in the country. Legal legislative corruption as defined by the researchers is "the political gains in the form of campaign contributions or endorsements by a government official, in exchange for providing specific benefits to private individuals or groups, be it by explicit or implicit understanding."[55] Prior to this 2018 survey, in 2014 Fox News in Oklahoma City ranked Oklahoma as the eleventh-most corrupt state in the country."[56]

This brief overview of Oklahoma politics suggests the prevalence of systemic political malfeasance, a sharp contrast to the dominant historical paradigm that describes only an incomplete list of discrete political scandals since statehood. These so-called political scandals have frequently ended in short prison terms for those few individuals held responsible by the criminal justice system in place. Quite often facilitators of these criminal acts have gone free.

With notable exceptions, a reframed history of Oklahoma politics delineates a list of political decisions and actions as representative of purposeful political corruption in the executive, legislative, and judicial branches of state government. These events have often been trivialized or intentionally censored, as is the case of the Tulsa race massacre and the decades of murders of the Osage tribe for their headrights. Frequently ignored or downplayed, these institutionalized and individual acts of economic, physical, and psychological violence frequently target those least able to sustain themselves.

One example among many still to be addressed is the alarmingly high rates of incarceration for Oklahoma women. Inexplicably, it would seem, these incarcerated women include a disproportionate percentage of minorities. A second under-researched topic is the historical use of juvenile detention centers as revenue streams for private industry.

At the other end of the spectrum stand elected and appointed officials of both parties seeking to follow the Oklahoma constitution to the best of their abilities. Oddly, some who studiously avoid political corruption in its various forms can end up themselves accused of trumped-up allegations. Republican OCC commissioner Bob Anthony, for instance, was openly denounced by some for his cooperation with the FBI. Nevertheless, Oklahoma voters have returned Anthony to office for thirty-six straight years. As part of his oath to serve as a commissioner at the OCC, Anthony upheld the interests of the public as articulated in Article IX of the Oklahoma constitution.

In 1995, FBI director Louis J. Freeh gave Anthony the Louis E. Peters Memorial Award, the FBI's highest award to a civilian. The words of Director Freeh at the award ceremony honoring Anthony are well worth remembering with regard to what reasonably should be expected of all elected officials and their appointees in Oklahoma, regardless of their party affiliation: "I am very, very delighted and pleased to welcome and to congratulate Mr. Anthony and to tell you sir that you are a worthy recipient of the Peters Award, and that you have our gratitude and respect for your courage and dedication."[57]

7

Networks of Care

Thou shalt love thy neighbor as thyself.
—Matthew 22:39

When evidence-based truths about the poor and poverty are placed within a reframing of the historical record, a different Oklahoma narrative emerges. The influence of certain social, political, and economic institutions and organizations embedded in Oklahoma culture has resulted in direct and often adverse consequences for those below the poverty line. In spite of these findings, however, it would be hypercritical not to explore with equal rigor a fact-based history of Oklahomans treating the poor with kindness and care. It is true those who are poor still confront a cluster munch of social myths, oppressive inequalities, stunt politics, and hapless sloganeering. Still, that does not rule out the possibility of examples, like Thy Will Be Done, of caring and compassionate Oklahomans concerned with the needs of the poor.

Acknowledging the declining religiosity of Oklahomans, there must be in the past significant examples of Oklahomans following Matthew 22:39. Could there also be contemporary examples of this same social phenomena? When I first began this research, I did not know enough about my home state to pose this question, let alone suggest answers.

TWBD is, in fact, one small part of a much larger network of food assistance programs throughout the state. There are two major food banks, the Regional Food Bank of Oklahoma and the Community Food Bank. The first serves fifty-three counties in the western part of the state, the second twenty-four counties in the eastern part. A significant number of food pantries are supported at least in part by churches, but others may be more secular in their support while housed in private or public buildings.[1]

Oklahoma food pantries may be supported in partnership with governmental food assistance programs and the private business sector. Many of the nongovernmental programs often operate with the help of commitments made by mom-and-pop operations along with local, state, and national food chains. Together various combinations of faith-based and secular food pantries throughout the state, along with the help of city, county, and state government resources and programs, form a network to address food insecurity.

In this sense, TWBD is a very small part of a relatively understudied network of Oklahomans demonstrating their care for those less fortunate than themselves. The exact approach to meeting the needs of those in poverty may, however, differ from one church-based, secular, or governmental entity to another. At the same time, some providers who address the needs of the poor do not always target food insecurity. This brief overview excludes the considerable contributions of nationwide or international organizations such as the Salvation Army as well as the key roles many Oklahoma volunteers play in these organizations.

Indeed, some faith-based approaches to serving those in poverty have focused on the health needs of the poor. Others have targeted the broader consequences of poverty based upon the ideas and strategies of reformer Jane Addams. Prominent in Oklahoma as well are labor-based movements providing support to workers who were often foreign-born. There is, last but not least, a vital philanthropic tradition in Oklahoma aimed at those in poverty.[2] The geographic focus in this brief historical overview rests upon Oklahoma City because it is where I was born, raised, and have spent a significant portion of my adult life.

For more than a century, the good works of the Catholic Sisters of Mercy have remained a largely unexamined model of caring for impoverished Oklahomans. Originally founded in 1831 by Catherine Elizabeth McAuley in Dublin, Ireland, the Sisters of Mercy dedicated themselves to leading lives of voluntary poverty, chastity, and obedience. As defined by their founder, the overriding purpose of the Sisters of Mercy is to serve those who are most in need. To that end, a handful of nuns from the order first traveled in the late 1890s from their base in St. Louis to the panhandle of Oklahoma. This region, where my maternal grandfather was born and raised, was commonly referred to as No Man's Land because of the lawlessness and violence that abounded there.[3]

The lifelong commitments by the Sisters of Mercy to public service eventually focused on establishing health care facilities in several states. In addition to Oklahoma, the Sisters also served the poor in nearby Arkansas, Kansas, Louisiana, Mississippi, Missouri, and Texas. Although this same Catholic order established and operated schools and colleges, in Oklahoma it specifically focused on the health and well-being of those not served by the medical establishment.

I was born at Sisters of Mercy Hospital in the same year, 1947, the Sisters took over the ownership and operation of this formerly private hospital. Mercy Hospital under that supervision quickly became an example of faith-based medical care intended for anyone in need. For the first time in the history of this major medical facility in Oklahoma City, Mercy Hospital began to serve all members of the community—not just those who were White and could afford to pay their medical bills. Instead, the objective of the Sisters of Mercy and their hospital was to provide professional medical care to all residents of Oklahoma City who sought it.

When I was old enough, my father used to take me with him to the hospital, where he practiced after returning from World War II. Starting in the mid-1950s, when I was six or seven, I rode along with him to Mercy while enjoying the rare opportunity of sitting in the front seat where my mother usually sat instead of with my brother and sister in the back. As I remember it, every Sunday morning my father had regular morning rounds at Mercy.

At Mercy there was a small parking lot for doctors steps away from the covered entrance where the ambulances unloaded patients to the emergency room. We entered through the ER and first headed for the nurses station. I was always dressed for Sunday morning services at my family's church, which was right across the street. I am aware now as an adult that the nuns at Mercy Hospital showered me and the hospital staff with genuine attention and concern, one of whom became our baby-sitter and a trusted member of our extended family. I still remember the genuine kindness of these sisters and the comfort of their voices. Soon thereafter, I was enrolled by my parents in a private religious school in the suburbs. At that private religious school it eventually became clear to me, in sharp contrast to the nuns at Mercy Hospital, who did and who did not practice what they preached.

My father never directly spoke to any of us children about the nuns and their mission of health care in Oklahoma City. He was not a talker at the dinner table or, for that matter, anywhere else. But I do know that on the weekends there were one or more phone calls from the Mercy ER looking for my father, who was an orthopedist. After speaking to Mercy, he always placed his napkin carefully on the table, then grabbed his black medical bag, which was never far from his sight. We could hear him revving the engine of his car before he sped away at all hours of the day and the night, weekends, holidays, any time he was needed.

What my father did say on rare occasions, enough times so my brother and I clearly remember: "One-third of the money I make goes to taxes, one-third to my family, and one-third to charity." Charity included not only donating annually to our church across the street from Mercy Hospital even, if truth be told, he rarely attended. It also meant personally giving of his time and skills, like many of the other physicians at Mercy Hospital, to those patients who could not afford to pay. It was called "Charity Call."

Another order of nuns founded St. Anthony Hospital in 1898, but I discovered no evidence that they served minorities as early on as Mercy Hospital. (If there is such evidence, I stand both corrected and apologetic.)

Prior to the nuns at Mercy Hospital, the closest hospital to treat Black residents of the largest city in Oklahoma was built and operated by Black doctors beginning in 1922. But the Okmulgee Colored Hospital, as it was named, was too far to travel for most Blacks living in Oklahoma City.[4]

Another major influence upon medical care to underserved populations in Oklahoma City about this same time in the 1940s was Opaline Deveraux Wadkins. She, along with the Oklahoma Negro Medical Society, was successful in forcing Oklahoma City's University Hospital to treat Black patients in a special wing called South Ward.[5]

But in 1947, prior to Mercy Hospital, there were very few Oklahoma City medical facilities serving either minorities or impoverished Whites, let alone at discounted rates or pro bono. According to my father and my uncle, Dr. William David Maril, the goal at Mercy Hospital was that everyone, White and minority, poor and nonpoor, receive the same medical care from the docs. Unfortunately, in spite of numerous attempts, it was not possible for me to interview any Sisters of Mercy nuns who worked at Mercy Hospital, because those few who remain are in their late nineties and older.[6]

Dr. Charles N. Atkins was one of only a handful of Black physicians serving Blacks in Oklahoma City beginning in the 1960s. I know he was highly respected by many in both the Black and White medical communities. I was fortunate enough to have a conversation with Hannah Atkins, his wife, on this topic. I had been a college friend of her son and spoke with her at length when she was invited to give a presentation at Oklahoma State University around 1993.

Hannah D. Atkins had the distinction of being the first African American woman to serve in the Oklahoma House of Representatives, then later on as secretary of state. She was elected to the Oklahoma House in 1968, where she served for twelve years. As an Oklahoma legislator she supported legislation that promoted not only "women's rights and civil rights, but health care, child welfare, and mental health reform" for those in poverty.[7]

Health activists Opaline Deveraux Watkins, Edward Atkins, and state politician Hannah Atkins were not alone in providing basic services for the general health and well-being of poor Oklahomans in Oklahoma City. According to the research of Elizabeth B. Anthony, as early as the 1920s members of the Methodist churches in Oklahoma City played an active role in several impoverished neighborhoods.[8]

Methodists from churches in Oklahoma City founded Wesley House in 1924 and Neighborhood Clubs in 1936. Both were established based upon the settlement house model championed first in Great Britain by Jane Addams and her colleagues including Ellen Gates Starr. Jane Addams's model of care for those in poverty differed in several ways from other approaches at that time. She encouraged social workers, almost always women, to live in the same neighborhoods as those they served. This led to a closer relationship and understanding on the part of the social workers of the daily lives of those they served. Another major objective of the settlement house movement in Oklahoma City was to provide pathways out of poverty.[9]

At the settlement houses in Oklahoma City, community members received not only religious instruction but food, shelter, vocational training, lessons in nutrition, sewing classes, day care, and early childhood education. Many were first- or second-generation immigrants. If employed, they worked low-wage jobs no one else would consider because of the working conditions and abysmal compensation for their labor. One other crucial objective of these providers was to help the poor become U.S. citizens who were active contributors to the welfare of their communities.

Methodist leaders of the settlement house movement in Oklahoma in 1922 included Grace Mercer of Norman, Bernice Morgan from Chickasha, Cella Hyde of Oklahoma City's St. Luke's Methodist Church, and Lillian McKeehen of Epworth Methodist Church. With the approval of the Oklahoma City Mission Board, this group of women soon began plans to build a facility in Southtown on the southern banks of the North Canadian River. This area was also known as "The Flats" or "Mulligan Flats." It was inundated by the river in 1923, and the flooding killed five and displaced an estimated 15,000, who lived in dilapidated housing with no city services. Years before the start of the Great Depression, the 1923 flood temporarily delayed the efforts of all those helping this Oklahoma City poverty population.[10]

Bernice Morgan, a leader in the Methodist support of settlement houses in Oklahoma City, wrote that, even though the flood temporarily delayed their best efforts, "we have been busy nevertheless in friendly visitation and feel that much good has been accomplished, for we realize that the friendship and confidence of the people among whom we are to work is of prime importance. There is much poverty and distress as a result of the flood, and we find the field a very needy one."

The Methodists were not alone in their efforts to aid those in poverty in Oklahoma City. Soon after the flood of 1923, female congregants at St. Paul's Episcopal Church established the Churchwomen's Community House. In 1927 the Junior League of Oklahoma City also built a community center in the adjacent low-income neighborhood of Walnut Grove. Miners and their families in McAlester, Dow, and Hartshorne in the southeastern part of the state were also aided at this time by a state branch of a national group named the Woman's Missionary Society of the East Oklahoma Conference. Those targeted were first-generation immigrants working in Oklahoma mines who came from Italy, Ireland, Poland, Lithuania, and Mexico.[11]

Traditional philanthropy aimed at poor Oklahomans also remains an understudied topic. In Oklahoma City, among other notable philanthropic endeavors, is the Oklahoma City Community Foundation. At the time it was incorporated in 1969, it had just two employees. One of the objectives of the OCCF at that time was to support the educational attainment of all community residents. Another was to help grow and sustain community nonprofits serving those in need.[12]

By 1985 the OCCF had $20 million in assets. Under the thirty-eight-year direction of Nancy Anthony, it increased its assets to $1.6 billion by 2022. On average the OCCF provides $46 million each year to individuals and social service providers in Oklahoma City.[13] In 2023 this philanthropic effort, now with forty-six employees, handed out almost $80 million in grants, scholarships, and other kinds of distributions. Grants to nonprofits included, among others, Oklahoma City organizations focusing on improving access to health care, services for older adults, increased opportunities for children, and improved parks and public spaces. President and CEO Trisha Finnegan stated, "We work with non-profits. We work with civic leaders. We work with individuals families and businesses and bring all of those parties together for one reason—to share and invest in a place and the people who live here."[14]

Another noteworthy philanthropic effort toward improving the lives of Oklahomans statewide, including Oklahoma City, is the Communities Foundation of Oklahoma, initiated by Tom McCasland Jr. and Gene Rainbolt.[15] In Tulsa, the Tulsa Community Foundation and the George Kaiser Family Foundation have similar goals.[16] While these are among the largest philanthropic foundations in Oklahoma, there are also many private foundations whose contributions are more modest but also aimed directly or indirectly at benefiting Oklahomans in poverty.

By the late 1980s business leaders and their elected representatives and appointees had already faced a series of economic setbacks. Predicated in part by the failure of the Penn Square Bank in 1982, the Oklahoma banking system faltered. Not surprisingly, the state's oil and gas industry's glorious boom reversed its course, a glut of cheaper foreign oil forcing the price of domestic oil into a downward spiral.

The Oklahoma City bombing could have been the final nail in the coffin for downtown Oklahoma City and the entire metroplex. It was the downtown area that was the biggest disappointment to the leadership. They had tried to revive it for years through various unsuccessful iterations. I had witnessed these failures in urban renewal when I worked several different summer jobs in downtown Oklahoma City through the 1960s. First the city leaders bought heavily into that decade's national urban renewal philosophy of tearing down buildings and, as necessary, disassembling existing neighborhoods. Then these same neighborhoods would receive civic projects and modest dollars aimed at revitalization.

In all of the greater metroplex, relatively few residents took interest with the exception of those whose neighborhoods had been leveled. Those who relished the process were likely to be devoted to high culture and upscale shoppers from the suburbs. Historic downtown buildings were demolished and most frequently replaced with parking lots. Fewer and fewer Oklahoma City residents had less and less reason to do business or shop downtown.

Ultimately, downtown Oklahoma City was saved by an unexpected sector of the community. City government, under the astute leadership of Republican mayor Ron Norick, began in the late 1980s to develop an innovative plan to increase and stabilize public funding for both old buildings in need of repair and brand-new projects intended, for the first time, to serve diverse interests.

When Mayor Norick first took office in the spring of 1987, he had this to say about the vital needs of a deteriorating Oklahoma City downtown: "The first thing we've got to do, has really been since '76, where we hadn't passed any bond issues, our streets are deteriorating, our bridges are deteriorating, our parks are getting run down cause there's nothing good. I said, 'we've got to have a long-term plan.'" He called his innovative attempt to revitalize downtown Oklahoma City economically the Metropolitan Area Projects (MAPS). "And it was the first one that had even been proposed in a number of years, and it passed. It was $127 million."[17]

Norick's development plan debunked the perpetual dream of city planners before him that relied on luring an outside industry to relocate to the metroplex in exchange for attractive tax benefits. According to that scenario, in spite of repeated failures, this industry was then supposed to attract other major industries to Oklahoma. But the dream never worked very well, at least not in Oklahoma City and throughout most of the state.[18]

The son of a former Oklahoma City mayor, Ron Norick served from 1988 to 1998. During the early part of his administration, he was instrumental in convincing not only the city council but a voting majority of the citizens that his MAPS was a viable solution to the redevelopment of a devasted downtown. A tipping point facilitating MAPS was the failure of previous political leadership, in spite of their best efforts, to convince United Airlines to locate its new maintenance center in Oklahoma City. United Airlines unceremoniously turned town Oklahoma City in favor of Indianapolis, Indiana. The decision, according to United, came because it was going to be a hard sell to convince their employees, both old and new, to relocate to Oklahoma. United couched its reservations about Oklahoma City in terms of quality-of-life indicators, indicators that Oklahoma City sorely lacked. This wasn't surprising. A younger generation of Oklahomans had already stampeded toward the city exits during the recession of the 1980s and early 1990s, leaving for better jobs with higher-paying salaries as well as a quality of life that in Oklahoma City was affordable only to the city's affluent already entrenched in some of the suburbs.[19]

Mayor Norick's political wisdom was expressed in a simple idea that made sense to voters. MAPS projects were not just directed toward meeting the agendas of the business community and the high-culture crowd. Instead, they required the participation of all stakeholders in and around downtown Oklahoma City and the rest of the metroplex—including those in poverty, including Blacks and low-income Whites. From the get-go, a majority vote for MAPS was captured by bringing together a variety of diverse groups who would benefit by projects appealing to their own specific interests. In effect, Norick went outside the traditional system of political patronage, both Republican and Democrat, to offer benefits to many who were disenfranchised and held little political power. True compromise would be required when these newcomers at the table finally had a horse in the race.

MAPS 1, the first phase, was an innovative and ambitious proposal and a real turning point for downtown Oklahoma City and the surrounding metroplex. With an eventual price tag of $350 million for public projects, it attracted a wide range of many different kinds of supporters. What sealed the deal for many traditionally conservative voters was Norick's promise that MAPS 1 would be debt free. No MAPS 1 project would get under way, according to the mayor, until voters approved a 1 percent sales tax increase and all the funds necessary to initiate and complete the project were raised.

Another compelling point to voters typically excluded from benefiting from their own tax dollars was that MAPS 1 would not be overseen by the usual political appointees and bureaucrats. Waste, graft, and corruption would be closely monitored. A separate city staff would be hired and placed under the direction of a group of citizens from across the political spectrum.

At a crucial time in the metroplex's history, the late 1980s and early 1990s, MAPS offered both a pathway to economic recovery and a taste of democratic engagement to those traditionally excluded. After intense public interest and review, a list of nine different public projects was finally accepted prior to the vote for MAPS 1. These public projects included extensive renovations to the Civic Center Music Hall, expansion of the convention center including a home for the Oklahoma City Barons hockey team, improvements to the popular Oklahoma City Fairgrounds, construction of the Triple-A Chickasaw Bricktown Ballpark, construction of the facility to house the NBA's new Oklahoma City Thunder, building the Bricktown Canal to support a burgeoning entertainment district, damming the North Canadian River in such a way that its waters could be used for recreational boating, building a new downtown library and learning center to replace the forty-five year old, obsolete library, and creating a downtown trolley bus system. In this list there was, for a change, something for everyone.[20]

MAPS 1 specifically began to address the needs of low-income residents who did not have an efficient system of public transportation to their workplace. In area, Oklahoma City is one of the larger cities in this country. If you do not own or have access to a dependable vehicle, it is challenging to hold down a job. Also, the MAPS 1 new public library was a preliminary attempt to address the broader problem of the public education of a skilled labor force. The same aging public library where I spent many hours as a child had been a gloomy facility for decades, ignored and underfunded.

To the surprise of some cynics, 55 percent of the voters supported MAPS 1. It was so popular that voters passed MAPS for Kids in 2001. MAPS 2 was dedicated to public education projects, again financed by a 1 percent sales tax. This time voters supported the project by a margin of 62 percent to 38 percent. It appealed to both Oklahoma City shareholders used to getting their way and newbie Oklahoma City stakeholders who directly benefited from projects they themselves had proposed.[21]

Following Norick from 1998 to 2004, a new Republican mayor, Kirk Humphrey, abided by the MAPS objectives his predecessor had established. Sales tax was collected over a period of years, so each project carried zero debt. Eventually $700 million was targeted to school districts. Oklahoma City school districts received 70 percent, and 30 percent went to suburban schools. This financial support of public education was in addition to a separate bond issue of $180 million targeting childhood obesity and new gyms for public school children.

Under the administration of Republican mayor Mick Cornett, 54 percent of the voters supported MAPS 3. Beginning in 2010, the extra sales tax was collected until 2017, and eight projects were selected. As before, varied constituencies expressed their needs and justified their choices at a series of public meetings.

When the dust settled, the eight projects selected for MAPS 3 were a downtown convention center, downtown 70-acre public park, streetcar and public transit system along with an intermodal hub, senior health and wellness center, improvements in the river system adjacent to Bricktown, improvements to the Oklahoma City Fairgrounds, expansion of walking and biking trails, and expansion of sidewalks to improve community walkability. Again, MAPS had appealed to a wide variety of not only stakeholders, including middle-income voters and the poor, but also shareholders, those more affluent and in general used to getting their way. As before, some of the most important needs of the underserved, as defined by their representatives, were addressed directly.

Approved by the city council in September 2021, MAPS 4, under the direction of Republican mayor David Holt, gained the largest public support of any of the previous economic development plans. Sixteen public projects were proposed and supported by 72 percent of voters. Close to $1 billion will be collected from 2019 to 2027 through the same 1 percent sales tax structure created for the previous three MAPS projects.

One MAPS 4 project earned $38 million for a Family Justice Center "dedicated to survivors of domestic violence and sexual abuse." Voters also funded the Henrietta B. Foster Center for Northeast Small Business Development and Entrepreneurship; the northeastern part of the metroplex, one of the historically segregated areas of the city, has endured environmental racism, questionable police practices, inconsistent public health services, and a dearth of city services other areas of the city had not experienced.

MAPS 4, when completed, will also include $17 million to "accelerate growth for minority-owned small businesses" and $60 million for a rapid transit bus system reaching underserved metroplex neighborhoods. Also on the list of new MAPS 4 projects are crisis centers serving those with mental health problems and addiction. This project, budgeted at $45 million, will specifically address those who are homeless: $8 million for "temporary housing for those experiencing mental illness and homelessness while transitioning out of crisis centers." Also planned are four new youth centers and a new senior wellness center. Along with these projects is a museum and center on civil rights with an allocation of $26 million. The museum will be named in honor of Clara Luper, one of the most respected activists in the history of Oklahoma civil rights.[22]

MAPS was already in place by the time of the Oklahoma bombing on April 19, 1995. Much of the downtown area was destroyed, but in response to this tragedy there was an enormous outpouring of caring and loving kindness to all Oklahomans who suffered.

The legacy of the bombing is seen today in a revitalized urban area that continues to grow and thrive with each passing year. What happened in Oklahoma City can justifiably serve in the future as a model for other American communities. One small example of this legacy is Dan Straughan. After retiring as a manager at the Federal Reserve Bank of Oklahoma City, Straughan created a not-for-profit entity to address the needs of the homeless. For twenty years his Homeless Alliance has served the unhoused in the capital city. When asked about the motivation for his involvement with the homeless in Oklahoma City, Straughan said, "Honestly, you know, it was the bombing."[23]

It was just after nine in the morning of April 19 when I first heard the jet. I was working at my home in Stillwater. I assumed the plane was coming from the direction of Oklahoma City, fifty miles to the south as the crow flies. But my assumption made little sense. The Stillwater airport had no jet service in 1995 except special private charters for the university's athletic teams and private corporate jets. What I distinctly heard that morning sounded like a passenger jet far too big for Stillwater's airport. I did not give it another thought as I returned to my screen.

Within seconds I heard the jet again. Puzzled and a little frustrated by the intrusive noise, I went outside to discover what the odd sound was. But I could see no sign of a jet or any other kind of plane. I still remember in detail the speckled gray and black asphalt in my driveway juxtaposed against the evergreens bordering our property. Tall spring grass sprouted in the pasture where our two horses and two mules quietly grazed near the barbed wire fence protecting my large garden.

An hour later I was on my way to Tulsa by way of the Cimarron Turnpike to meet with another researcher. I was playing the radio as loudly as possible because my jeep was so noisy. Out of nowhere they interrupted the country song I was trying to listen to. A male voice devoid of emotion announced that there had been a gas line explosion in downtown Oklahoma City. The area was closed to all local traffic.

I believe now that what I heard was not an aberrant jet but the reverberations of the Ryder truck bomb being detonated in front of the Alfred P. Murrah Federal Building on 5th Street in downtown Oklahoma City. One of the perpetrators behind this horrendous act of violence detonated the bomb, then jumped into his car to escape by driving north up Interstate 35. A wary Oklahoma state trooper stopped the truck bomber because the car he was driving bore an old license plate. The trooper, seeing that the suspect carried a gun, arrested him without making any connection to the devastation in downtown Oklahoma City. The closest jail to this arrest was Perry, Oklahoma, about twenty-five miles from my house.

That evening on the local news I watched and listened to the mob outside the Perry jail. Individuals in the mob had apparently heard rumors that one of the bombers was being held in their jail. Facts about the victims, which included the number of children who were murdered, were beginning to emerge. Some in the mob wanted to hang the baby killer then and there.

Many Americans unfortunately seem to have forgotten about this heinous act of violence committed by domestic terrorists. The official count was at first 168 killed, including nineteen children who were at the day care center on the second floor of the federal building.[24] An additional 684 Oklahomans were injured. More than three hundred buildings in downtown Oklahoma City were damaged. The Oklahoma City bombing was the most violent act of terrorism against the United States since the attack on Pearl Harbor. Then, of course, six years after the bombing in downtown Oklahoma City came the events of 9/11 by foreign terrorists. The Oklahoma City bombers' destruction reduced the Murrah Building, which took up an entire block, to a giant pile of exposed concrete, steel beams, and office furniture sliced into unrecognizable pieces.

The two bombers eventually convicted said they sought revenge for the deaths of the Branch Davidians in Waco, Texas, by federal authorities two years earlier. The individual who detonated the truck bomb, the same suspect jailed in Perry, was found guilty of all federal charges against him. He had virtually nothing to say to the court that found him guilty of killing 169 human beings.

In a later interview before the convicted domestic terrorist was executed, he referred to the nineteen children murdered as "collateral damage."[25] After the bombing and subsequent trials, after the national media rather quickly turned their attention elsewhere, many Oklahomans were left to confront the magnitude of the tragedy and subsequent suffering. To a great degree, Oklahomans were left by themselves to contend with this slaughter of residents and decimation of their downtown. Resilient, they transformed their suffering, grief, and neglect by the mass media and the majority of national politicians into organizing a permanent institution that would both honor and document all those touched by the terrorist bombing.

In response to the devastation, Mayor Ron Norick took a leadership role along with many other community leaders from all walks of life.

Under the mayor, a committee of 350 was soon selected to develop "an appropriate memorial to honor those touched by the event." This first committee included family members of those who were murdered, injured survivors, first responders, as well as representatives of the legions of fellow Oklahomans who spontaneously sought to help those in need. Locally and nationally, "people of all colors, ages, religions, and political philosophies reached out in love."[26]

Five years after the bombing, the Oklahoma City National Memorial Museum was officially commemorated by President Clinton. The memorial is located at 200 N.W. 5th Street on the former site of the Murrah Building. What first catches the visitor's eye is the Field of Empty Chairs next to the Reflecting Pool and a large clock. The hands on the clock remain at the exact time, two minutes after nine, when the six-ton truck bomb exploded. There is one chair in the Field of Empty Chairs for each victim of this mass slaughter. Nineteen diminutive and starkly empty chairs represent the life of each child taken by this cowardly act. The children's chairs stand next to one hundred and fifty larger chairs, each representing an adult also murdered.

As a rule, I do not cry easily. But I felt hopeless, as hopeless as I did when the barricades around the downtown blast area were removed. At my father's request, I drove him and my uncle around downtown, at one point stopping across the street from the old Skirvin Hotel. My father and uncle wanted to see if the building that once housed their clinic for more than forty years was still intact. The two old men—my father was eighty-six and walked with a cane, my uncle a few years younger—never spoke a word when they returned to the car or on the ride back to my uncle's house.

Opposite the Field of Empty Chairs are these words: "We come here to remember those who were killed, those who survived, and those changed forever. May all who leave here know the impact of violence. May the memorial offer comfort, strength, peace, hope, and serenity."

In spite of MAPS, the Oklahoma City bombing could have become the final nail in the coffin for Oklahoma City. Not just for the downtown area, but for the entire city. But instead, what soon emerged from this blatant act of disregard for human life by domestic terrorists was a new and stronger sense of community engagement. This was bolstered by an increased participation by diverse groups, not only from the capital city but from across the state, in the remaking and rebuilding of the metroplex. The synergy of MAPS along with this unique outpouring of civic engagement created a determination to succeed that could not be denied. This is referred to by many residents of Oklahoma as "the Oklahoma standard."[27]

The achievements of the congruency of MAPS and the Oklahoma City bombing have, of course, not been easy or perfect. Three decades after the Oklahoma City bombing on April 19, 1995, there is still much to accomplish.

Thy Will Be Done in Hereford is one small part of a largely understudied history of Oklahomans caring in multiple ways for the needs of poor Oklahomans. In Oklahoma City, this private and public network includes a variety of providers of services extending far beyond the reach of food pantries and food banks. Even a brief historical glance focusing upon Oklahoma City reveals the contributions of the Catholic Sisters of Mercy, the Methodists, the Episcopalians, the Junior League of Oklahoma City, and the Woman's Missionary Society of the East Oklahoma Conference. There have also been major contributions from the leadership of individuals including Opaline Deveraux Watkins, Hannah D. Atkins, and many others. Finally, the Oklahoma City Community Foundation, an effective and growing philanthropic community, is committed to providing significant annual funds to the general welfare of those in poverty.

These historical achievements in response to the needs of the poor should be both acknowledged and given further study. But even when added to the congruence of MAPS and all those Oklahomans who have come forward to help because of the Oklahoma City bombing, there still remains much to be accomplished to improve the lives of the poor in Oklahoma City.

8

The Future of the Poor and Poverty in Oklahoma

Things are tough. Folks broke. Kids hungry.
Sick. Everything.
—Woody Guthrie

Woody Guthrie's plain-spoken description of the poor and their poverty in *Bound for Glory*, originally published in 1943, resonates today in the Oklahoma heartland because of pervasive and persistent poverty. Born and raised in Okema, Oklahoma, Woody well knew the challenges poor Oklahomans faced in his own small town. He also traveled with Dust Bowl Okies on their way to the promised lands of California. In California there were supposed to be plentiful jobs guaranteeing Okies a fair wage for their hard labor.

The blunt truth is that it is still tough for Oklahomans who are poor. In the 2020s one of every six adults and one of every five children fall below the poverty line. The guests who come to Thy Will Be Done do not have enough food to eat and neither do their children. They may also have to confront many of the other fundamental problems associated with poverty.

The U.S. Census documents a population of poor people in Oklahoma, the greatest number of whom are White, who endure a variety of related issues over which they often have limited control or influence. This has developed within a historical tradition since statehood tainted by political corruption directly impacting the daily lives of the state's most vulnerable citizens. At the same time, there is a relevant history of Oklahoma communities of care directly addressing the consequences of poverty confronted by many who are poor.

What lessons can be learned in studying the Oklahoma poor? What, if anything, can be done to eliminate poverty in Oklahoma? What does the future of the poor and poverty in Oklahoma resemble if we choose to ignore the truths about our state?

Chapters 1 and 2 describe the specific characteristics and qualities of the guests at TWBD in detail. At this food pantry we meet a number of individuals and their families who do not always have enough food to eat. Yet not having enough food on the table is frequently only one of the fundamental necessities of life faced by the guests at TWBD. There are many others throughout Hereford and Wells County who face food insecurity as well as other consequences of poverty. For example, one food pantry guest had a heart attack while working at Walmart and was summarily fired. Another faces the challenging circumstances of contending with the health of her two grandchildren.

Single adults and seniors do walk through the TWBD doors seeking more food, but the majority are middle-aged Whites with families. Given their slim numbers in Hereford and Wells County, minorities are overrepresented at this food pantry. Some of the female and male guests are currently employed, but they often earn a minimum wage of $7.25 or slightly higher. One earns twice the minimum wage while working six days a week at a local factory, yet he is still very concerned about the future of his family. His needs are modest. He would like to spend more time with his family. He and his wife would like an additional bedroom for the baby. But in Hereford this young couple cannot afford an apartment with a second bedroom because they cannot afford the high rents.

In spite of the prevalent stereotypes ascribed to the poor by others throughout Hereford and Wells County, the guests at TWBD in general do not have personality characteristics or flaws that cause them to be poor. In general, these guests are indistinguishable from anyone else except perhaps for their clothes, along with their initial distrust of service providers they do not know. This distrust, in part the result of the ways they are regularly treated by those who are supposed to help them, soon disappears when they realize that TWBD volunteers are there to help them. As a result, by the end of their shopping experience many of the guests smile, joke, and often express their thanks for the food they received.

These guests in general are friendly, pensive, loving toward family members and friends, and possessing a wide range of traditional Oklahoma values. Nevertheless, they are understandably worried about the multiple problems confronting them. Like the nonpoor, these people are far from perfect human beings. A few are openly vain, wallowing in memories of a better past life.

The minimum wage for employed guests at TWBE appears to barely sustain them in poverty. The Oklahoma hourly wage was set in 2014 and more than a decade on has not increased.[1] Part-time work is also common among guests, especially women with children. Reliable transportation is a job killer. High rents do not hide the low quality of some housing in Hereford and Wells County and all the problems associated with it. Available low-income housing does not meet the existing demand. Health issues are a burden for many guests. Problematic relationships, including abuse, are not uncommon. Overweight and obesity can make the daily lives of guests much more difficult. The causes of overweight and obesity are not well understood by the scientific community, but they are not signs of a weak will—one of the typical stereotypes about the poor—and do not necessarily keep guests from enjoying a relatively normal life.

The issues the poor must face frequently do not come one at a time but often all at once. They can become overwhelmed. For example, some guests say they are not hired for jobs because of a perceived stigma among employers—employers who assume that those in poverty must be flawed in some way or would not be poor in the first place. The reality for guests at TWBD is that often they are full-time caregivers for others in their household. These household members may suffer from a variety of health issues including cancer, cognitive impairment, and other physical disabilities in addition to or simultaneous with overweight and obesity.

Guests at TWBD often have no other income than Social Security payments or, extremely rarely, retirement and pension funds. Social Security Disability Insurance is, guests say, often very difficult to qualify for regardless of need. Many guests say trying to live off state and federal programs specifically targeting the poor is very difficult. Some guests are homeless and worried about getting dependable and secure housing; others may be homeless but are reluctant to discuss it because of the stigma attached. Single parents face a barrage of issues including, for starters, the lack of affordable day care so they have the time to work.

Many TWBD guests are not familiar enough with work culture to understand what conditions and benefits their employers should provide them. Limited education and job skills appear not to provide access to higher-paying jobs even if those jobs are available. Those who are not documented citizens, including Latinos whose labor is much in demand, face different kinds of discriminatory issues, including being underpaid for their labor.

Although there are exceptions, these guests at TWBD are not poor because of personality flaws. In and of itself, not having much money creates insurmountable problems and consequences. Poverty summarily leaves the guests with a list of bad choices.

At the same time, TWBD guests possess and act with admirable values. When possible, for example, they try to lead lives based upon their faith and other traditional values widely shared by many in this heartland. Most guests believe, for example, that they should take care of their own whatever the cost, help others outside their families less fortunate than themselves, raise their children to get good educations they themselves never received, pay off their debts when and if they can, and, if given the chance, work hard at their jobs in spite of a prevailing low wage.

Guests come to this food pantry from small towns and communities throughout Wells County in addition to the small city of Hereford. The needs of the poor throughout the county have increasingly been recognized and addressed by the TWBD staff. Chapter 3 highlights the fact that most poverty rates are the same or higher in some Wells County rural communities than in Hereford. To meet that need, TWBD has begun to send freezer trucks filled with food packages to several of the different rural communities, including Macon.

Macon has one of the highest poverty rates in Wells County. Its economy has been stagnant since it first experienced several decades of oil booms followed by economic busts. Like almost every community in Wells County, Macon was founded upon an agricultural economy dependent upon the surrounding farms and ranches. Farming and ranching, however, changed dramatically in the 1980s. Food and animal producers all across the state found it difficult to compete in a marketplace dominated by national and international corporations able to benefit by their economies of scale.

In spite of the high poverty rate, negative stereotypes about the poor thrive in Macon along with general misinformation about the poor. White Oklahomans, the vast majority of the poor, far outnumber all other minorities, as is generally true in Wells County with the exception of the small communities of Evers and Lone Pony; Lone Pony is adjacent to Wells County. Evers, a predominantly Black community with no casinos, has the highest poverty rate in Wells County. In contrast Lone Pony reflects the recent economic benefit of casinos employing Native Americans along with Whites. Poverty in Lone Pony is declining.

The small group of religious leaders in Macon, although thankful that TWBD sends its freezer truck to a local church for food distribution, resist the idea that poverty is a serious problem in their community. Poverty rates to the contrary, political leadership in Macon also acts as if there is little need for public housing or infrastructure improvements. Some Macon leaders also assert that their public school system is outstanding, though a closer examination finds little to substantiate the claim. In the same manner, most local leaders assert that local business is thriving, jobs are plentiful for residents, the crumpling downtown is on the rise, violence and drugs are not community problems, and all those requiring health services not available in Macon can easily travel thirty minutes to the facilities in Hereford.

As chapter 4 demonstrates, there are serious flaws in the system of care for those in poverty in Hereford and throughout Wells County. Mission of Care in Hereford, the only emergency housing available in Wells County, falls far short of its stated goals. Funded primarily by HUD, the staff of MOC seem to have developed a set of rules and expectations for applicants that are inconsistent with HUD's stated goals and objectives.

The MOC director realizes that the organization cannot provide all the services they have been tasked with, including finding applicants jobs that pay enough for them to afford the high rents in Hereford. Job skills among MOC applicants are in general not in high demand. Part of the housing dilemma is that the market in Hereford predominantly targets students at Hereford State College. Local apartment owners and national investors profit more from renting to students and their families than to those in poverty. Those poor working full- and part-time are excluded from the market by high rents and other add-on costs, which may include a required month's rent as a pet deposit or a similar charge at the end of the lease for a clean-up inspection.

On one of the coldest days of the year a mother and her baby are kicked out of MOC because the mother loses her temper and curses at one of the staff; the director justifies this action. Common sense does not play a part in the director's decision late at night to throw the mother and her baby out into the frigid streets of Herford.

A close look at the MOC annual report suggests that the needs of the unhoused, in spite of the variety of programs offered on paper and federally funded, are not being adequately met in Wells County. At the same time, political leadership representing the business community clearly does not want the homeless to be seen on the streets of downtown Hereford. Instead, the homeless are invisible and, when possible, encouraged by law enforcement to leave town. The voices of residents of the meager number of low-income housing units are seldom considered. Some students at Hereford State are unhoused as well, and their needs do not yet seem to have been adequately addressed or even clearly defined.

The problems facing the poor in Hereford and the rest of Wells County are undeniable. Those who are poor here simply do not have the fundamental necessities to live, including enough food to eat. In general, public and private attempts to meet those needs vary from inadequate to grossly negligible. On the other hand, TWBD stands out as an exceptional provider of food to those in need. Led by a board that year in and year out supplies consistent financial backing, TWBD attempts to fill a large gap in the network of public and private providers in Hereford and throughout Wells County.

The poverty encountered in Hereford and the county is far from exceptional in Oklahoma. Chapter 5 documents unusually high poverty rates in Oklahoma since U.S. Census statistics first began measuring the economic status of its population in 1959. High rates of poverty in Oklahoma spanning more than sixty years are closely correlated with the negative consequences facing large percentages as well as numbers of Oklahomans who are poor. This census data, along with additional federal government research in more recent decades, examines not only the percentages and numbers of poor in Oklahoma but also a variety of other poverty measurements and correlations. These include comparisons of Oklahoma poverty rates to all other states, race and poverty, gender and poverty, children and the elderly in poverty, education and poverty, the disabled poor, and the impact of medical insurance and COVID-19 on the poor.[2]

U.S. Census facts along with additional scientific research undermine many of the stereotypes about the poor and poverty prevailing in Oklahoma. At the same time, these facts suggest ways poverty can be systemically addressed less as personality flaws and more as the product of certain societal forces.

When first measured in 1959, the poverty rate in Oklahoma was 30 percent of all residents. The census counted 679,517 men, women, and children who were poor out of a total population of 2,274,988. The poverty rate substantially declined by 1979, but there were still almost 400,000 poor Oklahomans. The state poverty rate sixty years after the first U.S. Census hovers at around 15 percent, but the number of Oklahomans in poverty is about the same as in 1979.

Oklahoma ranked eighth in the nation in poverty rates in 2019, before the COVID-19 pandemic, only by a slim margin better than the sixth-poorest state. In fact, in 1999 Oklahoma was the sixth-poorest state.

Today in Oklahoma poverty remains remarkably pervasive and persistent in spite of significant state natural resources and a strong work ethic across the population. This work ethic is especially to be found among those in poverty, as evidenced by many of the guests at TWBD along with interviews with experts across the state.

Contrary to the dominant stereotype, the majority of Oklahoma poor are White, with a poverty rate of 12.6 percent, compared to the rate for Blacks of 26.1 percent, more than double. Whites in poverty number 361,088, and Blacks 75,015. Latinos have a poverty rate of 23.4 percent and have become the largest number of poor in Oklahoma, at 102,516 individuals. Native American poverty rates have fallen substantially in the past two decades, from 28.1 percent in 1999 to 18.1 percent. However, even at a rate of 18.1 percent Natives in Oklahoma are much more likely to be poor than Whites.

While female adults of all races are about the same number in Oklahoma as male adults, female adult women have a poverty rate of 16.9 percent compared to 14.3 percent for males. Minority women, including Blacks and Native Americans, have much higher poverty rates than do White women, about 13 percent of whom fall below the poverty line. The poverty rate for Native American women has fallen to 22 percent but remains high when compared to both White women and Native men.

One of every five Oklahoma children, 20 percent, is poor. Oklahoma children in poverty number about 186,000. Of older adults in the state, 15 percent do not have enough food to eat. Seniors in Oklahoma also face severe housing problems, high suicide rates, poor-quality nursing homes, and an early-death rate that is the second-worst in the nation.

About 28 percent of all disabled Oklahomans are poor. The largest number of disabled are White. Disabled veterans have a poverty rate of 35.8 percent, although this is declining compared to previous years.

Oklahoma ranks second-worst in the nation in terms of the population having medical insurance. Prior to 2021, 14.3 percent of all Oklahomans lacked health insurance. When finally given a chance to voice their opinion, in 2021, Oklahomans voted for Medicaid expansion to the noninsured. During the subsequent year, comprehensive health insurance for all, Wellcare, was provided to adults between the ages of eighteen and sixty-four. With the end of the COVID-19 pandemic, funds for this program and its medical insurance ceased. Research suggests that thousands of Oklahoma lives could have been saved if existing vaccines and other tools had been fully utilized.

U.S. Census data show a strong correlation between the years of education earned by Oklahomans and poverty. Those with the least education—no high school degree—have the highest poverty rate, at 26.1 percent. Oklahomans whose education ended with high school graduation have the next-highest poverty rate, 15.9 percent. At the other end of the scale, those with a bachelor's degree or higher have a poverty rate of 4.8 percent.

The quality of Oklahoma public school education, which serves 90 percent of all children within the state, is suspect. Consistent support from state legislative earmarks has historically been absent. Other factors also influence the quality of education in Oklahoma schools, among them the quality of teaching and teachers' salaries. There is a long history of low teachers' salaries in Oklahoma in conjunction with teaching shortages.

Oklahoma's economy is commonly described as a boom-or-bust affair dependent to a great degree on the global market prices for oil and gas. If individuals are unemployed or poorly paid at the minimum wage of $7.25 an hour, according to the prevailing myth they only have to wait until the boomtime cycle comes round once again. Nevertheless, poverty in Oklahoma has shown itself to be both pervasive and persistent. Poor Oklahomans do not suddenly join the middle class when the price of crude exceeds $100 a barrel.

In addition, different poverty rates between men and women reported by the U.S. Census call into question the nature of the free Oklahoma market economy. For example, women in Oklahoma are better educated than their male counterparts, yet according to one researcher Oklahoma women earn 74.5 cents for every dollar earned by men, and women will not reach earnings equality with men until 2076. Complaints of the high costs of child care in Hereford and the rest of Wells County are borne out by statewide statistics. This same researcher found that in 2020 child care cost an average of $8,940 annually, an insurmountable employment barrier for many single parents and working couples.

The chapter 6 reframing of Oklahoma history since statehood in 1907 demonstrates that political corruption scandals involving state, county, and city government from both political parties as well as the business community are much more than one-and-done aberrations from the norm. From the perspective of the poor, these so-called scandals instead resemble institutionalized and systemic violence. Over this period, systemic violence of all forms against the least powerful has been normalized, especially in the eyes of those committing the violence. The scale of corruption suggests that there is often a direct relationship between it and poverty.

Just two of many examples, Okscam and the Oklahoma Corporation Commission scandals, each major programs of corruption over decades of Oklahoma history, involved massive numbers of elected public officials misusing public funds to the detriment of those most in need. These two historical examples of political corruption—Okscam at the county level, Oklahoma Corporation Commission multistate, both also involved the business sector. In both cases the misappropriation of hundreds of millions of dollars, perhaps much more, over decades of political corruption was accepted as normal and tolerated. These large sums in one way or the other involved the misuse of public tax dollars and other ways of scamming the public. Perpetrators rarely saw the inside of a jail cell. The societal damage created by these white-collar criminals appears to be unaccountable.

At the same time, normalizing the theft and misuse of public and private funds to the benefit of elected politicians, their appointees, and the private sector is somehow frequently blamed on the poor or on elected politicians and appointees who serve as their public voice. When elected officials do stand up for those in poverty because they are part of their constituencies, they themselves can become the victims of stigmatization. This was certainly the case for federal district attorney William Price and Oklahoma County Corporation commissioner Bob Anthony.

Equally notable is the remarkable criminal theft effected by Penn Square Bank. The eventual loss to investors, in excess of hundreds of millions of dollars, shook the national banking system as well as the state oil and gas industries. Somehow this corruption among the Oklahoma banking community with national repercussions was reduced to the conviction of a single white-collar banker, who served token time in a prison cell. The vast majority of Oklahoma's elected politicians remained unusually silent.

Since statehood, Democrat and Republican parties have shared responsibility for this systemic political corruption—corruption that has at times fostered the ideas of the KKK and other far-right groups that permeate Oklahoma's political history. Rarely justified and frequently dismissed as tangential to the history of the state, far-right conclaves and their impact on political corruption have received little attention from researchers.[3]

Chapter 7 outlines a neglected history of Oklahoma City institutions and dedicated individuals stepping forward to help the poor. In doing so these communities of care have helped to combat the prevailing cultural stereotypes about the poor. There is indeed an underexplored history of caring and compassionate professional groups, community leaders, and citizens who form communities of kindness designed to address the fundamental needs of poor residents of the capital city metroplex.

The Sisters of Mercy is but one example in Oklahoma City of institutional providers of health care to those who did not have access to the existing medical systems. After World War II, the Sisters purchased a private hospital in Oklahoma City to provide professional medical care to all residents of Oklahoma City, regardless of race or income. Undoubtedly there remain untold accounts of other hospitals performing similar acts of compassion.

Professional organizations and individuals in Oklahoma City prominent in their efforts to help include the Oklahoma Negro Medical Society, Opaline Deveraux Wadkins, Dr. Charles N. Atkins, Hannah Atkins, and churches of several denominations in Oklahoma City. There is a history as well of women's organizations that established settlement houses based on the model of Jane Addams. The Woman's Missionary Society of the East Oklahoma Conference served the needs of blue-collar workers, many of whom were immigrants. There have also been significant private efforts by the Oklahoma City Community Foundation and the Communities Foundation of Oklahoma.

The MAPS program initiated by Oklahoma City mayor Ron Norick is about political power and the use of public resources for the many rather than the few. From this perspective, MAPS becomes another community of caring, this one politically based. The synergy of the MAPS projects along with the determination of the residents of Oklahoma City and throughout the state to respond in positive ways to the agony of the Oklahoma City bombing by American terrorists have helped rebuild downtown Oklahoma City and parts of the greater metroplex.

Issues and concerns remain—there are still unmet fundamental political, economic, and social needs among residents—but the positive changes occurring in Oklahoma City are to some degree unprecedented. Together both stakeholders and some shareholders have demonstrated kindness and care in this heartland through their participation and support in MAPS in addition to their response and leadership after the domestic terrorist bombing.

As is true of the majority of volunteers who work at Thy Will Be Done, volunteers in Oklahoma City continue to benefit from being in the same room with both the poor and volunteers often with different agendas. In this process, for example, faith-based and nonreligious volunteers influence and in turn can be influenced by each other, and by the poor, who may or may not share their same level of religiosity.

Persistent and pervasive poverty does not have to be a part of Oklahoma's future. Oklahoma does not have to fall into the company of Mississippi, Arkansas, Louisiana, Alabama, and New Mexico, all states with notoriously high poverty rates for many decades. Voters and their elected and appointed representatives do not have to ignore the rule of law or devise ways to circumvent it. Heinous events in Oklahoma history should not and need not be written only from the perspective of the most powerful shareholders, as was the case with the Tulsa race massacre, until a century later they are rediscovered by historians.

Regardless of political party affiliation over the course of Oklahoma history, hardworking and honest politicians with demonstrated leadership skills have often been superseded by those claiming to represent a form of shareholder capitalism. Political corruption can and has led to different forms of violence applied without mercy against targeted groups including the poor. In shareholder capitalism the poor can be ignored, unless they are seen as possible customers, because the focus is only upon maximizing the bottom line. Tax allocations to specific groups become defined as legitimate revenue streams to be captured by businesses representing their shareholders' best interests.[4] From this perspective, bribery and other costs may be seen merely as the price of doing business. This can especially occur when rival shareholder businesses or the public's best interests may be the competition.

The question from a shareholder perspective can then become not whether the next generation of William L. "Taters" Anderson and others like him continue to bribe the Oklahoma Corporation commissioners. It becomes instead whether all three commissioners need to be bribed, how much the bribe should be, and how the bribe should be delivered in such a way as to appear perfectly legal.

In contrast, stakeholder capitalism can place the interests of key players—customers, suppliers, employees, and communities—before profits to shareholders. Stakeholder capitalism, in contrast to shareholder capitalism, chooses to ignore the favored groups and instead aims to maximize the advantages to all affected parties—including the poor.

Eliminating Oklahoma's culture of political corruption can lead to improving the well-being of the poor. Economic violence in the form of giving unfair advantage to certain private businesses over others, or excessive tax cuts to these same businesses, does great harm to those with the least political power. Other forms of violence can be just as devasting when the public's best interests are ignored.

Oklahoma's democratic roots grow stronger when the rule of law applies not only to the poor but to all others, including those elected or appointed to work for the public good. In Tater's political corruption case involving the Oklahoma Corporation Commission, again to highlight one of the most egregious examples, one elected politician who received bribes also was convicted and sent to prison. It is believed that he was the first and only OCC commissioner since statehood to be imprisoned because of corruption.[5]

Oklahomans share a common past and present, both of which can take on new meanings when seen from the perspectives of the poor. Our future with those in poverty will also be shared. What kind of better future lies ahead for Oklahomans who are poor?

A better Oklahoma future would be a future in which poor Whites, the majority of all those in poverty, are no longer stigmatized by misleading stereotypes. These stereotypes frequently blame everyone who is poor for their own poverty. Poor Oklahomans should never be blamed, ignored, or treated by service providers as if they are less than human.

A better Oklahoma future would be a future in which the poverty rate of Oklahoma minorities did not double that of Whites. Natives, in fact, have a declining poverty rate primarily because of casino revenues, though it is still much higher than that of Whites. The notable decline in Native poor again demonstrates that poverty is less about the personal flaws of the poor than it is about the consequences of not having enough money. A minimum wage of $7.25 does not keep the poor from poverty; rather, it sustains their poverty status.

Ignoring the rule of law as it applies to the executive, judicial, and legislative branches of Oklahoma government reinforces a culture of corruption. A better future, therefore, is one that champions the rule of law at all levels of state government. The same rule of law must also apply to the public and private business sectors. Public resources including tax revenue, often limited, are not just another part of the fiefdom of one Oklahoma private industry or another. Tax revenues are intended by law to serve the general welfare of the public.

Poverty in Oklahoma should be about sharing the benefits of the Oklahoma economy with all classes rather than filling the pockets of shareholders. The vast majority of Oklahomans remain stakeholders with no place at the bargaining table.

A better Oklahoma future would be a future in which children are educated in public schools to meet the demands of our changing economy. In this Oklahoma all young workers would have an opportunity to climb up the salary ladder rather than languish at the bottom for lack of marketable skills. In this Oklahoma future, as well, single parents could afford licensed day care while they worked. In this future Oklahoma, the disabled would be provided for and accepted for both who they are and who they want to be. In this future elderly Oklahomans could expect to live out the last years of their lives in dignity.

In an Oklahoma future like the one suggested here, the nonpoor benefit as well. Simultaneously, absent the varied harsh consequences of high poverty rates, moral and fiscal resources can be targeted at societal problems other than pervasive and persistent poverty.

A better future for the poor, including falling poverty rates for all races regardless of gender, disability, age, and geography, is attainable. Poor Oklahomans are not "them," poor Oklahomans are "us." Whether faith-based, governmental, or individual efforts, or new programs as yet untested serving those in poverty, many Okies already know and believe they should treat all their neighbors with compassion and love.

In his songs and writings Woody Guthrie described the real dilemmas the Oklahoma poor face on a daily basis. He also offered a solution to poverty. Not only did Woody observe through his experience that "things are tough. Folks broke. Kids hungry. Sick. Everything." He also knew that "there's a spirit of some kind we've all got. That's got to draw us together."[6]

In our Oklahoma, heartland communities of care can enrich our individual spirit and, at the same time, draw us together. Communities of care in our state already offer proven solutions to the needs of those living in persistent and pervasive poverty. But we can do much more. My fellow Oklahomans, there is no reason to hesitate.

Research Approach

To accomplish the objectives of this research, I developed an approach based upon my familiarity with methodological triangulation—frequently referred to as "mixed methods." This research approach can enhance an understanding of multidimensional human phenomena. Since 1980 I have used mixed methods to study poverty and its consequences upon the poor in a variety of different contexts.[1]

I follow the efforts of Norman Denzin's seminal work *The Research Act: A Theoretical Introduction to Sociological Methods*. Denzin suggests the utility of an approach that relies upon at least three different methods. Triangulation requires a blend of at least one or more inductive qualitative methods and one or more deductive quantitative methods as determined by the social phenomena under study.

To better comprehend the various aspects of the poor and poverty in this research, I used five different research methods, three qualitative and two quantitative. Beginning in the summer of 2019 and continuing through the fall of 2023, I conducted participant observation at an Oklahoma food pantry for five and a half months. To some degree the demands of the COVID-19 pandemic dictated the terms of this inductive qualitative method, including who was contacted, under what conditions information was gathered, questions asked, and follow-up discussions.

As volunteers at this food pantry during this study, my research assistant and I collected data from 146 guests. This number does not include all of the household members who may have been present, friends, or others who were accompanying guests while they shopped. Data were also collected from volunteers and staff.

In addition, I completed thirty semi-structured, open-ended interviews with individuals across the state. Some were collected while doing the participant observation at the above-mentioned food pantry, others during six additional trips to Oklahoma that varied in duration from three days to one week. This nonrandom sample consisted of those who worked directly with the poor, had in the past studied them, or both. One group of respondents included academics at different educational institutions throughout Oklahoma. I also interviewed elected politicians and appointees, health care providers, members of law enforcement agencies, private and public supervisors of social service providers, secondary school teachers, members of state, county, and local government, and religious leaders.

Autoethnography is the third qualitative component of this research effort.[2] My general understanding of the research findings is interpreted within my perspective of having lived for many years in Oklahoma. I was born and raised in Oklahoma, then eventually returned to my home state to work for a decade at Oklahoma State University. This total time period encompasses thirty years of living and working in my home state. Even in the years when I did not reside in Oklahoma, I never stopped returning to see family and friends, witness important events, or touch base with my colleagues around the state. My return visits often involved maintaining contacts with certain institutions, agencies, departments, and individuals with whom over the years I have established professional relationships.

This study of Oklahoma is also, of course, informed by my previous research on the poor and poverty primarily in the U.S.-Mexico borderlands and the American Southwest. It includes studying migrant farm workers, residents of border *colonias*, documented and undocumented commercial fishermen and fisherwomen, and a wide variety of other individuals who are poor but work part or full time. I have also studied the nonpoor in these same and other regions, including elected politicians, defense contractors, employees at different levels of state and federal government, bankers, insurance representatives, customs and border patrol agents, real estate developers, public and private school teachers, and the members of mass media.[3]

My ten years as a research associate at the Institute of Research on Poverty at the University of Wisconsin-Madison also contributed to both my strong belief in the utility of mixed methods and my perspectives about the poor and poverty.[4]

The first deductive quantitative method I employ is an analysis of longitudinal Oklahoma state, county, and city data collected by the U.S. Census. I use census data to demonstrate that pervasive and persistent poverty prevails not just in the towns and cities of one investigated Oklahoma county but statewide. I also compare Oklahoma poverty over time to poverty in other states and national rates. The census provides a virtual goldmine of data about the Oklahoma poor and about poverty. I previously analyzed these same data from 1959 to 1995.[5] In the present research I analyze the relevant data from 1959 to the present. I welcome other social scientists to appraise these same data.

My second deductive method is to employ these census data on poverty and the consequences of poverty as a fact-based guide to reframing Oklahoma history. In particular I use these data to explore, however briefly, the impact of systemic political corruption upon the poor since statehood in 1907, but with particular emphasis on the period covering more than sixty years from 1959 to the present. I also rely at times on other fact-based studies by national experts based upon these same data sets. In this exploratory historical reframing, based in part upon U.S. Census data, my objective is to better comprehend the perspective of the poor on the systemic criminal acts throughout Oklahoma history most often excused as unrelated scandals.

In spite of growing up in Oklahoma, I began knowing more European history than Oklahoma history. Only at Washington University–St. Louis, where I completed a doctorate in sociology, did I first have the opportunity to consider the importance of history through the teaching and research of Alvin Gouldner, Irving M. Zeitlin, Richard Radcliff, and George Rawick, among others.[6] I was also fortunate at Washington University–St. Louis to be mentored in my dissertation research by David J. Pittman, chair of the sociology department, whose research focused upon social-historical aspects of alcoholism.[7]

Only when I began teaching at Oklahoma State University in 1989 did I begin seriously to study the history of my own home state. This effort led, with the very capable help of sociology graduate student Jackie Burns, to my first analysis of U.S Census materials focusing upon the economic status of Natives in Oklahoma.[8] This research soon directed me to the scholarly work of Angie Debo. She unfortunately passed in 1988.

Throughout the research for this book, every effort has been made to protect the privacy and confidentiality of those associated with the participant observation at TWBD, the nonrandom sample, and the other three methodologies described and employed in this research. This effort included changing names and changing, when necessary, other individual characteristics that might identify respondents. As needed, institutional and organizational characteristics at which these individuals were employed were fictionalized, as were place names and other unique descriptors. None of these efforts change in any substantive way the data from my mixed methods research approach nor the conclusions based upon this data.

Conducting research on the poor during the COVID-19 pandemic was challenging in ways for which I was not prepared. For example, my coresearcher at the food pantry where we volunteered and I were both exposed to COVID-19 on numerous occasions and, in spite of being vaccinated, eventually caught it. Few guests or staff at the pantry, as true of many Oklahomans, wore masks or were vaccinated. I also contacted a serious case of bronchitis during my research in Oklahoma, which led to further delays. Doing research during the pandemic, nevertheless, served to spotlight various consequences of poverty faced daily by the poor that otherwise may have been underemphasized.

Acknowledgments

This book required a great amount of support from numerous individuals, the majority of whom unfortunately must remain anonymous. I owe a debt of gratitude to the scholarly contributions of Jayme Hall Johnson, coauthor of chapter 6, who also helped edit several drafts of the manuscript. Sarah Watson is coauthor of chapter 5. Elizabeth B. Anthony graciously shared her unpublished research on the history of Oklahoma City churches discussed in chapter 7.

Morgan Cloud, Charles Howard Candler Professor of Law Emeritus at the Emory University School of Law, provided his lucid appraisal of various drafts. I also owe much to Michael Voors, Professor of Art Emeritus at the East Carolina University School of Art Design. Our numerous conversations during the COVID-19 years, fueled by my consumption of quad espressos, forced me to rethink certain parts of the manuscript. Sociologist Gene Summers, Professor of Sociology Emeritus at the University of Wisconsin–Madison, patiently and generously provided encouragement throughout this endeavor. I am once again indebted to his mentorship. Wanda DeBruler, of DeBruler, Inc., thoughtfully shared her insightful appraisal of Oklahoma, as she has for many years. My thanks, too, to both the Oklahoma Council of Public Affairs and the Oklahoma Policy Institute.

Ronald R. Thrasher, former director of the forensic psychology program at the Oklahoma State University Center for Health Sciences, School of Forensic Sciences, once again served as a sounding board for many of my conclusions. I remain grateful for his steady judgment throughout the years, his sense of fairness, and his friendship. A special thanks also to Sr. Debbie Kern, RSM, of the Sisters of Mercy.

I am as well most grateful for the editorial encouragement and skills of Andrew Berzanskis at the University of Oklahoma Press, and to J. Kent Calder, whose initial interest in a new study of the poor and poverty in Oklahoma proved pivotal. I want to especially thank Alice Stanton for her generosity. Thanks go out, too, to the anonymous reviewers for their suggestions.

At East Carolina University, I am indebted to the collegiality of Mamadi Corra, Kristen Myers, Arunas Juska, Jermaine McNair, Susan Pearce, Colin Campbell, Joe Luczkovich, and David Griffith. John Lawrence, Assistant Director of Special Collections at Joyner Library, was always especially helpful. Lily Philbrook and Grace Osusky facilitated the completion of the notes and bibliography.

I owe much to the lasting influence and memory of sociologist Kathy Jones, who was officed across the hall from me on the fourth floor of the Brewster Building. She was always willing to listen and comment.

I want to personally thank Rebecca Powers at East Carolina University for her scholarly support over the past twenty-five years and her friendship during challenging times.

At Oklahoma State University, I would like to thank Tamara Mix, chair and professor of the Department of Sociology, for her support. I also am appreciative of the longtime patience of administrative associate Barbie Teel. At the University of North Carolina Chapel Hill, I am grateful for the inspiration of Erin Siegal McIntyre, Hussman School of Journalism and Media, and the ongoing work of Professor Gene R. Nichol, director of the Poverty Research Fund.

My deepest gratitude and respect to my coresearcher during the participant-observation stage of this project and my life partner, Dindy Reich. She provided an invaluable depth of understanding and support from the beginning to the end of this project.

I would be remiss if I did not give special thanks to the guests at Thy Will Be Done along with the staff. This book also would not have been possible without all the other individuals throughout Oklahoma who generously shared their expertise but who also must remain anonymous.

Notes

Introduction

1. Based on data from a publicly available source and/or a source in the author's possession. Details are withheld to protect pseudonymity. In reference to subsequent such cases, the endnote will state, "Sources details withheld to protect pseudonymity."
2. Oklahoma Department of Transportation, "Oklahoma Capitol Complex Maps."
3. Oklahoma City National Memorial Museum, "Safe Place for History."
4. Institute for Research on Poverty, "Research."
5. Gibson, *Oklahoma.*
6. Saunt, *Unworthy Republic*; Debo, *And Still the Waters Run.*
7. Hightower, *1889*; Thompson, *Closing the Frontier.*
8. Debo, *And Still the Waters Run*; Grann, *Killers of the Flower Moon.*
9. Maril, *Waltzing with the Ghost of Tom Joad.*
10. Hill, *1921 Tulsa Race Massacre.*
11. White House, "Remarks by President Biden."
12. Bell and Maril, "Longitudinal Analysis"; Burns and Maril, "Socio-economic Status."
13. Maril, *Waltzing with the Ghost of Tom Joad.*
14. Benson, *Poverty in States and Metropolitan Areas.*
15. Lipka and Wormald, "How Religious Is Your State?"
16. Jones, "Conservatives Greatly Outnumber Liberals."
17. Mitchell, *Race against Time.*
18. U.S. Census Bureau, "Race and Hispanic Origin."
19. Mitchell, *Race against Time.*
20. Federal Bureau of Investigation, "Medgar Evers."

21. Toobin, *Homegrown.*
22. Ellis, Adams, and Bochner, "Autoethnography."
23. Annie E. Casey Foundation, *2024 Kids Count Data Book.*
24. Grann, *Killers of the Flower Moon*; Hill, *1921 Tulsa Race Massacre.*
25. Hightower, *At War with Corruption*; Holloway and Meyers, *Bad Times for Good Ol' Boys.*
26. Benson, *Poverty in States and Metropolitan Areas.*

Chapter 1

1. Oklahoma Medical Marijuana Authority, "FY 2023 Annual Report."
2. Bink, "MAP."
3. Economic Research Service, "Food Insecurity in the U.S."
4. Data drawn from the Current Population Survey Food Security Supplements for 2019–2021.
5. Schweitzer, Mix, and Esquibel, "Negotiating Dignity and Social Justice."
6. U.S. Department of Labor, "Minimum Wage Laws."
7. National Archives, "Servicemen's Readjustment Act (1944)."
8. Social Security Administration, "Understanding Supplemental Security Income (SSI) Overview."

Chapter 2

1. Institute for Research on Poverty, "What Are Good Sources of Information?"; Maril, *Waltzing with the Ghost of Tom Joad*; Agee and Evans, *Let Us Now Praise Famous Men*; Harrington, *Other America*; Elman, *Poorhouse State*; Snow and Anderson, *Down on Their Luck*; Griffith, *Jones's Minimal*; Desmond, *Evicted.*
2. Friends Committee on National Legislation, "Top 10 Hungriest States."
3. Oklahoma State University Extension, "Health and Hunger."
4. Debo, *And Still the Waters Run.*
5. U.S. Department of Housing and Urban Development, "About HUD."
6. National Academies of Sciences, Engineering, and Medicine, *Reducing Intergenerational Poverty.*
7. U.S. Centers for Disease Control and Prevention, "Body Mass Index."
8. Warren, West, and Beck, *State of Obesity.*
9. U.S. Centers for Disease Control and Prevention, "How Overweight and Obesity Impacts Your Health."
10. Campbell et al., "Consequences of Living in a Small-Town Food Desert"; Longo et al., "Adipose Tissue Dysfunction."
11. National Initiative for Children's Healthcare Quality, "Oklahoma State Fact Sheet."
12. Institute for Research on Poverty, "Child Obesity."
13. U.S. Centers for Disease Control and Prevention, "Type 2 Diabetes"; Mayo Clinic, "Type 1 Diabetes in Children."

14. Romich and Hill, "Boosting the Poverty-Fighting Effects"; Godøy and Romich, "Anna Godøy and Jennie Romich on the Impacts"; Shamsuddin and Campbell, "Housing Cost Burden."
15. Barber and Wilson-Hartgrove, *White Poverty.*
16. Behrman and Taubman, "Intergenerational Earnings Mobility"; Becker and Tomes, "Human Capital"; Smeeding et al., "American Poverty and Inequality"; Spartz and Siers-Poisson, "Classroom Supplement"; Kim and Henly, "Social Support"; Agee and Evans, *Let Us Now Praise Famous Men.*

Chapter 3

1. Statistics drawn from U.S. Census data tables: https://data.census.gov/table?q=Oklahoma%20Income%20and%20Poverty.
2. Carter, Todd, and Pearson, "Crews Shift from Rescue to Recovery."
3. Source details withheld to protect pseudonymity.
4. Source details withheld to protect pseudonymity.
5. Gross and Stelzenmuller, "Research: Europe's Messy Russian Gas Divorce."
6. Swanson, *Agriculture and the Economy.*
7. Schneider, "Rash of Suicides."
8. Stull, Broadway, and Griffith, *Any Way You Cut It.*
9. Oklahoma State University Extension, "County Agricultural Land Value Changes."
10. Maril, *Waltzing with the Gost of Tom Joad*, 130–42.
11. Oklahoma Department of Commerce, "Oklahoma Main Street."
12. Google, "Mayes County, Oklahoma."
13. The following report is based on Charles, "Sewage Spill."
14. Source details withheld to protect pseudonymity.
15. Source details withheld to protect pseudonymity.
16. Swanson, *Agriculture and the Economy.*
17. Campbell et al., "Consequences of Living in a Small-Town Food Desert."
18. Source details withheld to protect pseudonymity.
19. National Assessment of Educational Progress, "NAEP Data Explorer."
20. U.S. Census Bureau, "American Community Survey."
21. World Population Review, *Perkins.*
22. DATA USA, "Glencoe, OK"; DATA USA, "Ripley, OK."
23. Aveilhe, "Oklahoma."
24. DATA USA, "Langston, OK."
25. DATA USA, "Pawnee, OK"; U.S. Census Bureau, *Quick Facts, Pawnee County, Oklahoma.*
26. Carter, "Tribes Pushing Minimum Wage Higher."
27. Dean, "Oklahoma Native Impact." Economic data about Natives are very challenging to find; these data are based upon fifteen of the thirty-eight tribes.
28. Peachman, "Meet America's Best Employers by State."

Chapter 4

1. Salvation Army International, "Salvation Army."
2. World Population Review, "Per Pupil Spending by State."
3. Oklahoma State Department of Education, "Child Nutrition."
4. National Center for Education Statistics, "Digest of Education Statistics."
5. Fife, "As Universal Free Lunch Program Ends"; Thomas, "Oklahoma Loses Federal Programs."
6. Olivas, "Marlow Public Schools."
7. McKee, "8 Facts About Human Services." The Oklahoma Health Care Authority is the largest recipient of state tax dollars, the Department of Transportation second.
8. U.S. Department of Housing and Urban Development, "2022 Annual Homelessness Assessment Report"; Saadi, "Homeless Youth Walk a Hidden Path."
9. Healthy Minds Policy Initiative, "About Healthy Minds."
10. Healthy Minds Policy Initiative, "Programs of Assertive Community Treatment."
11. Bryan, "Lawsuit Alleges Widespread Abuse"; Adcock and Goforth, "Oklahoma Officials Claim the Okmulgee Jail"; Stitt, Holt, and Broyles, *2021 Three-Year Plan.*
12. Belusko, "Pendulum of Change."
13. U.S. Department of Housing and Urban Development, "Continuum of Care Program FAQs"; National Center for Homeless Education, "Determining Eligibility."
14. Source details withheld to protect pseudonymity.
15. Federal Reserve Bank of St. Louis, "Oklahoma."
16. National Institute on Minority Health and Health Disparities, *Oklahoma Poverty—Table.* Pacific Islanders record the highest poverty rate, 53 percent in Wells County. But they are not considered here because there are only thirty-four individuals residing in the county.
17. NewsPress Staff, "Our View."
18. Source details withheld to protect pseudonymity.

Chapter 5

1. Barber II and Wilson-Hartgrove, *White Poverty*; Maril, *Waltzing with the Ghost of Tom Joad.*
2. U.S. Census Bureau, "How the Census Bureau Measures Poverty."
3. U.S. Census Bureau, "Poverty in States and Metropolitan Areas."
4. Bailey and Duquette, "How Johnson Fought the War on Poverty"; Maril, *Waltzing with the Ghost of Tom Joad*, 90–106.
5. Shrider et al., "Income and Poverty"; U.S. Census Bureau, "Poverty in States and Metropolitan Areas."
6. National Institute on Minority Health and Health Disparities, *Oklahoma Poverty—Table.*
7. Shrider et al., "Income and Poverty."
8. Maril and Bisping, "Four Decades of Poverty."
9. Benson, *Poverty in States and Metropolitan Areas.*

10. Oklahoma Geological Survey, "Oil and Gas."
11. U.S. Bureau of Labor Statistics, "Economy at a Glance"; Transparent Oklahoma Performance, "Performance-Informed Budgeting."
12. Oklahoma Department of Commerce, "Oklahoma Top Employers."
13. U.S. Census Bureau, "American Community Survey Data."
14. U.S. Census Bureau, "American Community Survey Data."
15. Oklahoma Office of State Finance Gaming Compliance Unit, "Frequently Asked Questions."
16. National Indian Gaming Commission, "Frequently Asked Questions."
17. Dean, *Economic Impact of Tribal Nations.*
18. Carter, "Tax Commission."
19. Oklahoma Historical Society, "Latino History in Oklahoma."
20. U.S. Census Bureau, "American Community Survey Data."
21. U.S. Census Bureau, "American Community Survey Data."
22. Ahlstrom and Dass, *Status of Women in Oklahoma*, 2.
23. Ahlstrom and Dass, *Status of Women in Oklahoma*, 3.
24. U.S. Census Bureau, "Poverty in States and Metropolitan Areas"; U.S. Census Bureau, "American Community Survey Data."
25. Annie E. Casey Foundation, *2021 Kids Count Data Book.*
26. Annie E. Casey Foundation, *2022 Kids Count Data Book.*
27. Oklahoma Department of Human Services, "Oklahoma Pinnacle Plan"; Wertz, "Outside Monitoring."
28. Wertz, "Continuing Oklahoma's Improvement."
29. Perry, "In the Know."
30. Shyers, "Senior Hunger"; UnitedHealth Group, "United Health Foundation."
31. The following relative rankings related to the elderly in Oklahoma are drawn from America's Health Rankings, United Health Foundation, "2022 Annual Report."
32. See also Oklahoma Department of Mental Health and Substance Abuse Services, "Reports."
33. See also Oklahoma Rehabilitation Services, "Oklahoma Disability Statistcis"; and U.S. Department of Veterans Affairs, "Special Reports."
34. ILR Yang-Tan Institute on Employment and Disability, "Disability Statistics."
35. Maril, *Waltzing with the Ghost of Tom Joad.*
36. Wellcare Oklahoma, see Wellcare homepage.
37. Monies, "Nearly 300,000 Are Poised to Lose SoonerCare."
38. Radley, Baumgartner, and Collins, "2022 Scorecard."
39. Polansky, "New Study"; University of Oklahoma Health, "Dr. Dale Bratzler."
40. Brown University, School of Public Health, "New Analysis"; Simmons-Duffin and Nakajima, "This Is How Many Lives."
41. Oklahoma State Department of Health, "COVID-19 Data."
42. The following discussion of education in Oklahoma is based on U.S. Census Bureau, *American Community Survey Data 2022*, except where otherwise noted.

43. Annie E. Casey Foundation, "2022 Kids Count Data Profile."
44. U.S. Department of Health and Human Services, "Making a Difference."
45. Cox, *Caste, Class, and Race*; Oliver and Shapiro, *Black Wealth/White Wealth*.
46. Oklahoma Education Association, "Latest Rankings"; Shelton, "Oklahoma Teacher Salaries."
47. Maril, *Waltzing with the Ghost of Top Joad*, 123–29.
48. Greenberg, "Are Oklahoma Teachers the Lowest Paid?"
49. Oklahoma Education Association, "Latest Rankings"; Felder, "State of Oklahoma."
50. ABC News, "Oklahoma Teacher Panhandles"; Oklahoma Education Association, "About OEA"; Polansky, "Stitt, Walters Slam 'Liberal Teachers' Unions.'"
51. Sanchez, "Oklahoma Governor Compares Teachers"; 2 News Oklahoma, "Edison Preparatory School Students."
52. Oklahoma Education Association, "Latest Rankings."
53. Oklahoma State Department of Education State, "Comprehensive Teacher Pay Reform."

Chapter 6

1. Mills, *Power Elite*; Rose, *Power Structure*; Dahrendorf, *Class and Class Conflict*; Domhoff and Dye, *Power Elites*; Kelley, *America's Inequality Trap*; Piketty, *Capital and Ideology*; Reich, *System*.
2. Maril, *Waltzing with the Ghost of Tom Joad*; Steinbeck, *Grapes of Wrath*; Maril, *Poorest of Americans*.
3. Military Bases.US., "Fort Sill"; U.S. Air Force, "Tinker Air Force Base."
4. The following brief review of Hamon is drawn from New York Times, "Says Jake Hamon"; This and That Newsletter, "Glimpse into the Past"; and Lackmeyer, "Meet the Oklahoma Flapper."
5. Grann, *Killers of the Flower Moon*; Burns and Maril, "Socio-economic Status of Native Americans"; Bel and Maril, "Longitudinal Analysis of Poverty."
6. U.S. Census Bureau, "American Community Survey".
7. Debo, *Geronimo*; Debo, *And Still the Waters Run*.
8. Madigan, *Burning*; Oklahoma Commission to Study the Race Riot of 1921, *Tulsa Race Riot*; Parrish, *Nation Must Awake*.
9. Krehbiel, "Third Gunshot Victim Exhumed"; Hassan, "Total of 27 Graves."
10. O'Dell, "Walton, John Calloway."
11. Duren, "'Klanspiracy' or Despotism?"; Oklahoma City Government Archives and Records, "John C. Walton."
12. Oklahoman, "Opposing Jack Walton."
13. Bryant, "Murray, William Henry David."
14. Jacobs, "William H. 'Alfalfa Bill' Murray."
15. Bryant, "Murray, William Henry David."
16. Davis, "Edmonson, James Howard."
17. Peterson-Veatch, "Kerr-McGee Corporation."

18. Selcraig, "Worst Newspaper in America."
19. National Governors Association, "Governor David Hall."
20. Burke, "From the Ashes of Scandal."
21. Berry and Alexander, *Justice for Sale*.
22. Holloway, "Political Scandals"; Citizens Overseeing Oklahoma, "Oklahoma's History of Corruption."
23. Feaver, "Oklahoma Scandal."
24. Hightower, *At War with Corruption*.
25. English, "Funeral Home Owner Vondel Smith."
26. United Press International, "Former Oklahoma House Speaker J. D. McCarty Dead"; Tulsa World, "Knowing the Territory Paid Off"; Daily Oklahoman, "McCarty Guilty 2 Counts"; Holloway and Meyers, *Bad Times for Good Ol' Boys*.
27. The following review of the crimes, investigations, and consequence is drawn from Hightower, *At War with Corruption*, except where otherwise noted
28. Oklahoman, "Toll 230 as Book Closes"; Holloway, "Political Scandals."
29. Holloway, "Political Scandals."
30. Oklahoman, "Toll 230 as Book Closes"; Hogan, "Salesman Indicted."
31. Weaver, "Former DA Gets Out of Prison."
32. 270 to Win, "Oklahoma: Recent Presidential Elections."
33. Krehbiel, "1980s County Commissioners Scandal."
34. The following Penn Square Bank story is drawn from Singer, *Funny Money*, in addition to sources otherwise noted.
35. Hogan, "Key Figure in Penn Square Collapse"; Doti, "Penn Square Bank."
36. Oklahoman, "Civic Leader Bill Jennings Dies."
37. U.S. House of Representatives, "Penn Square Bank Failure."
38. Zweig, *Belly Up*.
39. On the OCC, see Oklahoma Corporation Commission, "About the Oklahoma Corporation Commission."
40. Maril, "Impact of Utility Rate Increases."
41. Frontline, Interview with Robert Anthony.
42. Vandewater, "Anthony's Case Pursued."
43. Wilmoth, "Commissioner Files Recording."
44. Hightower, *At War with Corruption*, 355.
45. Ulsperger, "Greed, Ghosts, and Grand Juries"; Ellis, "Health Department Scandal."
46. CBSNews.com staff, "Culture of Corruption."
47. Ellis and Palmer, "Health Department Scandal."
48. News on 6, "VanMeter, Jiles Indicted"; Clay, Ellis, and Killackey, "Pair Guilty in Bribery Case"; Hurt, "Scandal Brings State Agency under Scrutiny."
49. Killackey, "Health Department Scandal."
50. Clay, "VanMeter Admits He Took Bribes"; CBSNews.com staff, "Investigators."
51. Ellis and Clay, "2 Indicted."
52. Oklahoma Geological Survey, "Oil and Gas."

53. U.S. Geological Survey, "Oklahoma Has Had a Surge of Earthquakes."
54. KFOR-TV and Querry, "Gov. Fallin Transfers $1.4 Million."
55. Dincer and Johnston, "Measuring Illegal and Legal Corruption in American States"; Holloway and Meyers, *Bad Times for Good Ol' Boys*, 34–98.
56. Kristen, "Oklahoma Ranked 11th Most Corrupt."
57. Oklahomans for Anthony, "FBI Presents Bob Anthony."

Chapter 7

1. Regional Food Bank of Oklahoma, "Our History."
2. Shields, Hamington, and Soeters, *Oxford Handbook of Jane Addams*; Knight, *Citizen*.
3. Daigler, *Through the Windows*; Sisters of Mercy, "Our History"; Sister Debbie Kern, personal communication, September 21, 2023.
4. Cowan, "Okmulgee Black Hospital."
5. Oklahoma Historical Society, "African Americans in Oklahoma."
6. Kern, personal communication.
7. Decker, "Atkins, Hanna Diggs."
8. The following review of church efforts for the poor is based on Elisabeth B. Anthony's unpublished research of 2021, except where otherwise noted.
9. Linn, *Jane Addams*.
10. Smith, "1923 Flood Also Inundated City"; Mead and Hawley, "Map of the North Canadian River."
11. Maril, *Waltzing with the Ghost of Tom Joad*.
12. Oklahoma City Community Foundation, "About."
13. Journal Record Staff, "Longtime OKC Advocate Anthony Plan Retirement."
14. Oklahoma City Community Foundation, "About."
15. Communities Foundation of Oklahoma, "About CFO."
16. Tulsa Community Foundation, "What We Do"; Oklahoma City Community Foundation, "Our Donors."
17. Erling, "Ron Norick."
18. Maril, *Waltzing with the Ghost of Tom Joad*; Lyson and Falk, *Forgotten Places*.
19. Nelson, "United to City"; Renn, "Doing OK in OKC."
20. For details of the several MAPS projects, see Oklahoma City Government, *MAPS 3*; and Oklahoma City Government, *MAPS 4*.
21. McLean, *Case for Shareholder Capitalism*; Freeman et al., *Stakeholder Theory*.
22. Lowell Milken Center for Unsung Heroes, "Meet the Hero"; Oklahoma Hall of Fame, "Life of Clara Luper"; Uncrowned Community Builders, "Clara Mae Shepard Luper."
23. Homeless Alliance, "Together, We Can End Homelessness."; Korth and Poppe, "Oklahoma City's Homeless Alliance Director Reflects."
24. Linenthal, "Oklahoma City Bombing."
25. Los Angeles Times Archives, "McVeigh Labels Young Victims."

26. Oklahoma City National Memorial Museum, "Safe Place for History."
27. Oklahoman, "Take the Oklahoman Survey."

Chapter 8

1. Casteel, "Congressional Panel Hears about Workforce Issues."
2. America's Health Rankings, United Health Foundation, "2022 Annual Report"; Benson, *Poverty in States and Metropolitan Areas*"; Maril, *Waltzing with the Ghost of Tom Joad*, 90–106; Maril and Bisping, "Four Decades of Poverty"; Shrider et al., "Income and Poverty"; Annie E. Casey Foundation, *2021 Kids Count Data Book.*
3. Toobin, *Homegrown.*
4. Chomsky and Waterstone, *Consequences of Capitalism*; McLean, *Case for Shareholder Capitalism.*
5. Holloway, "Political Scandals."
6. Guthrie, *Bound for Glory.*

Research Approach

1. Maril, *Texas Shrimpers*; Maril, *Poorest of Americans*; Maril, *Bay Shrimpers of Texas*; Maril, *Waltzing with the Ghost of Tom Joad.*
2. Adams, Jones, and Ellis, *Handbook of Autoethnography.*
3. Maril, "Teaching Domestic Terrorism"; Maril, "Methodological Approaches"; Maril, "Impact of Mandatory Car Insurance"; Maril and Asaad, "Mismanagement of Federal Contracts"; Maril, "Methodological Considerations"; Maril, "Through a Shrimper's Eye"; Maril, "Oklahoma in Poverty."
4. Maril, *Fence.*
5. Maril, *Waltzing with the Ghost of Tom Joad*, 130–43.
6. Gouldner, *Coming Crisis of Western Sociology*; Zeitlin and Ratcliff, *Landlords and Capitalists*; Rawick, *From Sundown to Sunup.*
7. Maril and Zavaleta, "Drinking Patterns."
8. Burns and Maril, "Socio-economic Status of Native Americans."

Bibliography

2 News Oklahoma. 2018. "Edison Preparatory School Students Walked Out of Class to Protest amid School's Recent Scandals." February 15. Accessed September 26, 2024. www.kjrh.com/news/local-news/edison-preparatory-school-students-walked-out-of-class-to-protest-amid-schools-recent-scandals.

270 to Win. n.d. "Oklahoma: Recent Presidential Elections." Accessed August 28, 2024. www.270towin.com/states/Oklahoma.

ABC News. 2017. "Oklahoma Teacher Panhandles to Raise Money for School Supplies." July 25. Accessed September 26, 2024. https://abcnews.go.com/Lifestyle/oklahoma-teacher-panhandles-raise-money-school-supplies/story?id=48815271.

Adams, Tony E., Stacy Holman Jones, and Carolyn Ellis. 2021. *Handbook of Autoethnography.* 2nd. Routledge.

Adcock, Clifton, and Dylan Goforth. 2023. "Oklahoma Officials Claim the Okmulgee Jail Illegally Held Juveniles." *The Frontier,* December 18. Accessed September 13, 2024. www.readfrontier.org/stories/oklahoma-officials-claim-the-okmulgee-jail-illegally-held-juveniles.

Agee, James, and Walker Evans. 1941. *Let Us Now Praise Famous Men.* Houghton Mifflin.

Ahlstrom, Laura J., and Malabi Dass. 2022. *Status of Women in Oklahoma: A Summary Report to United WE.* Spears School of Business, Oklahoma State University. Accessed July 31, 2025. https://oklahoma.gov/content/dam/ok/en/ocsw/documents/Status+of+Women+in+Oklahoma+Report.pdf.

America's Health Rankings, United Health Foundation. 2022. "2022 Annual Report: Oklahoma." Annual Summary report. Accessed September 26, 2024. www

.americashealthrankings.org/learn/reports/2022-annual-report/state-summaries-oklahoma.

———. n.d. "Early Death—Ages 65–74 in Oklahoma." Accessed September 26, 2024. www.americashealthrankings.org/explore/measures/premature_death_sr/OK.

Annie E. Casey Foundation. 2021. *2021 Kids Count Data Book.* June 21. Accessed September 26, 2024. www.aecf.org/resources/2021-kids-count-data-book.

———. 2022. *2022 Kids Count Data Book.* August 8. Accessed September 26, 2024. www.aecf.org/resources/2022-kids-count-data-book.

———. 2022. "2022 Kids Count Data Profile: Oklahoma." Accessed September 26, 2024. https://assets.aecf.org/m/databook/2022KCDB-profile-OK.pdf.

———. 2024. *2024 Kids Count Data Book.* Accessed September 26, 2024. www.aecf.org/resources/2024-kids-count-data-book.

Aveilhe, Tara. 2018. "Oklahoma: Home to More Historically All-Black Towns Than Any Other U.S. State." Oklahoma Center for the Humanities, University of Tulsa. March 16. Accessed October 5, 2024. https://humanities.utulsa.edu/oklahoma-home-historically-black-towns-u-s-state.

Bailey, Martha J., and Nicolas J. Duquette. 2014. "How Johnson Fought the War on Poverty: The Economics and Politics of Funding at the Office of Economic Opportunity." *Journal of Economic History* 74 (2): 351–88.

Barber II, Reverend Dr. William J., and Jonathan Wilson-Hartgrove. 2024. *White Poverty: How Exposing Myths about Race and Class Can Reconstruct American Democracy.* Liveright.

Bartfeld, Judi, Craig Gundersen, Timothy Smeeding, and James Ziliak. 2015. *SNAP Matters: How Food Stamps Affect Health and Well-Being.* Institute for Research of Poverty, University of Wisconsin–Madison. December 2. Accessed October 5, 2024. www.irp.wisc.edu/resource/snap-matters-how-food-stamps-affect-health-and-well-being.

Becker, Gary S., and Nigel Tomes. 1986. "Human Capital and the Rise and Fall of Families." *Journal of Labor Economics* 4 (3): 1–39.

Behrman, Jere, and Paul Taubman. 1985. "Intergenerational Earnings Mobility in the United States: Some Estimates and a Test of Becker's Intergenerational Endowments Model." *Review of Economics and Statistics* 67 (1): 144–51.

Bell, Patricia, and Robert Lee Maril. 1991. "A Longitudinal Analysis of Poverty in Oklahoma." Annual Meeting of the Rural Sociological Society, Columbus, OH.

Belusko, Jan Wallace. 2006. "The Pendulum of Change: Oklahoma's Juvenile Justice System." M.S. thesis, University of Tulsa. May. Accessed September 13, 2024. https://openresearch.okstate.edu/server/api/core/bitstreams/8ceb0508-c08f-49ac-8f45-a125777e9495/content.

Benson, Craig. 2023. *Poverty in States and Metropolitan Areas: 2022.* American Community Survey Briefs, U.S. Census Bureau. Accessed September 26, 2024. www.census.gov/content/dam/Census/library/publications/2023/acs/acsbr-016.pdf.

Berry, William A., and James Edwin Alexander. 1996. *Justice for Sale.* Macedon.

Bink, Addy. 2023. "Map: These Oklahoma Counties Are Home to the Most Excessive Drinkers, Study Finds." *KFOR*. Oklahoma News Channel 4, November 12. Accessed September 2, 2024. https://kfor.com/news/local/map-these-oklahoma-counties-are-home-to-the-most-excessive-drinkers-study-finds.

Brown University, School of Public Health. 2022. "New Analysis Shows Vaccines Could Have Prevented 318,000 Deaths." May 13. Accessed September 26, 2024. https://globalepidemics.org/2022/05/13/new-analysis-shows-vaccines-could-have-prevented-318000-deaths.

Bryan, Max. 2024. "Lawsuit Alleges Widespread Abuse, Cover-Up at Tulsa Juvenile Center." KWGS Public Radio Tulsa, May 29. Accessed September 13, 2024. www.publicradiotulsa.org/local-regional/2024-05-29/lawsuit-alleges-widespread-abuse-cover-up-at-tulsa-juvenile-center.

Bryant, Keith L., Jr. n.d. "Murray, William Henry David (1869–1956)." *Encyclopedia of Oklahoma History and Culture*. Accessed August 16, 2024. www.okhistory.org/publications/enc/entry.php?entry=MU014.

Burke, Bob. 2023. "From the Ashes of Scandal Came Court Reform." *Oklahoma Bar Journal* 94 (5). Accessed August 28, 2024. www.okbar.org/barjournal/may-2023/from-the-ashes-of-scandal-came-court-reform.

———. n.d. "Hall, David (1930–2016)." *Encyclopedia of Oklahoma History and Culture*. Accessed August 28, 2024. www.okhistory.org/publications/enc/entry?entry=HA007.

Burns, Jackie, and Robert Lee Maril. 1992. "The Socio-economic Status of Native Americans in Oklahoma." Annual Meeting of the Rural Sociological Society, University Park, PA.

Campbell, Colin, Monica Maria Calderon Pinedo, Willa Midgette, and Justin Vieira. 2020. "The Consequences of Living in a Small-Town Food Desert: Mixed Methods Evidence from a Quasi-experiment." *Social Currents* 76: 563–81. doi:https://doi.org/10.1177/2329496520928428.

Caplovitz, David. 1967. *The Poor Pay More*. Free Press.

Carter, Chelsea J., Brian Todd, and Michael Pearson. 2023. "Crews Shift from Rescue to Recovery a Day after Oklahoma Tornado, Officials Say." May 22. Accessed October 5, 2024. www.cnn.com/2023/05/22/weather/oklahoma-tornado-recovery/index.html.

Carter, M. Scott. 2014. "Tribes Pushing Minimum Wage Higher." Oklahoma Watch. Updated September 8, 2020. Accessed October 5, 2024. https://oklahomawatch.org/2014/09/12/tribes-pushing-minimum-wage-higher.

Carter, Ray. 2022. "Tax Commission: Indians Not Exempt from Oklahoma Tax." October 12. Oklahoma Council of Public Affairs. Accessed September 26, 2024. https://ocpathink.org/post/independent-journalism/tax-commission-indians-not-exempt-from-oklahoma-tax.

Casteel, Chris. 2023. "Congressional Panel Hears about Workforce Issues in 'Heartland' Oklahoma." *Oklahoman*, March 8. Accessed October 8, 2024. www.oklahoman.com/story/news/politics/2023/03/08/oklahoma-business-owners-describe-problems-getting-workers-to-show-up/69981242007.

CBSNews.com staff. 2001. "A Culture of Corruption." *CBS News*, May 23. www.cbsnews.com/news/a-culture-of-corruption.

———. 2002. "Investigators: Culture of Corruption in Some Nursing Homes." *CBS News*, January 31. www.cbsnews.com/news/investigators-culture-of-corruption-in-some-nursing-homes.

Chomsky, Noam, and Marv Waterstone. 2021. *Consequences of Capitalism: Manufacturing Discontent and Resistance.* Haymarket Books.

Citizens Overseeing Oklahoma. n.d. "Oklahoma's History of Corruption." Citizens Overseeing. Accessed August 28, 2024. www.citizensoverseeing.com/oklahoma/history-of-corruption-ok.

Clay, Nolan. 2002. "VanMeter Admits He Took Bribes Ex-health Official Pleads Guilty, Agrees to Testify." *Oklahoman,* November 23. www.oklahoman.com/story/news/2002/11/23/vanmeter-admits-he-took-bribes-ex-health-official-pleads-guilty-agrees-to-testify/62069753007.

Clay, Nolan, Randy Ellis, and Jim Killackey. 2000. "Pair Guilty in Bribery Case: FBI Tape Seals Convictions in Health Department Case." *Daily Oklahoman,* October 19.

Communities Foundation of Oklahoma. n.d. "About CFO." Communities Foundation of Oklahoma. Accessed September 18, 2024. www.cfok.org/about-us.

Cowan, Emily. 2021. "Okmulgee Black Hospital." Abandoned OK. February 21. Accessed September 18, 2024. https://abandonedok.com/okmulgee-black-hospital.

Cox, Oliver C. 1948. *Caste, Class, and Race: A Study in Social Dynamics.* Monthly Review Press.

Dahrendorf, Ralf. 1959. *Class and Class Conflict in Industrial Society.* Stanford University Press.

Daigler, Mary. 2005. *Through the Windows: A History of the Sisters of Mercy of the Americas.* University of Scranton Press.

Daily Oklahoman. 1967. "McCarty Guilty 2 Counts." *Daily Oklahoman*, July 3.

DATA USA. n.d. "Cushing, OK." Accessed October 5, 2024. https://datausa.io/profile/geo/cushing-ok.

———. n.d. "Glenco, OK." Accessed July 31, 2025. https://datausa.io/profile/geo/Glenco-ok.

———. n.d. "Langston, OK." Accessed July 31, 2025. https://datausa.io/profile/geo/langston-ok.

———. n.d. "Pawnee, OK." Accessed July 31, 2025. https://datausa.io/profile/geo/pawnee-ok.

Davis, Billy Joe. n.d. "Edmonson, James Howard (1925–1971)." *Encyclopedia of Oklahoma History and Culture.* Accessed August 16, 2024. www.okhistory.org/publications/enc/entry?entry=ED005.

Dean, Kyle. 2019. "Oklahoma Native Impact." Oklahoma Native Impact Study. Accessed October 5, 2024. www.oknativeimpact.com.

———. 2019. *The Economic Impact of Tribal Nations in Oklahoma.* doi:10.13140/RG.2.2.19733.27365.

Debo, Angie. 1989. *And Still the Waters Run.* University of Oklahoma Press.

———. 1976. *Geronimo: The Man, His Time, His Place.* University of Oklahoma Press.

Decker, Stefanie Lee. n.d. "Atkins, Hanna Diggs (1923–2010)." *Encyclopedia of Oklahoma History and Culture.* Accessed September 18, 2024. www.okhistory.org/publications /enc/entry?entry=AT002.

Denzin, Norman K. 1989. *Research Act: A Theoretical Introduction to Sociological Methods.* Prentice-Hall.

———. 2023. *The Sage Handbook of Qualitative Research.* 6th ed. Sage.

Desmond, Matthew. 2017. *Evicted: Poverty and Profit in the American City.* Crown.

Dincer, Ogushan, and Michael Johnston. n.d. Institute for Corruption Studies at Illinois State University. "Measuring Illegal and Legal Corruption in American States." Accessed July 31, 2025. https://greasethewheels.org/cpi.

Domhoff, William D., and Thomas R. Dye. 1987. *Power Elites and Organizations.* Sage.

Doti, Lynne Pierson. n.d. "Penn Square Bank." *Encyclopedia of Oklahoma History and Culture:* Accessed August 28, 2024. www.okhistory.org/publications/enc/entry ?entry=PE009.

Duncan, Cynthia M. 1999. *Worlds Apart: Poverty and Politics in Rural America.* Yale University Press.

Duren, Brad L. 2002. "'Klanspiracy' or Despotism? The Rise and Fall of Governor Jack Walton, Featuring W. D. McBee." *Chronicles of Oklahoma* 80 (4): 468–85. https:// gateway.okhistory.org/ark:/67531/metadc2016876.

Economic Research Service. n.d. "Food Insecurity in the U.S.: Measurement." Economic Research Unit, USDA. Accessed September 4, 2025. www.ers.usda.gov/topics /food-nutrition-assistance/food-security-in-the-us/measurement/#:~:text=Food%20 insecurity%20is%20the%20limited,foods%20in%20socially%20acceptable%20ways.

Ehrenreich, Barbara. 2001. *Nickel and Dimed: On (Not) Getting by in America.* Metropolitan Books.

Ellis, Carolyn, Tony E. Adams, and Arthur P. Bochner. 2011. "Autoethnography: An Overview." *Historical Social Research* 12 (1): 273–90.

Ellis, Randy. 2000. "Health Department Scandal: FBI Focuses on Bribery Affidavit Says Health Chief Used Money for Gambling." *Oklahoman,* May 4. www.oklahoman .com/story/news/2000/05/04/health-department-scandal-fbi-focuses-on-bribery -affidavit-says-health-chief-used-money-for-gambling/62199796007.

Ellis, Randy, and Nolan Clay. 2000. "2 Indicted in Health Agency Scandal Ex-official Nursing Home Owner Accused of Bribery." *Oklahoman,* May 18. www.oklahoman .com/story/news/2000/05/18/2-indicted-in-health-agency-scandal-ex-official-nursing -home-owner-accused-of-bribery/62197704007.

Ellis, Randy, and Griff Palmer. 2000. "Health Department Scandal: 'Ghosts' Got More Than Paychecks Expense Claims Exceed $50,000: All Agencies Must Check Payrolls." *Oklahoman,* June 24. www.oklahoman.com/story/news/2000/06/24/health -department-scandal-ghosts-paychecks-expense-claims-exceed-50000-agencies -must-check-payrolls/62192729007.

Elman, Richard M. 1966. *The Poorhouse State: The American Way of Life on Public Assistance.* Pantheon Books.

English, Paul. 1989. "Funeral Home Owner Vondel Smith Dies of Complications from Stroke." *Oklahoman,* July 26. www.oklahoman.com/story/news/1989/07/26/funeral-home-owner-vondel-smith-dies-of-complications-from-stroke/62606571007.

Erling, John. 2009. "Ron Norick, Mayor during the Oklahoma City Bombing." Interview transcript. Voices of Oklahoma, July 28. Accessed September 18, 2024. https://d1fi48u691x62i.cloudfront.net/wp-content/uploads/2013/10/Norick_Transcript.pdf.

Everett, Dianna. n.d. "Hennessey." *Encyclopedia of Oklahoma History and Culture.* Accessed October 5, 2024. www.okhistory.org/publications/enc/entry.php?entry=HE016.

Feaver, Douglas B. 1981. "Oklahoma Scandal." *Washinton Post,* October 22. www.washingtonpost.com/archive/politics/1981/10/22/oklahoma-scandal/d82ddfdd-aab6-47e3-b9dd-1e6139f38cd3.

Federal Bureau of Investigation. n.d. "Medgar Evers." Accessed August 14, 2024. www.fbi.gov/history/famous-cases/medgar-evers.

Federal Reserve Bank of St. Louis. n.d. "Oklahoma." *FRED.* Accessed September 13, 2024. https://fred.stlouisfed.org/release/tables?eid=341692&rid=416.

Felder, Ben. 2018. "State of Oklahoma: Schools Plagued by Low Funding as Student Needs Increase." *Oklahoman,* May 6. Accessed September 26, 2024. www.oklahoman.com/story/news/education/2018/05/06/state-of-oklahoma-schools-plagued-by-low-funding-as-student-needs-increase/60526413007.

Fife, Ari. 2022. "As Universal Free Lunch Program Ends, Obstacles Return for Some Families." Oklahoma Watch. September 7. Accessed September 13, 2024. https://oklahomawatch.org/2022/09/07/as-universal-free-lunch-program-ends-obstacles-return-for-some-families.

Floyd, Larry C. 2009. "Jake Hamon: The Man Who Made Harding President." *Chronicles of Oklahoma* 87 (3): 294–319. https://gateway.okhistory.org/ark:/67531/metadc2006487/m2/1/high_res_d/4_294_Floyd_Jake_Hamon_MSS.pdf.

Freeman, R. Edward, Jeffrey S. Harrison, Andrew C. Wicks, Bidan L. Parmar, and Simone de Colle. 2010. *Stakeholder Theory: The State of the Art.* Cambridge University Press.

Friends Committee on National Legislation. 2024. "Top 10 Hungriest States in the U.S." September 17. Accessed October 5, 2024. www.fcnl.org/updates/2023-11/top-10-hungriest-states-us.

Frontline. n.d. Interview with Robert Anthony. Accessed August 28, 2024. www.pbs.org/wgbh/pages/frontline/shows/fixers/interviews/anthony.html.

Gibson, Arrell M. 1965. *Oklahoma: A History of Five Centuries.* University of Oklahoma Press.

Godøy, Anna, and Jennie Romich. 2024. "Anna Godøy and Jennie Romich on the Impacts of Increasing the Minimum Wage for Working Parents and Child-Care Workers." Institute for Research on Poverty, University of Wisconsin–Madison. August 16. Accessed October 5, 2024. www.irp.wisc.edu/resource/anna-godoy-and-jennie-romich-on-the-impacts-of-increasing-the-minimum-wage-for-working-parents-and-child-care-workers.

Google. n.d. "Mayes County, Oklahoma." Google Data Centers. Accessed October 5, 2024. www.google.com/about/datacenters/locations/mayes-county.

Gouldner, Alvin. 1970. *The Coming Crisis of Western Sociology.* Basic Books.

Grann, David. 2017. *Killers of the Flower Moon: The Osage Murders and the Birth of the FBI.* Doubleday.

Greenberg, Jon. 2018. "Are Oklahoma Teachers the Lowest Paid? Nearly." *Politifact,* March 7. Accessed September 26, 2024. www.politifact.com/factchecks/2018/mar/07/good-jobs-first/are-oklahoma-teachers-lowest-paid-nearly.

Griffith, David. 2019. *Jones's Minimal.* Pennsylvania State University Press.

Gross, Samantha, and Constanze Stelzenmuller. 2024. "Europe's Messy Russian Gas Divorce." Brookings Institution. June 18. Accessed October 5, 2024. www.brookings.edu/articles/europes-messy-russian-gas-divorce.

Guthrie, Woody. 1983. *Bound for Glory: The Hard-Driving, Truth-Telling, Autobiography of America's Great Poet-Folk Singer.* Plume.

Harrington, Michael. 1997. *The Other America: Poverty in the United States.* Scribner.

Hassan, Carma. 2021. "A Total of 27 Graves Have Been Found So Far at 1921 Tulsa Massacre Search Site." *CNN,* June 8. www.cnn.com/2021/06/08/us/tulsa-race-massacre-coffins-found/index.html.

Healthy Minds Policy Initiative. n.d. "About Healthy Minds." Accessed September 13, 2024. www.healthymindspolicy.org/about.

———. 2024. "Programs of Assertive Community Treatment: Oklahoma's Unmet Needs and Opportunities to Expand Intensive Services." January 31. Accessed September 13, 2024. www.healthymindspolicy.org/research/pact-programs-of-assertive-community-treatment-oklahoma.

Hightower, Michael J. 2021. *At War with Corruption: A Biography of Bill Price, U.S. Attorney for the Western District of Oklahoma.* 2 Cities Press.

———. 2018. *1889: The Boomer Movement, the Land Run, and Early Oklahoma City.* University of Oklahoma Press.

Hill, Karlos K. 2021. *The 1921 Tulsa Race Massacre: A Photographic History.* University of Oklahoma Press.

Hogan, Gypsy. 1982. "Salesman Indicted in Kickback Probe." *Oklahoman,* April 9. www.oklahoman.com/story/news/1982/04/09/salesman-indicted-in-kickback-probe/62888472007.

———. 1992. "Key Figure in Penn Square Collapse Keeps Long Silence." *Oklahoman,* July 12. Accessed August 6, 2025. www.oklahoman.com/story/news/1992/07/12/key-figure-in-penn-square-collapse-keeps-long-silence/62487967007.

Holloway, Harry. n.d. "Political Scandals." *Encyclopedia of Oklahoma History and Culture.* Accessed August 16, 2024. www.okhistory.org/publications/enc/entry?entry=SC001.

Holloway, Harry, and Frank S. Meyers. 1993. *Bad Times for Good Ol' Boys: The Oklahoma County Commissioner Scandal.* University of Oklahoma Press.

Homeless Alliance. n.d. "Together, We Can End Homelessness." Accessed September 19, 2024. www.homelessalliance.org.

Hurt, Kelly. 2000. "Scandal Brings State Agency under Scrutiny." *Oklahoman,* July 9.

ILR Yang-Tan Institute on Employment and Disability. n.d. "Disability Statistics." Accessed September 26, 2024. www.ilr.cornell.edu/yti/work/disability-statistics.

Institute for Research on Poverty. 2017. "Childhood Obesity." *Fast Focus* (University of Wisconsin-Madison: Institute for Research on Poverty) (28): 1–2. Accessed October 5, 2024. www.irp.wisc.edu/wp/wp-content/uploads/2018/05/FF28-2017.pdf.

———. n.d. "Research." Accessed August 14, 2024. www.irp.wisc.edu/research.

———. n.d. "What Are Good Sources of Information on Basic Trends in Poverty and Related Issues?" Accessed September 4, 2024. www.irp.wisc.edu/resources/what-are-good-sources-of-information-on-basic-trends-in-poverty-and-related-issues.

Institute of Education Statistics. 2022. "The Nation's Report Card: 2022 Mathematics State Snapshot Report: Oklahoma, Grade 4, Public Schools." Oklahoma State Department of Education. Accessed September 26, 2024. https://sde.ok.gov/sites/default/files/2022%20Grade%204%20and%208%20Math%20%26%20Reading%20Results.pdf.

Jacobs, Ron. 2024. "William H. 'Alfalfa Bill' Murray, Part 2." *Marietta Monitor,* July 15. Accessed August 2, 2025. www.mariettamonitor.com/society/william-h-alfalfa-bill-murray-part-2/article_479c6f2e-3fc6-11ef-a2fb-e3f2f75875f2.html.

Jones, Jeffrey M. 2019. "Conservatives Greatly Outnumber Liberals in 19 U.S. States." *Gallup*, February 22. Accessed August 14, 2024. https://news.gallup.com/poll/247016/conservatives-greatly-outnumber-liberals-states.aspx.

Journal Record Staff. 2022. "OCCF President, Longtime OKC Advocate Anthony Plans Retirement." *Journal Record,* February 2. Accessed September 18, 2024. https://journalrecord.com/2022/02/occf-president-longtime-okc-advocate-anthony-plans-retirement.

Kelley, N.J. 2019. *America's Inequality Trap.* University of Chicago Press.

KFOR-TV and K. Querry. 2016. "Gov. Fallin Transfers $1.4 Million to Corporation Commission, OGS to Understand Earthquakes." *Oklahoma News Channel 4,* January 28. https://kfor.com/news/gov-fallin-transfers-1-4-million-to-corporation-commission-ogs-to-understand-earthquakes.

Killackey, Jim. 2000. "Health Department Scandal: Watchdog Sees Risk to Patients 40 Centers Require Immediate Attention, DHS Official Says." *Oklahoman,* May 9. Accessed June 2, 2025. www.oklahoman.com/story/news/2000/05/09/health-department-scandal-watchdog-risk-patients-centers-require-immediate-attention-official-says/62199053007.

Kim, Jaeseung, and Julia R. Henly. 2021. "Social Support Can Mitigate Material Hardship for Families Facing Unstable Child Care Subsidy Use." *Journal of Family Issues* 42 (2): 368–90. doi:https://doi.org/10.1177/0192513X20930410.

Knight, Louise W. 2005. *Citizen: Jane Addams and the Struggle for Democracy.* University of Chicago Press.

Korth, Robby, and Nathan Poppe. 2024. "Oklahoma City's Homeless Alliance Director Reflects on 20 Years at Nonprofit." *KOSU,* April 2. Accessed September 19, 2024. www.kosu.org/news/2024-04-02/oklahoma-citys-homeless-alliance-director-reflects-on-20-years-at-nonprofit.

Krehbiel, Randy. 2020. "1980s County Commissioners Scandal Lives on in Oklahoma's Tight Control on Counties, and Tulsa County Lobbyist Urges Loosening the Grip." *Tulsa World*, September 8. https://tulsaworld.com/news/state-and-regional/govt-and-politics/1980s-county-commissioners-scandal-lives-on-in-oklahomas-tight-control-on-counties-and-tulsa-county/article_8506208c-f1e9-11ea-8244-4351a45e7c81.html.

———. 2024. "Third Gunshot Victim Exhumed in Search for Race Massacre Graves, Researchers Announce." *Tulsa World*, August 3. https://tulsaworld.com/news/local/racemassacre/third-gunshot-victim-exhumed-in-search-for-race-massacre-graves-researchers-announce/article_291286c2-5116-11ef-9d88-631af334a240.html.

Kristen. 2014. "Oklahoma Ranked 11th Most Corrupt State in the Country." *Fox News Channel 25*, July 3. Accessed August 6, 2025. https://okcfox.com/archive/oklahoma-ranked-11th-most-corrupt-state-in-the-country.

Lackmeyer, Steve. 2023. "Meet the Oklahoma Flapper Who Wowed Crowds with 18 Instruments—while Escaping a Notorious Past." *Oklahoman*, July 16. Accessed July 31, 2025. www.oklahoman.com/story/news/2023/07/16/oklahoma-flapper-loma-worth-olive-belle-hamon-history-scandal/65935080o1.

Linenthal, Edward Tabor. n.d. "Oklahoma City Bombing." *Encyclopedia of Oklahoma History and Culture*. Accessed September 19, 2024. www.okhistory.org/publications/enc/entry?entry=OK026.

Linn, James Weber. *Jane Addams: A Biography*. 2000. University of Illinois Press.

Lipka, Michael, and Benjamin Wormald. 2016. "How Religious Is Your State?" Pew Research Center, February 29. Accessed August 14, 2024. www.pewresearch.org/short-reads/2016/02/29/how-religious-is-your-state/?state=alabama.

Longo, Michele, Federica Zatterale, Jamal Naderi, Luca Parrillo, Pietro Formisano, Gregory Alexander Raciti, Francesco Beguinot, and Claudia Miele. 2019. "Adipose Tissue Dysfunction as Determinant of Obesity-Associated Metabolic Complications." *International Journal of Molecular Sciences* 20 (9): 2358–81. doi:https://doi.org/10.3390/ijms20092358.

Los Angeles Times Archives. 2001. "McVeigh Labels Young Victims 'Collateral Damage.'" *Los Angeles Times*, March 29. Accessed September 19, 2024. www.latimes.com/archives/la-xpm-2001-mar-29-mn-44250-story.html.

Lowell Milken Center for Unsung Heroes. n.d. "Meet the Hero: Clara Luper." Accessed September 19, 2024. www.lowellmilkencenter.org/programs/projects/view/clara-luper-a-leader-in-desegregations-sit-in-movement/hero.

Lyson, Thomas A., and William W. Falk. 1993. *Forgotten Places: Uneven Development in Rural America*. University Press of Kansas.

Madigan, Tim. 2013. *The Burning: The Tulsa Race Massacre of 1921*. Thomas Dunne Books.

Maril, Robert Lee. 1995. *The Bay Shrimpers of Texas: Rural Fishermen in a Global Economy*. University of Kansas Press.

———. 2011. *The Fence: National Security, Public Safety, and Illegal Immigration along the U.S.-Mexico Border*. Texas Tech University Press.

———. 1992. “The Impact of Mandatory Car Insurance upon Low Income Drivers.” National Association of Independent Insurers, Unpublished.

———. 2001. “The Impact of Utility Rate Increases on Poor Oklahomans.” Oklahoma Corporation Commission.

———. 1986. “Methodological Approaches to the Study of American Commerical Fishermen.” *Proceeding of the Workshop on Fisheries Sociology.* Edited by Conner Bailey, Craig Harris, Clayton Heaton, and Rosamund Ladner. Woods Hole Oceanographic Institution.

———. 2004. “Methodological Considerations in the Study of the United States Border Patrol.” Annual Meeting of the Society for Applied Anthropology, Dallas, TX.

———. 1996. “Oklahoma in Poverty: A Telephone Survey of Poor Oklahomans.” Government report, Oklahoma Department of Commerce.

———. 1998. “Opinions and Attitudes of Social Service Providers: A Phone Survey.” Government report. Oklahoma Department of Commerce.

———. 1989. *Poorest of Americans: The Mexican Americans of the Lower Rio Grande Valley of Texas.* University of Notre Dame Press.

———. 1999. “Poverty in Oklahoma.” Government report. Oklahoma Department of Commerce.

———. 1995. “Poverty in Oklahoma: Survey of Poor Oklahomans.” Government report. Oklahoma Department of Commerce.

———. 2014. “Teaching Domestic Terrorism in the Classroom.” *Times Higher Education,* June 14.

———. 1983. *Texas Shrimpers: Community, Capitalism, and the Sea.* Texas A&M University Press.

———. 1990. “Through a Shrimper’s Eye: A Knowledge of Place in Coastal Texas.” Biannual Meeting of the Coastal Society, San Antonio, TX.

———2000. *Waltzing with the Ghost of Tom Joad: Poverty, Myth, and Low-Wage Labor in Oklahoma.* University of Oklahoma Press.

Maril, Robert Lee, and Anas Asaad. 2016. “Mismanagement of Federal Contracts and Employees in the Department of Homeland Security.” Annual Meeting of the Society for Applied Anthropology, Vancouver, BC.

Maril, Robert Lee, and Timothy Bisping. 1996. “Four Decades of Poverty in Oklahoma.” Government report. Oklahoma Department of Commerce.

Maril, Robert Lee, and A. N. Zavaleta. 1979. “Drinking Patters of Low-Income Mexican American Women.” *Journal of Studies on Alcohol* 40 (5): 480–84.

Mayo Clinic. n.d. “Type 1 Diabetes in Children.” Accessed October 5, 2024. www.mayoclinic.org/diseases-conditions/type-1-diabetes-in-children/symptoms-causes/syc-20355306.

McKee, Kara Joy. 2017. “8 Facts about Human Services Funding in Oklahoma.” *TogetherOK,* January 31. Accessed September 13, 2024. https://togetherok.okpolicy.org/8-facts-human-services-funding-oklahoma-betterok-budget-bootcamp.

McLean, R. David. 2023. *The Case for Shareholder Capitalism: How the Pursuit of Profit Benefits All.* Cato Institute.

Mead, Daniel W., and John B. Hawley. 1930. "Map of the North Canadian River through Oklahoma City Showing Overflow by the FLood of October 1929 and Proposed Floodway and Levees." Map from Consulting Engineers, Oklahoma Department of Transportation, U.S. Geological Survey. Accessed September 18, 2024. https://webapps.usgs.gov/dbflood/ODOTdatabase/NewsClips/Oklahoma40109-NewsClip.pdf.

Military Bases.US. n.d. "Fort Sill." Accessed August 16, 2024. www.militarybases.us/army/fort-sill/#:~:text=Fort%20Sill%20is%20a%20United%20States%20Army%20post,Marin%20Corps%E2%80%99%20site%20for%20Field%20artillery%20MOS%20school.

Mills, C. Wright. 1956. *The Power Elite.* Oxford University Press.

Mitchell, Jerry. 2021. *Race against Time: A Reporter Reopens the Unsolved Murder Cases of the Civil Rights Era.* Simon and Schuster.

Monies, Paul. 2023. "Nearly 300,000 Are Poised to Lose SoonerCare Following COVID Pandemic." *Oklahoman*, November 6. Accessed September 26, 2024. www.oklahoman.com/story/news/2023/11/08/soonercare-oklahoma-ending-thousands-covid-medicaid-medicare-protections/71493653007.

National Academies of Sciences, Engineering, and Medicine. 2024. *Reducing Intergenerational Poverty.* National Academies Press. https://doi.org/10.17226/27058.

National Archives. n.d. "Servicemen's Readjustment Act (1944)." Accessed September 4, 2024. www.archives.gov/milestone-documents/servicemens-readjustment-act.

National Assessment of Educational Progress. n.d. NAEP Data Explorer (website portal): Oklahoma. Accessed October 5, 2024. www.nationsreportcard.gov/ndecore/landing.

National Center for Education Statistics. n.d. "Digest of Education Statistics, Table 204.10." Accessed September 13, 2024. https://nces.ed.gov/programs/digest/d18/tables/dt18_204.10.asp.

National Center for Homeless Education. 2015. "Determining Eligibility for Rights and Services under the McKinney-Vento Act." SERVE, March. www.brunswick.k12.me.us/wp-content/uploads/2014/09/NCHE-Determing-Eligibility-of-McKinney-Vento.pdf.

National Governors Association. n.d. "Governor David Hall." Accessed August 16, 2024. www.nga.org/governor/david-hall-2.

National Indian Gaming Commission. n.d. "Frequently Asked Questions." Accessed September 26, 2024. www.nigc.gov/commission/faqs-detail/what-is-the-difference-between-class-ii-and-class-iii-gaming.

National Initiative for Children's Healthcare Quality. n.d. "Oklahoma State Fact Sheet." http://childhealthdata.org.

National Institute on Minority Health and Health Disparities. n.d. *Oklahoma Poverty—Table.* U.S. Department of Health and Human Services. Accessed September 26, 2024. https://hdpulse.nimhd.nih.gov/data-portal/social/table?socialtopic=080&socialtopic_options=social_6&demo=00007&demo_options=poverty_3&race=00&race_options

=race_7&sex=0&sex_options=sexboth_1&age=001&age_options=ageall_1&statefips =40&statefips_options=area.

Nelson, Mary Jo. 1991. "United to City: No Thanks Indianapolis Wins Aircraft Center: Norick 'Very Proud' of Proposal." *Oklahoman*, October 24. Accessed September 19, 2024. https://www.oklahoman.com/story/news/1991/10/24/united-to-city-no-thanks -indianapolis-wins-aircraft-center-norick-very-proud-of-proposal/62513085007.

News on 6. 2002. "VanMeter, Jiles Indicted by Federal Grand Jury." *News on 6, Tulsa, OK.* February 21. www.newson6.com/story/5e3680512f69d76f620944e2/vanmeter -jiles-indicted-by-federal-grand-jury.

New York Times. 1920. "Says Jake Hamon Told Woman to Flee: Clara Smith's Attorneys Assert She First Heard of Death at El Paso." *New York Times*, December 25. www .nytimes.com/1920/12/25/archives/says-jake-hamon-told-woman-to-flee-clara-smiths -attorneys-assert.html.

O'Dell, Larry. n.d. "All-Black Towns." *Encyclopedia of Oklahoma History and Culture.* Accessed October 5, 2024. www.okhistory.org/publications/enc/entry.php?entry=AL009.

———. n.d. "Walton, John Calloway (1881–1949)." *Encyclopedia of Oklahoma History and Culture.* Accessed August 16, 2024. www.okhistory.org/publications/enc/entry ?entry=WA014.

Oklahoma City Community Foundation. n.d. "About." Accessed September 18, 2024. https://occf.org/about.

———. n.d. "Our Donors." Accessed September 18, 024. https://occf.org/donors.

Oklahoma City Government Archives and Records. n.d. "John C. Walton." Accessed August 16, 2024. www.okc.gov/government/archives-records/oklahoma-city-history /previous-mayors/john-c-walton.

Oklahoma City Government. n.d. *MAPS 3*. Accessed September 19, 2024. www.okc.gov /government/maps-3/maps-history.

———. n.d. *MAPS 4*. Accessed September 19, 2024. www.okc.gov/government/maps-4.

Oklahoma City National Memorial Museum. n.d. "A Safe Place for History." Accessed September 19, 2024. https://memorialmuseum.com/experience/collections-and -archives.

———. n.d. "Looking Back. Thinking Forward." Accessed August 14, 2024. https:// memorialmuseum.com/experience.

Oklahoma Commission to Study the Race Riot of 1921. 2001. *Tulsa Race Riot.* Government Commission study. CreateSpace Independent Publishing Platform.

Oklahoma Corporation Commission. n.d. "About the Oklahoma Corporation Commission." Accessed August 28, 2024. https://oklahoma.gov/occ/about.html.

Oklahoma Department of Commerce. n.d. "Oklahoma Main Street." Accessed October 5, 2024. www.okcommerce.gov/oklahoma-main-street.

———. n.d. "Oklahoma Top Employers by # of Employees." Accessed September 26, 2024. www.okcommerce.gov/wp-content/uploads/Oklahoma-Largest-Employers-List.pdf.

Oklahoma Department of Human Services. n.d. "Oklahoma Pinnacle Plan Home." Accessed September 26, 2024. https://oklahoma.gov/okdhs/services/child-welfare-services/the-oklahoma-pinnacle-plan/pinnacle-plan-home.html.

———. n.d. "Welcome! How Can We Help?" Accessed September 4, 2024. https://oklahoma.gov/okdhs.html.

Oklahoma Department of Mental Health and Substance Abuse Services. n.d. "Reports." Accessed September 26, 2024. https://oklahoma.gov/odmhsas/research/reports.html.

Oklahoma Department of Transportation. n.d. "Oklahoma Capitol Complex Maps." Accessed August 14, 2024. www.odot.org/cmplxmap.

Oklahoma Education Association. n.d. "About OEA." Accessed September 26, 2024. https://okea.org/about-oea.

———. n.d. "Latest Rankings Help Explain Teacher Shortage." Accessed September 26, 2024. https://okea.org/latest-rankings-help-explain-teacher-shortage.

Oklahoma Geological Survey. n.d. "Oil and Gas." University of Oklahoma. Accessed August 28, 2024. www.ou.edu/ogs/research/energy/oil-gas.

Oklahoma Hall of Fame. 2021. "The Life of Clara Luper: A Pioneer of the American Civil Rights Movement." Gaylord-Pickens Museum exhibit. August 7. Accessed September 19, 2024. www.oklahomahof.com/museum/exhibit/the-life-of-clara-luper-a-pioneer-of-the-american-civil-rights-movement.

Oklahoma Historical Society. n.d. "African Americans in Oklahoma before 1954." Accessed September 18, 2024. www.okhistory.org/learn/african-americans9.

———. n.d. "Latino History in Oklahoma." Accessed September 26, 2024. www.okhistory.org/learn/latino6.

Oklahoma Medical Marijuana Authority. 2023. "FY 2023 Annual Report." https://oklahoma.gov/content/dam/ok/en/omma/content/publications/annual-report/fy-2023/OMMA%20Annual%20Report%20FY%202023.pdf.

Oklahoma Office of State Finance Gaming Compliance Unit. n.d. "Frequently Asked Questions." Accessed September 26, 2024. www.ok.gov/OGC/Frequently_Asked_Questions.

Oklahoma Rehabilitation Services. n.d. "Oklahoma Disability Statistics." Accessed September 26, 2024. https://oklahoma.gov/okdrs/information/about-us/ok-statistics.html.

Oklahoma State Department of Education. n.d. "Child Nutrition." Accessed September 13, 2024. https://oklahoma.gov/education/services/child-nutrition.html.

———. n.d. "Comprehensive Teacher Pay Reform." Accessed September 26, 2024. https://oklahoma.gov/education/services/teacher-leadership-development/comprehensive-teacher-pay-reform.html.

Oklahoma State Department of Health. n.d. "COVID-19 Data." Accessed September 26, 2024. https://oklahoma.gov/health/health-education/acute-disease-service/viral-view/covid-19.html.

Oklahoma State University Extension. n.d. "County Agricultural Land Value Changes." Accessed October 5, 2024. https://extension.okstate.edu/programs/farm-management-and-finance/oklahoma-land-values/county-agricultural-land-value-change.

———. n.d. "Health and Hunger." Accessed October 5, 2024. https://extension.okstate.edu/programs/family-and-consumer-sciences/health-and-hunger.

Oklahoman. 2003. "Civic Leader Bill Jennings Dies." *Oklahoman*, January 3. www.oklahoman.com/story/news/2003/01/03/civic-leader-bill-jennings-dies/62064683007/.

———. 2002. "Opposing Jack Walton." *Oklahoman*, May 17. www.oklahoman.com/story/news/2002/05/17/opposing-jack-walton/62094708007.

———. 2025. "Take the Oklahoman Survey: Is the Oklahoma Standard Still Alive and Well?" *Oklahoman*, April 8. https://www.oklahoman.com/story/opinion/columns/your-voice/2025/04/08/30-years-after-the-tragic-okc-bombing-what-have-we-learned-federal-building-oklahoma-standard/82888035007.

———. 1984. "Toll 230 as Book Closes on County Commissioner Scandal." *Oklahoman*, February 3. www.oklahoman.com/story/news/1984/02/03/toll-230-as-book-closes-on-county-commissioner-scandal/62815077007.

Oklahomans for Anthony. n.d. "FBI Presents Bob Anthony with Bureau's Highest Civilian Honor." Bob Anthony. Accessed August 28, 2024. www.bobanthony.com/bob/awards.htm.

Olivas, Kaylee. 2023. "Marlow Public Schools Send Text Threatening to Parents over Unpaid Lunch Debt." *Oklahoma's News 4*, July 13. Accessed September 18, 2024. https://kfor.com/news/local/marlow-public-schools-sends-text-threatening-to-not-place-elementary-students-who-have-unpaid-lunch-debt-in-class.

Oliver, Melvin, and Thomas M. Shapiro. 2006. *Black Wealth/White Wealth: A New Perspective on Racial Inequality.* Routledge.

Parrish, Mary E. Jones. 2021. *The Nation Must Awake: My Witness to the Tulsa Race Massacre of 1921.* Trinity University Press.

Peachman, Rachel Rabkin. 2022. "Meet America's Best Employers by State 2024. August 20. Accessed July 31, 2025. www.forbes.com/sites/rachelpeachman/2024/08/20/meet-americas-best-employers-by-state-2024/?ctpv=searchpage.

Perry, Gene. 2014. "In the Know: Court Monitors Find Oklahoma Has Not Made 'Good Faith Effort' to Fix Child Welfare." OKPolicy. October 20. Accessed September 26, 2024. https://okpolicy.org/know-court-monitors-find-oklahoma-made-good-faith-effort-fix-child-welfare.

Peterson-Veatch, Ross. n.d. "Kerr-McGee Corporation." *Encyclopedia of Oklahoma History and Culture.* Accessed August 28, 2024. www.okhistory.org/publications/enc/entry?entry=KE010.

Piketty, T. 2020. *Capital and Ideology.* Harvard University Press.

Polansky, Chris. 2022. "A New Study Finds Oklahoma Has One of the Highest Rates of Vaccine-Preventable COVID Deaths in the Country." *Public Radio Tulsa*, May 17.

Accessed September 26, 2024. www.publicradiotulsa.org/local-regional/2022-05-17/a-new-study-finds-oklahoma-has-one-of-the-highest-rates-of-vaccine-preventable-covid-deaths-in-the-country.

———. 2022. "Stitt, Walters Slam 'Liberal Teachers' Unions' in Executive Order." *Public Radio Tulsa,* August 22. Accessed September 26, 2024. www.publicradiotulsa.org/local-regional/2022-08-22/stitt-walters-slam-liberal-teachers-unions-in-executive-order.

Radley, David C., Jesse C. Baumgartner, and Sara R. Collins. 2022. "2022 Scorecard on State Health System Performance." Commonwealth Fund. June 16. Accessed September 26, 2024. www.commonwealthfund.org/publications/scorecard/2022/jun/2022-scorecard-state-health-system-performance.

Rawick, George. 1973. *From Sundown to Sunup: The Making of the Black Community.* Praeger.

Regional Food Bank of Oklahoma. n.d. "Our History." Accessed September 18, 2024. www.regionalfoodbank.org/about-us/history.

Reich, R. B. 2020. *The System: Who Rigged It, How We Can Fix It.* Alfred A. Knopf.

Renn, Aaron M. 2015. "Doing OK in OKC." *City Journal,* Autumn. Accessed September 19, 2024. www.city-journal.org/article/doing-ok-in-okc.

Romich, Jennifer, and Heather D. Hill. 2017. "Boosting the Poverty-Fighting Effects of the Minimum Wage." *Focus* 33 (3): 23–25. Accessed October 5, 2024. www.irp.wisc.edu/resource/boosting-the-poverty-fighting-effects-of-the-minimum-wage.

Rose, Arnold M. 1967. *The Power Structure: Political Process in American Society.* Oxford University Press.

Saadi, Yasmeen. 2023. "Homeless Youth Walk a Hidden Path in Rural Oklahoma." *Oklahoma Watch,* August 3. Accessed September 13, 2024. https://oklahomawatch.org/2023/08/03/homeless-youth-walk-a-hidden-path-in-rural-oklahoma.

Salvation Army International. n.d. "The Salvation Army." Accessed September 13, 2024. www.salvationarmy.org.

Sanchez, Ray. 2018. "Oklahoma Governor Compares Teachers to 'A Teenage Kid That Wants a Better Car.'" *CNN,* April 4. Accessed September 26, 2024. www.cnn.com/2018/04/04/us/oklahoma-governor-mary-fallin-teacher-comment/index.html.

Saunt, Claudio. 2020. *Unworthy Republic: The Dispossession of Native Americans and the Road to Indian Territory.* W. W. Norton.

Schneider, Keith. 2023. "Rash of Suicides in Oklahoma Shows That the Crisis on the Farms Goes On." *New York Times,* March 15. Accessed October 5, 2024. www.nytimes.com/2023/03/15/us/oklahoma-farm-suicides.html.

Schweitzer, Julie, Tamara L. Mix, and Jimmy J. Esquibel. 2024. "Negotiating Dignity and Social Justice in Community Food Access Spaces." *Safer Communities* 23 (2): 171–86. Accessed October 5, 2024. https://doi.org/10.1108/SC-08-2023-0036.

Selcraig, Bruce. 1999. "The Worst Newspaper in America." *Columbia Journalism Review* 37 (5): 46–51.

Shamsuddin, Shomon, and Colin Campbell. 2022. "Housing Cost Burden, Material Hardship, and Well-Being." *Housing Policy Debate* 32 (3): 413–32. Accessed October 5, 2024. https://doi.org/10.1080/10511482.2021.1882532.

Shelton, Curtis. 2023. "Oklahoma Teacher Salaries Have Risen Dramatically." Oklahoma Council of Public Affairs. November 10. Accessed September 26, 2024. https://ocpathink.org/post/analysis/oklahoma-teacher-salaries-have-risen-dramatically.

Shields, Patricia M, Maurice Hamington, and Joseph Soeters. 2022. *The Oxford Handbook of Jane Addams.* Oxford University Press.

Shrider, Emily A., Melissa Kollar, Frances Chen, and Jessica Semega. 2021. "Income and Poverty in the United States: 2020." U.S. Census Bureau, September. Accessed September 26, 2024. www.census.gov/data/tables/2021/demo/income-poverty/p60-273.html.

Shyers, Treba. 2019. "Senior Hunger." Hunger Free Oklahoma. May 14. Accessed September 26, 2024. www.hungerfreeok.org/senior-hunger.

Simmons-Duffin, Selena, and Koko Nakajima. 2022. "This Is How Many Lives Could Have Been Saved with COVID Vaccinations in Each State." *NPR*, May 13. Accessed September 26, 2024. www.npr.org/sections/health-shots/2022/05/13/1098071284/this-is-how-many-lives-could-have-been-saved-with-covid-vaccinations-in-each-sta.

Singer, Mark. 1985. *Funny Money.* Knopf.

Sisters of Mercy. n.d. "Our History." Accessed May 23, 2025. https://sistersofmercy.org/about-us/our-history-mercy-heritage-center.

Smeeding, Timothy, Maria Cancian, John Karl Scholz, Barbara Wolfe, Robert Haveman, Jennifer Noyes, Katherine Magnuson, et al. 2011. "American Poverty and Inequality: Key Trends and Future Research Directions." *Fast Focus* (University of Wisconsin-Madison: Institute for Research on Poverty) (12): 1–8. Accessed October 5, 2024. www.irp.wisc.edu/wp/wp-content/uploads/2018/05/FF12-2011.pdf.

Smith, George. 1987. "1923 Flood Also Inundated City." *Oklahoman,* May 31. www.oklahoman.com/story/news/1987/05/31/1923-flood-also-inundated-city/62688326007.

Snow, Mark, and Charles Anderson. 1993. *Down on Their Luck: A Study of Homeless Street People in New York City.* Continuum.

Social Security Administration. n.d. "Understanding Supplemental Security Income (SSI) Overview." Accessed September 4, 2024. www.ssa.gov/ssi/text-over-ussi.htm.

Spartz, James T., and Judith Siers-Poisson. 2021. "Classroom Supplement for Preventing Child Maltreatment and Neglect in the United States: Opportunities for Change." Focus on Poverty Classroom Supplement (University of Wisconsin-Madison: Institute for Research on Poverty) 37 (2). Accessed October 5, 2024. www.irp.wisc.edu/wp/wp-content/uploads/2021/09/Focus-on-Poverty-Classroom-Supplement-37-2.pdf.

Steinbeck, John. 1989. *The Grapes of Wrath.* Viking Press Reprint.

Stitt, J. Kevin, Rachel C. Holt, and Laura B. Broyles. n.d. *2021 Three-Year Plan.* Office of Juvenile Justice and Delinquency Prevention Program, U.S. Department of Justice, Oklahoma Office of Juvenile Affairs. Accessed September 13, 2024. https://oklahoma

.gov/content/dam/ok/en/oja/documents/sag-state-advisory-group/oklahoma-state-plan-information/2022%20Updates%20to%20OK%20Three%20Yr%20Prev%20Plan%20Narrative.pdf.

Stull, Donald D., Michael J. Broadway, and David Craig Griffith. 1995. *Any Way You Cut It: Meat Processing and Small-Town America.* University Press of Kansas.

Swanson, Krista. 2023. *Agriculture and the Economy: An Assessment of Our Current Situation versus the 1980s.* March 31. Accessed July 31, 2025. https://ncga.com/stay-informed/media/editorials/article/2023/03/agriculture-and-the-economy-an-assessment-of-our-current-situation-versus-the-1980s.

This and That Newsletter. 2022. "A Glimpse into the Past: Jake Lewis Hamon." *OklahomaHistory.net*, January 27. Accessed August 16, 2024. https://oklahomahistory.net/newsletters/TT1305.htm.

Thomas, Kilee. 2024. "Oklahoma Loses Federal Programs to Feed Many Hungry Kids during Summer Break." *KOCONews5*, July 31. Accessed September 13, 2024. www.koco.com/article/oklahoma-loses-summer-ebt-program-summer-break-feeding-sites/60779532.

Thompson, John. 1986. *Closing the Frontier.* University of Oklahoma Press.

Toobin, Jeffrey. 2023. *Homegrown: Timothy McVeigh and the Rise of Right-Wing Extremism.* Simon and Schuster.

Transparent Oklahoma Performance. n.d. "Performance-Informed Budgeting." Accessed September 26, 2024. https://oklahoma.gov/top.html.

Tulsa Community Foundation. n.d. "What We Do." Accessed September 18, 2024. https://tulsacf.org/whatwedo.

Tulsa World. 1992. "Knowing the Territory Paid Off for McCarty." September 28. https://tulsaworld.com/archives/knowing-the-territory-paid-off-for-mccarty/article_5c7845cb-082f-5120-bac4-782b65ae1e2e.html.

Ulsperger, Jason S. 2003. "Greed, Ghosts, and Grand Juries: The Formation of Nursing Home Law and Oklahoma's Health Department Scandal." *Free Inquiry in Creative Sociology* 31 (2): 113–24.

Uncrowned Community Builders. n.d. "Clara Mae Shepard Luper." Accessed September 19, 2024. https://uncrownedcommunitybuilders.com/person/clara-mae-shepard-luper.

United Press International. 1981. "Former Oklahoma House Speaker J. D. McCarty Dead." January 1. www.upi.com/Archives/1981/01/01/Former-Oklahoma-House-Speaker-JD-McCarty-dead/8540347173200.

UnitedHealth Group. n.d. "United Health Foundation." Accessed September 26, 2024. www.unitedhealthgroup.com/uhg/people-and-culture/our-foundations.html.

University of Oklahoma Health. n.d. "Dr. Dale Bratzler." Accessed September 26, 2024. www.ouhealth.com/find-a-doctor/dale-bratzler-do-mph-macoi-fidsa.

U.S. Air Force. n.d. "Tinker Air Force Base: FY 23 Economic Impact Statement." Accessed August 16, 2024. www.tinker.af.mil/Portals/106/Documents/Economic%20Impact

/Tinker%20Economic%20Impact%20Statement%20FY%2023%20Final.pdf?ver=fNEf_3_NBrkrxSM05VGP1Q%3d%3d.

U.S. Bureau of Labor Statistics. n.d. “Economy at a Glance: Oklahoma.” Accessed September 26, 2024. www.bls.gov/eag/eag.ok.htm.

U.S. Census Bureau. n.d. “About Poverty in the U.S. Population”. Accessed September 4, 2024. www.census.gov/topics/income-poverty/poverty/about.html.

———. n.d. “American Community Survey (ACS).” https://www.census.gov/programs-surveys/sapie/guidance/model-input-data/cpsasec.html.

———. n.d. “2021 ACS 1-Year Estimates.” Accessed September 26, 2024. www.census.gov/programs-surveys/acs/technical-documentation/table-and-geography-changes/2021/1-year.html.

———. n.d. “How the Census Bureau Measures Poverty.” Accessed September 26, 2024. https://www.census.gov/topics/incomepoverty/poverty/guidance/poverty-measures.html.

———. n.d. *Langston town, Oklahoma.* Accessed October 5, 2024. https://data.census.gov/profile/Langston_town_Oklahoma?g=160XX00US4041550.

———. 2022. “Poverty in States and Metropolitan Areas: 2022.” Accessed September 26, 2024. www.census.gov/library/publications/2023/acs/acsbr-016.html.

———. n.d. *Quick Facts: Pawnee County, Oklahoma.* Accessed October 5, 2024. www.census.gov/quickfacts/pawneecountyoklahoma.

———. 1992. “Race and Hispanic Origin: 1990.” Table 3 in *General Population Characteristics: Mississippi.* U.S. Department of Commerce, Economics and Statistics Administration. Accessed October 5, 2024. www2.census.gov/library/publications/decennial/1990/cp-1/cp-1-26.pdf.

———. 2020. “Race, Panola County.” Accessed October 5, 2024. https://data.census.gov/table/DECENNIALDHC2020.P8?g=050XX00US28107.

U.S. Centers for Disease Control and Prevention. 2011. “Body Mass Index: Considerations for Practitioners.” Accessed September 4, 2024. https://stacks.cdc.gov/view/cdc/25368.

———. n.d. “How Overweight and Obesity Impacts Your Health.” Accessed October 5, 2024. www.cdc.gov/healthy-weight-growth/food-activity/overweight-obesity-impacts-health.html.

———. n.d. “Type 2 Diabetes.” Accessed October 5. 2024. www.cdc.gov/diabetes/about/about-type-2-diabetes.html.

U.S. Department of Health and Human Services. 2002. “Making a Difference in the Lives of Infants and Toddlers and Their Families: The Impacts of Early Head Start.” Executive Summary. June 15. Accessed July 31, 2025. https://acf.gov/opre/report/making-difference-lives-infants-and-toddlers-and-their-families-impacts-early-head.

U.S. Department of Housing and Urban Development. 2022. “The 2022 Annual Homelessness Assessment Report (AHAR) to Congress.” Accessed September 13, 2024. www.huduser.gov/portal/sites/default/files/pdf/2022-AHAR-Part-1.pdf.

———. n.d. “About HUD.” Accessed October 5, 2024. www.hud.gov/about.

———. n.d. "Continuum of Care Program FAQs". Accessed September 13, 2024. www.hud.gov/program_offices/comm_planning/coc/faqs.

U.S. Department of Labor. n.d. "State Minimum Wage Laws: Oklahoma." Accessed October 5, 2024. www.dol.gov/agencies/whd/minimum-wage/state.

U.S. Department of Veterans Affairs. 2017. "Special Reports: State Summaries, Oklahoma." National Center for Veterans Analysis and Statistics. Accessed September 26, 2024. https://www.va.gov/vetdata/docs/SpecialReports/State_Summaries_Oklahoma.pdf.

U.S. Geological Survey. n.d. "Oklahoma Has Had a Surge of Earthquakers since 2009: Are They Due to Fracking?" Accessed August 28, 2024. www.usgs.gov/faqs/oklahoma-has-had-a-surge-earthquakes-2009-are-they-due-fracking.

U.S. House of Representatives. 1982. "Penn Square Bank Failure." Hearings before the Committee on Banking, Finance and Urban Affairs. Accessed via FRASER. https://fraser.stlouisfed.org/title/penn-square-bank-failure-748/part-2-23605.

Vandewater, Bob. 1993. "Anthony's Case Pursued by Loving." *Oklahoman*, April 17. https://www.oklahoman.com/story/news/1993/04/17/anthonys-case-pursued-by-loving/62461986007/.

Warren, Molly, Madison West, and Stacy Beck. 2023. *The State of Obesity: Better Policies for a Healthier America*. Trust for America's Health issue report. September. Accessed October 5, 2024. www.tfah.org/wp-content/uploads/2023/09/TFAH-2023-ObesityReport-FINAL.pdf.

Weaver, Patti. 1997. "Former DA Gets Out of Prison Today." *Tulsa World*, September 4. https://tulsaworld.com/archive/former-da-gets-out-of-prison-today/article_2b5268ce-6577-549e-9fca-601f344d8495.html.

Wellcare Oklahoma. n.d. Wellcare homepage. Accessed September 26, 2024. www.wellcareok.com.

Wertz, William C. 2023. "Continuing Oklahoma's Improvement in Child Protection: What Come's Next?" *Oklahoman*, March 26. Accessed September 26, 2024. www.oklahoman.com/story/news/politics/government/2023/03/26/oklahoma-child-welfare-services-tricia-howell-whats-next/69986238007.

———. 2023. "Outside Monitoring of Oklahoma's Troubled Child Welfare System May Soon End." *Oklahoman*, March 22. Accessed September 26, 2024. www.oklahoman.com/story/news/2023/03/22/child-welfare-oklahoma-department-human-services-court-ordered-monitoring-may-end-soon/70037903007.

White House. 2021. "Remarks by President Biden Commemorating the 100th Anniversary of the Tulsa Race Massacre." Accessed July 31, 2025. https://bidenwhitehouse.archives.gov/briefing-room/speeches-remarks/2021/06/02/remarks-by-president-biden-commemorating-the-100th-anniversary-of-the-tulsa-race-massacre.

Wilmoth, Adam. 2003. "Commissioner Files Recording in Case Alleging Bribery Attempt." *Oklahoman*, June 5. www.oklahoman.com/story/news/2003/06/05/commissioner-files-recording-in-case-alleging-bribery-attempt/62040655007.

World Population Review. n.d. "Per Pupil Spending by State 2024." Accessed September 13, 2024. https://worldpopulationreview.com/state-rankings/per-pupil-spending-by-state.

———. n.d. *Perkins.* Accessed October 5, 2024. https://worldpopulationreview.com/us-cities/oklahoma/perkins.

Zeitlin, Irving M. 2000. *Ideology and the Development of Sociological Theory.* Prentice Hall.

Zeitlin, Maurice, and Richard Earl Ratcliff. 1988. *Landlords and Capitalists: The Dominant Class of Chile.* Princeton University Press.

Zweig, Phillip L. L. 1986. *Belly Up: The Collapse of the Penn Square Bank.* Random House.

Index

www.ingramcontent.com/pod-product-compliance
Lightning Source LLC
Chambersburg PA
CBHW031538260326
41914CB00039B/2001/J
* 9 7 8 0 8 0 6 1 9 6 5 6 5 *